Shelby Foote

THE CIVIL WAR

A NARRATIVE

Shelby Foote

THE CIVIL WAR

A NARRATIVE

11

★ ★ ★

YELLOW TAVERN
TO COLD HARBOR

40th Anniversary Edition

BY SHELBY FOOTE
AND THE EDITORS OF TIME-LIFE BOOKS,
ALEXANDRIA, VIRGINIA

All these were honoured in their generations,
and were the glory of their times.

There be of them,
that have left a name behind them,
that their praises might be reported.

And some there be, which have no memorial;
who are perished, as though they had never been;
and are become as though they had never been born;
and their children after them.

But these were merciful men,
whose righteousness hath not been forgotten.

With their seed shall continually remain
a good inheritance,
and their children are within the covenant.

Their seed standeth fast,
and their children for their sakes.

Their seed shall remain for ever,
and their glory shall not be blotted out.

Their bodies are buried in peace;
but their name liveth for evermore.

— ECCLESIASTICUS XLIV

Contents

★ ★ ★

★

Prologue

*I*n the spring of 1864, the Union high command was not pleased with the recent course of the war. Nathaniel Banks's glory-seeking attempt to strengthen and stretch the Federal hold on Louisiana and Texas had come a cropper along the Red River, Confederate cavalryman Nathan Bedford Forrest had taken Fort Pillow in his latest raid into Kentucky, and the South's ironclad *Albemarle* was wreaking havoc in the North Carolina coastal waters. As Abraham Lincoln grew ever more gloomy about his chances for reëlection, Ulysses S. Grant, the man on whom the President had pinned his hopes to turn the military situation around (and thus turn the political situation to Lincoln's advantage) had left Washington for the Virginia front grumbling about the incoherent strategy of the armies he now headed.

Determined to reorganize not just the Army of the Potomac but the North's entire war effort, Grant had arrived at winter quarters and begun shaking things up. Shifting commanders and corps like so many playing cards, Grant had dragged into his fighting ranks every available soldier, from teamster to supply clerk, and issued new marching orders across the board. It was not just that Benjamin Butler was to lead an army up the James River or Franz Sigel to march through the Shenandoah Valley or William Tecumseh Sherman to head for Atlanta. They were to find the enemy and fight him, just as George Meade, directly under Grant, was to face Robert E. Lee wherever and whenever possible. And they were to fight regardless of the costs until the war was won.

In a sense, Lee welcomed Grant's grim approach, since he planned to make those costs so high for the Union army opposite him that the United States, if not Grant himself, would lose the stomach for battle and turn against Lincoln at the polls. Jefferson Davis, too, held to the desperate hope that the Confederacy could fight long enough and well enough to cause Lincoln to lose the presidency and the North to settle for peace. Emotionally distraught by the accidental death of his son Joe and worried by the cries of such domestic critics as Georgia Governor Joseph E. Brown for independent action, Davis would try to instill in Joseph E. Johnston the same fighting spirit against Sherman down in Georgia that Lee showed against Grant in Virginia.

In the long run, however, neither Grant nor Lincoln would be undone by the ever more massive spilling of Union blood. The first hints that such was the case came as Grant kept fighting after losing tens of thousands of men in the early days of the Wilderness Campaign. But the numbers would mount horribly as the Union armies slogged on in Virginia — at Spotsylvania, New Market, Bermuda Hundred, and along the North Anna — until Cold Harbor, where even Grant would fear the slaughter was too great a price to pay and after which Lincoln would caution him about the high casualties of his campaign. Some 75,000 Union soldiers would become casualties in the forty days of fighting, a number equal to that of Lee's entire army at the beginning the campaign. But the numbers would never mount high enough to provoke Lincoln into recalling this new general as he had every other commander. Nor would the numbers lead Grant to avoid fighting Lee as they had each of his predecessors.

The numbers for Sherman would not be so disproportionate because his approach would not be so head-on as he moved from Ringgold through Resaca and around Kennesaw Mountain and along the Chattahoochee, avoiding intrenched rebels where he could, fighting them where he must, till his menacing presence might flush them into open battle. So, while the South might celebrate the exploits of a Bedford Forrest, who continued his raiding in Tennessee, while it might exult in Franz Sigel's retreat down the Shenandoah Valley, while it might cheer P. G. T. Beauregard for bottling up Ben Butler between Richmond and Petersburg, and while it might even take solace in the bloody stalemate Lee had forced on Grant, it would not be able to ignore Sherman's inexorable march south. Thus, as spring turned to summer, instead of Lincoln replacing Grant, it would be Jeff Davis replacing Johnston that headlined the war's action.

There would be other causes for the South to worry or mourn. In the fighting around Yellow Tavern, the South's storied cavalry officer Jeb Stuart would lose his life at the hands of one of George Armstrong Custer's troopers. In the English Channel, the legendary C.S.S. *Alabama* would meet its match in the hitherto obscure U.S.S. *Kearsarge*. And ultimately Grant's dogged tenacity in the face of Lee's seemingly endless ability to inflict heavy casualties would prove troublesome. Where before Lee's superior generalship had always cheered the cause forward even as generals like Joe Johnston gave up ground in the western theater, such exceptional soldiering would increasingly offer less comfort as Grant fought on in Virginia and Sherman approached the outskirts of Atlanta.

★ ★ ★

*The Union suffered more than
35,000 casualties in the fighting in
the Wilderness and at Spotsylvania,
many of whom were taken to this
divisional hospital.*

O N E

Sheridan's Raid; A Race for the North Anna

1864 ★ ★ ★ ★ ★ ★ **D**irected by Grant, through Meade, to "cut loose from the Army of the Potomac, pass around Lee's army, and attack his cavalry and communications," Sheridan was determined not only to make the most of the opportunity, which came his way as a result of the high-tempered clash at headquarters earlier that same Sunday, May 8, but also to do so in a style that was in keeping with his claim that, left to the devices he had been urging all along, he could whip Jeb Stuart out of his boots. "We are going out to fight Stuart's cavalry in consequence of a suggestion from me," he told his three division commanders that evening, and he added, by way of emphasizing the highly personal nature of the challenge as he saw it: "In view of my recent representations to General Meade I shall expect nothing but success."

His method of assuring this was demonstrated at first light next morning, back near Fredericksburg, when the march began down the Telegraph Road, the main-traveled artery to Richmond. Riding four abreast, accompanied by all 32 of their guns and such forage and ordnance wagons as were needed, the 12,000 blue troopers comprised a column thirteen miles in length. They moved not at a run or trot, and not by separate, converging routes — both of which had been standard procedure on raids in the past — but at a walk and in a single inspissated column, compact as a fist clenched for striking on short notice. Not

★

much concerned with deception, and even less with speed, Sheridan's dependence was on power, the ability of his three combined divisions to ride through or over whatever got in their path. Previous raiders had sought to avoid the fast-moving rebel horsemen, lest they be delayed or thwarted in their attempt to reach their assigned objectives; but Sheridan's objective, so to speak, was just such a confrontation. He defined the raid as "a challenge to Stuart for a cavalry duel behind Lee's lines, in his own country," and the more there were of the gray riders when the showdown was at hand, the better he would like it, since that would mean there were more to be "smashed up." His confidence was in numbers and the superiority of his horses and equipment: as was shown within an hour of the outset, when the head of the column ran into brisk fire from an enemy outpost line and stopped to ponder the situation.

Little Phil, as his troopers had taken to calling him, came riding up and asked what was the matter. Skirmishers, he was told — apparently in strength. "Cavalry or infantry?" he demanded, and on being informed that they were cavalry, barked impatiently: "Keep moving, boys. We're going on through. There isn't cavalry enough in all the Southern Confederacy to stop us."

Southward the march led down across the Ni, the Po, the Ta, and around the mazy sources of the Mat — four streams that combined to contribute their waters and their names to the Mattaponi — until, well in the rear of Lee's far right, the column turned off the Telegraph Road and headed southwest for Chilesburg and the North Anna, three miles beyond which lay Beaver Dam Station, Lee's advance supply base on the Virginia Central Railroad. Stores of all kinds were collected there, drawn from the Carolinas and the Shenandoah Valley; Sheridan planned to "go through" them in the course of his move on Stuart and the Confederate capital itself, which he would approach by the front door, if it came within his reach, while Ben Butler's infantry was knocking at the back. Torbert's division, still under Wesley Merritt, had the lead, followed by Gregg and Wilson. Progress was steady all day long, mainly because Sheridan refused to be distracted, whether by threats or the rumor of threats, which were frequent, front and rear. When a rebel brigade launched an attack on his rear guard south of the Ta, for example, he simply detached one of Gregg's brigades as a reinforcement and kept the main body moving at the deliberate pace he had set at the start, on the far side of the Ni. Just before dusk the North Anna came in sight; Merritt crossed with his three brigades while the other two divisions went into camp on the near bank. Before long, the sky was aglow in the direction Merritt had moved and the night breeze was fragrant with the aroma of burning bacon, wafted northward all the way from Beaver Dam.

Much of the burning — close to a million rations of meat and better than half a million of bread, along with Lee's entire reserve of medical stores — had been done by the depot guards themselves, who fired the sheds to keep

★

The brigade of General George A. Custer burned Confederate railway cars and locomotives and freed 378 Union soldiers captured in the Wilderness.

their contents out of the hands of the raiders. First on the scene was the brigade of twenty-four-year-old Brigadier General George A. Custer, Michiganders as skilled in wrecking as they were in fighting. They added more than a hundred railway cars to the conflagration, as well as two locomotives — one fourth of all the Virginia Central had in operation at the time — and for lagniappe freed 378 Union soldiers, captured in the Wilderness and en route to prison camps. After the excitement of all this, the horsemen bedded down for a few hours' sleep by the fitful light of the fading embers of the station, and were roused before dawn to get to work on the railroad track. Ten miles in all were torn up, together with the telegraph wires and poles that ran beside it, before the whooping troopers fell back into column to resume their march. Like their comrades on the north bank, they were well rested despite their overnight carnival of destruction, having slept in one large bivouac that required few sentinels, rather than in scattered groups requiring many. Reconsolidated, the three divisions proceeded again at an energy-saving walk, a road-wide dusty blue serpent more than a dozen miles long and crawling inexorably south. So leisurely, so unperturbed was this horse-back saunter through the springtime greenness of Virginia — except of course for those engaged in the rear-guard fret of fending off the rebels snapping persistently at their heels — that the raiders had to remind themselves from time to time that they were deep in enemy country, out for blood.

By late afternoon (Tuesday, May 10: Upton was massing for his abortive penetration of Ewell's works, thirty air-line miles due north) the head of the column reached Ground Squirrel Bridge on the South Anna, and there in the grassy fields beside the river, well over halfway to Richmond, Sheridan called a halt for the night. He might have kept on; today's march had been a good deal shorter than yesterday's and there were still a couple of daylight hours left; but this was an excellent place to feed and water his mounts and rest his men. Besides, he not only was in no hurry, he also reasoned that Stuart by now, as he said later, was "urging his horses to the death so as to get in between Richmond and our column," and he preferred it so.

He wanted Jeb to win the race, since only in that way would it end in the confrontation he was seeking.

★ ★ ★ *S*tuart had accepted the gambit and was proceeding much as Sheridan supposed: with one exception. Unlike his opponent, who had stripped the Federal army of practically every horseman he could lay hands on, the southern cavalry commander had resisted the temptation to jump this latest adversary with everything he had, and instead of leaving Lee to grope as blind as Grant was going to be for the next week or two, had taken up the pursuit with only three of his six brigades, some 4500 sabers opposing 12,000 engaged in what might turn out to be an attempt to seize the scantly defended capital already menaced by Butler's army from the far side of the James. One factor in this decision to forgo a better chance at personal laurels was that he could not know, until the Yankees cleared Beaver Dam on the morning of the second day, whether their intention was to keep on riding south for Richmond or turn north for a strike at Spotslyvania from the rear, in which case Lee of course would need all the help he could get, especially from his cavalry. As a result of this limiting decision, made at the outset, Stuart knew as well as Sheridan did that, in light of the numerical odds prevailing, the confrontation could have only one result if it was head-on; Sheridan — whose three well-mounted divisions were equipped with rapid-fire carbines, whereas the three gray brigades were armed with single-shot muzzle loaders and mounted on crowbait horses — would ride right over him. Stuart's solution, in considering this dilemma, was not to avoid the confrontation, despite the likelihood that it would be disastrous on those terms, but rather to arrange for it to be something other than head-on and to get what assistance he could from the Richmond garrison, scant as it was, when the march of the two columns intersected in the vicinity of the threatened capital.

Whatever he lacked in comparative strength — even at the outset of the raid, before his underfed, short-winded horses started breaking down from the strain of the chase — there was at least no diminution of his accustomed vigilance and vigor. Pressing close in rear of the outsized blue formation with one of Fitz Lee's brigades, he sent for Fitz and his other brigade, as well as Brigadier General James B. Gordon's brigade of W.H.F. Lee's division, and with these three took up the pursuit in earnest, first down the Telegraph Road, then southeast to the North Anna, beyond which, as night came down, he saw to his distress the spreading reflection of the flames at Beaver Dam, where a three-week supply of food went up in smoke while the men for whom it had been intended went hungry in the Spotsylvania woods. In just one day, by this one blow, Sheridan had accomplished more than any of his predecessors had managed to do in the past three years. What was worse, with Richmond not much farther south than he had come already, he seemed likely to accomplish a great deal more, unless Stuart found some way to check or divert him.

Up to now, the grayjackets had been limited to attacks on the Union rear, since to have doubled the blue column for a strike at its head would have left the raiders free to turn for an unmolested dash against the rear of Lee's intrenchments. By next morning, though, with all the enemy horsemen over the North Anna, proceeding south past the charred base they had destroyed the night before, Stuart was free at least of that restriction; he could give his full attention to covering Richmond, since that now seemed without much doubt to be the Federal objective. Accordingly, he told Gordon to keep his brigade of North Carolinians close on the tail of the blue column, impeding it all he could, while Fitz Lee and his two Virginia brigades, under Brigadier Generals Lunsford Lomax and Williams Wickham, rode east along the Virginia Central to regain the Telegraph Road, just this side of Hanover Junction, and hurry down it to take up a position in which to intercept the raiders before they got to Richmond. A message went to Braxton Bragg, informing him of the danger to the capital in his charge. Stuart hoped to be reinforced from the city's garrison in time for the confrontation on its outskirts, but if Sheridan brushed past him, he told Bragg, "I will certainly move in his rear and do what I can."

So much for intention; execution, he knew, would be a larger order. However, before setting out to catch up with Fitz, Jeb took advantage of an opportunity Sheridan had unwittingly given him to call on his wife Flora and their two children, who were visiting on a plantation near Beaver Dam Station, thought until yesterday to be a place of safety from the Yankees. She came out to meet him on the front steps of the house, and though he did not take the time to dismount, he at least had the satisfaction of leaning down from the saddle to kiss her hello and goodbye before continuing on his way.

The parting had a somber effect on the normally jovial cavalier. So many goodbyes by so many soldiers had turned out to be last goodbyes in the course of the past three years, and today was the anniversary, moreover, of the death of his great and good friend Stonewall Jackson. Stuart rode in silence for a time before he spoke to his only companion, a staff major, on a theme he seldom touched. He did not expect to survive the war, he said, and he did not want to live anyhow if the South went down in defeat.

Sheridan's calculation that his adversary would be "urging his horses to the death so as to get in between Richmond and our column" was nearly confirmed quite literally that night. Tireless himself, Jeb was not inclined to have much patience with tiredness in others. "We must substitute *esprit* for numbers," he had declared in the early days of the war, adding in partial explanation, not only of his exuberant foxhunt manner, but also for the gaudy uniform — red-lined cape, bright yellow sash, black ostrich plume, and golden spurs — he wore with such flamboyance, on and off the field of battle: "I strive to inculcate in my men the spirit of the chase."

Overtaking Fitz Lee soon after dark near Hanover Junction, he learned from Gordon, who sent a courier cross country, that the Federals had made an early halt that afternoon at Ground Squirrel Bridge on the South Anna.

*Jeb Stuart was noted for his flamboyant uniform —
which made him an easy target — as well as
for his daring as a Confederate cavalry commander.*

★

This was within twenty miles of Richmond, five miles closer than Stuart himself was at the time; Jeb was all for pushing ahead on an all-night march, until Fitz persuaded him that unless he stopped to feed and rest his weary mounts he would arrive with no more than a handful of troopers, the remainder having been left behind to clutter the road with broken-down horses. Stuart relented, on condition that Fitz would have his men back in the saddle by 1 a.m., but rode on himself for another few miles before he lay down by the roadside to get a little sleep. Up and off again before the dawn of May 11 — unaware, of course, that this was to be his last day in the field — he crossed the South Anna at sunrise and passed the farm where he had bivouacked, one month less than two years ago tomorrow night, on the eve of his first "ride around McClellan," the exploit that had made his name a household word. Nearing Ashland, four miles south on the Richmond, Fredericksburg & Potomac, he found that a brigade of raiders, detached from the main column, had struck the place the night before, burning a locomotive and a train of cars, along with several government warehouses, while tearing up six miles of track. Stuart quickened his pace at this evidence of what might be in store for Richmond, fifteen miles away, unless he managed to head the marauders off or force them into retreat by pitching into their rear while they were attacking the works that ringed the city. Today as yesterday, however, a staff officer who rode with him found him inclined to speak of personal rather than of military matters. "He was more quiet than usual, softer and more communicative," the staffer observed, believing, as he later wrote, that Jeb somehow felt "the shadow of the near future already upon him."

Informed by another courier from Gordon that the Federal main body had resumed its march from Ground Squirrel Bridge this morning on the Mountain Road from Louisa, Jeb found his problem as to the choice of an interceptive position more or less solved before he got there. Less than half a mile below the junction of the Mountain and Telegraph roads, which came together to form Brook Turnpike, a macadamized thoroughfare running the last six miles into Richmond, was an abandoned stagecoach inn called Yellow Tavern, paintless now, made derelict by progress, and set amid rolling, sparsely wooded fields of grass and grain. Stuart arrived at 8 o'clock, ahead of his troops, and after sending word to Bragg that he had won the race, proceeded at once to plan his dispositions.

Sporadic firing up the Mountain Road confirmed that Gordon still was snapping terrierlike at the heels of the Union column, as instructed, and gave warning that Fitz Lee not only had no time to spare in getting ready to receive it, but also could expect no reinforcements from Bragg on such brief notice. Stuart's decision was to compromise between taking up a frontal and a flank position, since the former would invite the powerful enemy force to run right over him, while the latter would afford him little more than a chance to pepper the blue troopers as they galloped past him, bound for Richmond. He had Fitz put Wickham on the right, one mile north of Yellow Tavern, facing south into the V of the converging roads, and Lomax on the left, his left advanced so that the two brigades came together at an angle, presenting a concave front which allowed a concentration of fire upon whatever moved against them down the western arm of the V. By 10 o'clock these dispositions were completed; Stuart had his men in line, dismounted except for a single regiment, the 1st Virginia, which he held in reserve to be hurried wherever it was needed most. Within another hour the enemy too had come up and was massing for attack.

This was approximately what Sheridan had been wanting all along, and now that he had it he took care to make the most of it. Richmond lay just ahead, the prize of prizes, but he was in no hurry; Richmond would still be there tonight and tomorrow, whereas Stuart, with his reputation for hairbreadth extractions, might skedaddle. From noon until about 2 o'clock he reconnoitered the Confederate position, probing here and there to test its strength, then settled down in earnest, using one brigade to hold off Gordon in his rear, two more to block the turnpike escape route, and the remaining four against Fitz Lee, whom he outnumbered two-to-one in men and three-to-one in guns. For another two hours the fight was hot, sometimes hand to hand at critical points. By 4 o'clock Sheridan had found what he believed was the key to Lee's undoing, and orders went for Merritt to press the issue on the right, crumpling Lomax to fling him back on Wickham, after which the whole line would move forward to exploit the resultant confusion. Merritt passed the order on to Custer, who promptly attacked with two regiments mounted and the other two on foot as skirmishers, striking hard for the left of the rebel line just north of Yellow Tavern.

Stuart was there, having sensed the point of greatest danger from his command post near the center. A conspicuous target in his silk-lined cape and nodding plume, he laughed at an aide's protest that he was exposing himself unnecessarily. "I don't reckon there is any danger," he replied. For three years this had apparently been true for him, although his clothes had been slit repeatedly by twittering bullets and he once had half of his mustache clipped off by a stray round. Moreover, he was encouraged by a dispatch from Bragg expressing the opinion that he could hold the Richmond works with his 4000 local defense troops and the help of three brigades of regulars he had ordered to join him from the far side of the James, provided the raiders could be delayed long enough for these reinforcements to make it across the river. Jeb figured there had been time for that already, and once again was proudly conscious of having carried out a difficult assignment, though he was determined to gain still more by way of allowing a margin for error.

Arriving on the far left as the two Michigan regiments thundered past in a charge on a section of guns just up the line, he drew his big nine-shot LeMatt revolver and fired at the blue horsemen going by. They took the guns,

★

Before Jeb Stuart was shot at Yellow Tavern,
he fired his LeMatt revolver, like the one shown here,
into the ranks of the 5th Michigan troopers.

scattering the cannoneers, but soon came tumbling back, some mounted and some unhorsed by a counterattack from the 1st Virginia, which Fitz Lee threw at them. Stuart had ridden forward to a fence, putting his horse's head across it between two of his butternut soldiers in order to get as close as possible to the bluecoats coming back. "Steady, men, steady!" he shouted, still firing his silver-chased pistol at the enemy beyond the fence. "Give it to them!"

Instead, it was they who gave it to him: one of them anyhow. A dismounted private, trotting past with his revolver drawn — John A. Huff of the 5th Michigan, who had served a two-year hitch in a sharpshooter outfit, winning a prize as the best marksman in his regiment, then returned home and reënlisted under Custer, apparently out of boredom, though at forty-five he was old for that branch of the service — took time to fire, almost casually in passing, at the red-bearded officer thirty feet away. Jeb's head dropped suddenly forward, so that his plumed hat fell off, and he clapped one hand to his right side.

"General, are you hit?" one of the men alongside him cried as the blue trooper ran off down the fence line, pistol smoking from the fire of that one unlucky shot.

"I'm afraid I am," Stuart replied calmly when the question was asked again. "But don't worry, boys," he told the distressed soldiers gathering rapidly around him; "Fitz will do as well for you as I have done."

They got him off his horse and did what they could to make him comfortable while waiting for an ambulance. Fitz Lee came riding fast when he heard of the wound, but Jeb sent him back at once to take charge of the field. "Go ahead, Fitz, old fellow," he said. "I know you'll do what is right." Then the ambulance came and they lifted him into it, obviously in pain. Just as it started rearward a portion of the line gave way and a number of flustered gray troopers made off across the field. "Go back!" Stuart called after them, sitting up in his indignation despite the wrench to his hurt side. "Go back and do your duty, as I have done mine, and our country will be safe. Go back, go back!" Then he added, though in different words, what he had told the staff major yesterday about not wanting to survive the South's defeat: "I'd rather die than be whipped!"

Presently a surgeon and other members of his staff overtook the mule-drawn ambulance and stopped it, out of range of the Federals, for an examination of the wound. While his blood-stained sash was being removed and his bullet-torn jacket opened, Stuart turned to Lieutenant Walter Hullihen, a staff favorite, and addressed him by his nickname: "Honeybun, how do I look in the face?" Hullihen lied — for his chief was clearly in shock and getting weaker by the minute. "You are looking all right, General," he replied. "You will be all right." Jeb mused on the words, as if in doubt, knowing only too well what lay in store for a gut-shot man. "Well, I don't know how this will turn out," he said at last, "but if it is God's will that I shall die I am ready."

By now the doctor had completed his examination and ordered the ambulance to move on. He believed there was little chance for the general's survival, but he wanted to get him to Richmond, and expert medical attention,

*Waving his ostrich-plumed hat, Major General
Jeb Stuart leads his Confederate cavalry up an incline
in this symbolic painting by Charles Hoffbauer.*

★

as soon as possible. An eighteen-year-old private followed the vehicle for a time on horseback, looking in under the hood at the anguished Stuart until it picked up speed and pulled away. "The last thing I saw of him," the boy trooper later wrote, "he was lying flat on his back in the ambulance, the mules running at a terrific pace, and he was being jolted most unmercifully. He opened his eyes and looked at me, and shook his head from side to side as much as to say, 'It's all over with me.' He had folded arms and a look of resignation."

★ ★ ★   itz Lee by then had restored his line, and Sheridan, after prodding it here and there for another hour, decided the time had come to move on after all. Shadows were lengthening fast; moreover he had intercepted a rebel dispatch urging Bragg to send substantial reinforcements. So he broke off what he called "this obstinate contest" north of Yellow Tavern, and pushed on down Brook Turnpike, through the outer works of Richmond, to within earshot of the alarm bells tolling frantically in the gathering darkness. This was the route Kilpatrick had taken ten weeks ago, only to call a halt when he came under fire from the fortifications, and Little Phil had a similar reaction when he drew near the intermediate line of defense, three miles from Capitol Square. "It is possible that I might have captured the city of Richmond by assault," he would report to Meade, "but the want of knowledge of your operations and those of General Butler, and the facility with which the enemy could throw in troops, made me abandon the attempt." His personal inclination was to plunge on down the pike, over the earthworks and into the streets of the town, though he knew he lacked the strength to stay there long; "the greatest temptation of my life," he later called the prospect, looking back. "I should have been the hero of the hour. I could have gone in and burned and killed right and left. But I had learned this thing: that our men knew what they were about. . . . They would have followed me, but they would have known as well as I that the sacrifice was for no permanent advantage."

Forbearance came hard, but he soon had other matters on his mind. Withdrawal, under present circumstances, called for perhaps more daring, and certainly more skill, than did staying where he was or going in. Gordon was still clawing at his rear on Brook Turnpike, and Fitz Lee was somewhere off in the darkness, hovering on his flank; Bragg, for all he knew, had summoned any number of reinforcements from beyond the James, and presently the confusion was compounded by a howling wind- and rainstorm (the one that was giving Hancock so much trouble, out on its fringes, on the night march into position for his dawn assault on the toe of Ewell's Mule Shoe) so severe that the steeple of old St John's Church, on the opposite side of Richmond, was blown away. Sheridan turned eastward, headed for Meadow Bridge on the Chickahominy, which he intended to cross at that point, putting the river between him and his

★

pursuers, and then recross, well downstream, to find sanctuary within Butler's lines, as had been prearranged, at Haxall's Landing on the James.

In addition to the rain-lashed darkness, which made any sense of direction hard to maintain, the march was complicated by the presence of land mines in his path; "torpedoes," they were called, buried artillery projectiles equipped with trip wires, and the first one encountered killed a number of horses and wounded several men. Sheridan had an answer to that, however. Bringing a couple of dozen prisoners forward to the head of the column, he made them "get down on their knees, feel for the wires in the darkness, follow them up and unearth the shells." Despite the delay he reached Meadow Bridge at daylight: only to find that the rebels had set it afire the night before to prevent his get-away. At the same time he discovered this, Bragg's infantry came up in his rear and Fitz Lee's vengeance-minded troopers descended whooping on his flank.

He faced Wilson and Gregg about to meet the double challenge, and gave Merritt the task of repairing the bridge for a crossing. Fortunately, last night's rain had put the fire out before the stringers and ties burned through; a new floor could be improvised from fence rails. While these were being collected and put in place, the two divisions fighting rearward gave a good account of themselves, having acquired by now some of the foxhunt jauntiness formerly limited to their gray-clad adversaries. For example, when instructed by Sheridan to "hold your position at all hazards while I arrange to withdraw the corps to the north side of the river," James Wilson made a jocular reply. "Our hair is badly entangled in [the enemy's] fingers and our nose firmly inserted in his mouth. We shall, therefore, hold on here till something breaks." Nothing broke; not in the blue ranks anyhow, though James Gordon was mortally wounded on the other side, shot from his horse while leading a charge by his brigade. Merritt finished his repair work in short order and the three divisions withdrew, without heavy losses, to camp for the night down the left bank of the Chickahominy, near the old Gaines Mill battlefield. Proceeding by easy marches they rode past other scenes from the Seven Days, including Malvern Hill, to Haxall's Landing, which they reached on May 14.

The raid was over, all but the return, and Sheridan was greatly pleased with the results, not only because of the specific damage accomplished at Beaver Dam and Ashland, but also because of other damage, no less grave for being more difficult to assess. At a cost of 625 killed and wounded and missing, he had freed nearly 400 Union prisoners and brought them with him into Butler's lines, along with some 300 captive rebels. How many of the enemy he had killed or wounded in the course of the raid he could not say, but he knew at least of one whose loss to Lee and the Confederacy was well-nigh immeasurable. The killing of Jeb Stuart at Yellow Tavern, he declared, "inflicted a blow from which entire recovery was impossible."

After three days' rest with Butler he was off to rejoin Grant. The northward march was uneventful except for a rather spectacular demonstration, staged while crossing the high railroad bridge over Pamunkey River, of the indestructibility of the army pack mule. Falling from a height of thirty feet, one of these creatures — watched in amazement by a regiment of troopers whose colonel recorded the incident in his memoirs — "turned a somersault, struck an abutment, disappeared under water, came up, and swam ashore without disturbing his pack." On May 24 the three divisions rejoined the army they had left, two weeks and one day ago, near Spotsylvania.

Stuart by then had been eleven days in his grave, not far from the church that lost its steeple in the windstorm on the night he arrived from Yellow Tavern. After six mortal hours of being jounced on rutted country roads because the ambulance had to take a roundabout route to avoid the raiders on the turnpike, he reached his wife's sister's house on Grace Street at 11 o'clock that

---

"Our hair is badly entangled in [the enemy's] fingers and our nose firmly inserted in his mouth. We shall, therefore, hold on here till something breaks."

— James Wilson

---

evening, and there, attended by four of Richmond's leading physicians through another twenty hours of suffering, he made what was called "a good death" — a matter of considerable importance in those days, from the historical as well as the religious point of view. After sending word of his condition to his wife at Beaver Dam, in hope that she and the children would reach him before the end, he gave instructions for the disposition of his few belongings, including his spurs and various horses. "My sword I leave to my son," the impromptu will concluded.

The night was a hard one, with stretches of delirium, but toward morning he seemed to improve; an aide reported him "calm and composed, in the full possession of his mind." Shortly after sunrise on May 12, when the rumble of guns was heard from the north, he asked what it meant, and on being told that part of the capital garrison had gone out to work with the cavalry in an attempt to trap the raiders at Meadow Bridge: "God grant that they may be successful," he said fervently, then turned his head aside and returned with a sigh to the matter at hand: "But I must be prepared for another world." Later that morning the President arrived to sit briefly at his bedside. "General, how do you feel?" he asked, taking the cavalryman's hand. "Easy; but willing to die," Jeb said, "if God and my country think I have fulfilled my destiny and done my duty."

Davis could scarcely believe the thirty-one-year-old Virginian was near death; he seemed, he said afterward, "so calm, and physically so strong." But one of the doctors, seeing the Chief Executive out, told him there was no chance for Stuart's recovery. The bullet had pierced his abdomen, causing heavy internal bleeding, and probably his liver and stomach as well; "mortification" — peritonitis — had set in, and he was not likely to see another dawn. That afternoon Jeb himself was told as much. "Can I last the night?" he asked, realizing that his wife might not arrive before tomorrow because of the damage to the railroad north of Richmond, and received the doctor's answer: "I'm afraid the end is near." Stuart nodded. "I am resigned, if it be God's will," he said. "I would like to see my wife. But God's will be done." Near sunset he asked a clergyman to lead in the singing of "Rock of Ages," and it was painful to see the effort he made to join the slow chorus of the hymn. "I am going fast now, I am resigned; God's will be done," he murmured. That was shortly after 7 o'clock, and within another half hour he was dead.

Flora Stuart and the children did not arrive until four hours later, but were with him in plenty of time for the funeral next day at St James Church and the burial in Hollywood Cemetery. There was no military escort; the home guard was in the field and Lee could spare no soldiers from the Spotsylvania line. Davis and Bragg were there, along with other government dignitaries, but Fitz Lee's troopers were still out after Sheridan, down the Peninsula.

Such were the last rites for the man John Sedgwick, dead himself for four days now, had called "the greatest cavalry officer ever foaled in America."

★ ★ ★ *H*is achievements form a conspicuous part of the history of this army, with which his name and services will be forever associated," Lee was presently to declare in a general order mourning the fallen Jeb. This was the hardest loss he had had to bear since the death of Jackson, and coupled as it was with the disablement of Longstreet, the indisposition of A. P. Hill, and the increasing evidence that one-legged Ewell would never fulfill the expectations which had attended his appointment as Stonewall's successor, there was cause for despair in the Confederate army, near exhaustion from its twenty-hour struggle for the Mule Shoe. Fortunately, as if in respectful observation of Stuart's funeral fifty miles away in Richmond, the following day was one of rest. For the next two days, and into a third, rain fell steadily — "as if Heaven were trying to wash up the blood as fast as the civilized barbarians were spilling it," a South Carolina sergeant of artillery observed. Such killing as there was was mostly done at long range, by cannoneers and snipers on both sides. There was little actual fighting, only a lumbering shift by the Union army, east and south. Lee conformed to cover Spotsylvania, extending his right southward, beyond the courthouse, to the crossing of the Po. The blue maneuver seemed quite purposeless, not at all like Grant; Lee was puzzled. Unable to make out what the Federals were up to, if anything, he remarked sadly to a companion: "Ah, Major, if my poor friend Stuart were here I should know all about what those people are doing."

Grant was not as quiescent as he seemed; anyhow he hadn't meant to be. During the day of rest from his exertions of May 12 he considered what to do to break the stalemate his headlong efforts had produced. A move around Lee's left would draw the old fox into open country, but in the absence of

After the fighting at the Mule Shoe, Robert E. Lee extended his right beyond Spotsylvania Court House (above), 10 miles south of the Wilderness battlefield.

After reoccupying the Mule Shoe, John Gibbon's division of Hancock's II Corps prepares to attack the rebel line on May 18 in this sketch by Alfred Waud.

Sheridan's troopers Grant would be at a disadvantage, maneuvering blind against a foe who still had half his cavalry on hand. His decision, then, was to strike the enemy right by shifting Warren from his own right to his left on a night march that would end in a surprise attack at first light, May 14; Wright would follow to extend the envelopment which, if successful, would turn Lee out of his Spotsylvania works and expose him to destruction when he retreated.

Orders to effect this were issued before the day of rest was over; but all that came of them was lumbering confusion and the loss of many tempers. Floundering through roadless mud, rain-whipped underbrush, and swollen creeks, the V Corps did not reach its jump-off position on the Fredericksburg Road until 6 a.m., two hours behind schedule, and had to spend the rest of the day collecting the thousands of mud-caked stragglers left exhausted in its wake. The attack had to be called off, and instead there followed another day of rest.

This time it was Wright who had a notion. The Confederates having conformed to the Union movement by shifting Anderson to their right, Wright suggested that a sudden reversal of last night's march — left to right, instead of right to left — would provide a capital opportunity for a breakthrough on the rebel left, which had been thinned to furnish troops for the extension of the line down to Snell's Bridge on the Po. Grant liked and enlarged the plan to include Hancock, setting dawn of May 18 as the time of attack. Reoccupying the abandoned Mule Shoe in the darkness of the preceding night, Hancock and Wright were to assault

★

Barlow
V

May 18th 1864

the new works across its base, while Burnside made a diversionary effort on their left and Warren stood by to join them once the fortifications were overrun.

That gave two full days for getting ready; Grant wanted the thing done right, despite the mud. Moreover, on the first of these two days the rain left off, letting the roads begin to dry, and the second — May 17 — hastened the drying process with a sun as hot as summer. Everything went smoothly and on schedule: up to the point at which the six divisions moved into the Mule Shoe in the darkness, under instructions to take up positions for the 4 a.m. assault. So much time was spent occupying and moving through the first and second lines of the original intrenchments, undefended though they were, that it was 8 o'clock before the troops were in position to make the surprise attack that should have been launched four hours ago, at the first blush of dawn.

It would not have been a surprise in any case, even if the attackers had stayed on schedule. Rebel cavalry scouts, undistracted by the blue troopers taking their rest at Haxall's Landing, and lookouts in the Spotsylvania belfry, surveying the Union rear with glasses, had reported the countermovement yesterday. That left only the question of just where on the left the blow was going to land, and this in turn was answered by Ewell's outpost pickets, who came back in the night to announce that the assault would be delivered from the Mule Shoe.

At first the defenders could not credit their luck; this must be a feint, designed to cover the main effort elsewhere. An artillery major, whose battalion had lost eight of its twelve guns in the dawn assault six days ago, reported later that he and his cannoneers "could not believe a serious attempt would be made to assail such a line as Ewell had, in open day, at such a distance," but he added that "when it was found that a real assault was to be made, it was welcomed by the Confederates as a chance to pay off old scores." Pay them off they did, and with a vengeance, from the muzzles of 29 guns commanding the gorge of the abandoned salient and the shell-ripped woods beyond, first with round shot, then with case and canister as the Federals pressed forward "in successive lines, apparently several brigades deep, well aligned and steady, without bands, but with flags flying, a most magnificent and thrilling sight, covering Ewell's whole front as far as could be seen." The conclusion was foregone, but the gunners made the most of their opportunity while it lasted. Double-timing over the mangled corpses of the fallen, the attackers managed to reach the abatis at scattered points, only to find the fire unendurable at that range. They fell back with heavy losses and the worst wounds of the campaign, and when they reëntered the woods they had emerged from, such a short time back, the guns fell silent, not out of mercy, but simply to save ammunition in case the attack was resumed. It was not. "We found the enemy so strongly intrenched," Meade admitted in a letter to his wife, "that even Grant thought it useless to knock our heads against a brick wall, and directed a suspension." By 10 o'clock the one-sided carnage was over, and nowhere along the line had the opposing infantry come to grips. "This attack fairly illustrates the immense power of artillery well handled," Ewell's chief of artillery said proudly.

Perhaps by now, if not earlier, Grant had learned the error of his statement to Halleck, a week ago today: "I am satisfied the enemy are very shaky." By now perhaps he also had discovered the basis for what had seemed to him the overexaltation of Lee by many high-ranking Federals, who had not agreed with their new general-in-chief that the Virginian would be likely to fall back in haste from the Rapidan when he found the blue army on his flank. "Lee is not retreating," Colonel Theodore Lyman of Meade's staff wrote home that night. "He is a brave and skillful soldier and will fight while he has a division or a day's rations left." As for the troops who served the gray commander, wretchedly fed and clad though they were, Lyman considered them anything but shaky. "These rebels are not half starved," he added. "A more sinewy, tawny, formidable-looking set of men could not be. In education they are certainly inferior to our native-born people, but they are usually very quick-witted, and they know enough to handle weapons with terrible effect. Their great characteristic is their stoical manliness. They never beg or whimper or complain, but look you straight in the face with as little animosity as if they had never heard a gun fired."

Indeed, at this stage of the contest, there was a good deal more disaffection in the Union than there was in the Confederate ranks. "We fought here. We charged there. We accomplished nothing," a blue artillerist complained, while a disgruntled infantryman protested specifically, in the wake of this second Mule Shoe fiasco, that the army was being mishandled from the top. The Wilderness had been "a soldier's battle," he said, in which no one could see what he was doing anyhow. "The enlisted men did not expect much generalship to be shown. All they expected was to have battle-torn portions of the line fed with fresh troops. There was no chance for a display of military talent." But that was not the case at Spotsylvania, he went on. "Here the Confederates are strongly intrenched, and it was the duty of our generals to know the strength of the works before they launched the army against them." He was bitter, and the bitterness was spreading: not without cause. There was a saying in the army, "A man likes to get the worth of his life if he gives it," and the

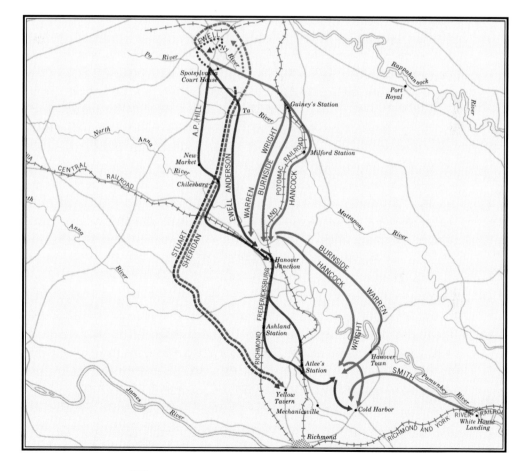

This map depicts movements of the Confederate and Union forces from Spotsylvania to Yellow Tavern, Hanover Junction, and Cold Harbor in May 1864.

★

survivors here could not see that their fallen comrades, shot down in close-packed masses flung off-schedule against impregnable intrenchments, had gotten the smallest fraction of the worth of theirs.

Whatever else he saw (or failed to see; he was admittedly not much given to engaging in hindsighted introspection) Grant saw clearly enough that something else he had said in the week-old letter to Halleck was going to have to be revised, despite the wide publicity it had received in the newspaper version: "I propose to fight it out on this line if it takes all summer." Stalemate was little better than defeat, in his opinion, and yet — having assaulted headlong twice, without appreciable success, and tried in vain to turn both enemy flanks — that seemed the best he could do in this location. Ten May days were a long way short of "all summer," yet they sufficed to show that he had nothing to gain from continuing the contest on "this line." So he decided, quite simply, to abandon it: not, of course, by retreating (retreat never entered his mind) but by shifting his weight once more with a wide swing around Lee's right, in the hope once more that he would catch him napping. Still without his cavalry to serve as a screen for the movement and keep him informed of his adversary's reaction — although it was true Sheridan had failed him in both offices before — he decided to try a different method of achieving Lee's destruction. He would mousetrap him.

Hancock was to be the bait. Grant's plan, as set forth in orders issued next morning, May 19, was for the II Corps to march that night to the Richmond, Fredericksburg & Potomac Railroad, six miles east, then down it on the far side of the Mattaponi River to Milford Station, well beyond Lee's flank and deep in his right rear. Lee could be expected to try to overtake and destroy Hancock, and this would mean that he would be exposed to the same treatment by Grant, who would give Hancock about a twenty-mile head start before moving out with the other three corps for a leap at the gray army whose attention would be fixed on the bright lure dangling off its flank, beyond the Mattaponi. That was the plan, and there was about it a certain poetic justice, since it was a fairly faithful reproduction of what Lee himself had done to Pope on the plains of Manassas — except that he had lacked the strength to follow it through to the Cannae he was seeking, whereas Grant did not, having just received about half of the more than 30,000 reinforcements sent from Washington over a ten-day period starting four days ago. By way of preparation for the move, he shifted Burnside around to the far left on May 18, returned Wright to his former position alongside Warren, and placed Hancock in reserve beyond the Ni, ready to take off promptly the following night on the march designed to lure Lee out of his Spotsylvania intrenchments and into open country, where he would be exposed to slaughter.

First, though, there was a delay involving bloodshed. On the day whose close was scheduled to see Hancock set out eastward, Lee lashed out at the denuded Federal right.

★

Richard Stoddard Ewell set out on a reconnaissance of Union positions near the Ni River on May 19.

Alert to the possibility that Grant might steal a march on him, the Confederate commander, on receiving word that morning that the Federals had resumed their ponderous sidle to his right, ordered Ewell, who held the left, to test the validity of the report by making a demonstration to his front. Though he was down to about 6000 effectives — considerably less than half his infantry strength two weeks ago, when he opened the fight in the Wilderness — Ewell, feeling perky as a result of his easy repulse of yesterday's assault, asked if he might avoid the risk of a costly frontal attack, in case the Yankees were still there, by conducting a flank operation. Lee was willing, and Ewell took off shortly after noon on a reconnaissance in force around the end of the empty-looking — and, as it turned out, empty — Union works. Accompanied by Hampton's two brigades of cavalry, he carried only six of his guns along because of the spongy condition of the roads, and even these he sent back when he reached the Ni, about 3 o'clock, and found the mud too deep for them to make it over, although Hampton managed to get his four lighter pieces across by doubling the teams. So far, Old Bald Head had encountered nothing blue; but presently, he reported, less than a mile beyond the river, on his own in what had been the Federal right rear, "I came upon the enemy prepared to meet me."

What he "came upon" was Warren's flank division, posted beyond the Ni as a covering force for Hancock, whose corps was getting ready to take off eastward after sundown. Responding to orders from headquarters to reinforce Warren instead, Hancock sent his largest division first — a new one, just arrived the day before from Washington, under Brigadier General Robert Tyler — and followed with Birney's three bled-down brigades. Tyler had been a heavy artilleryman until recently, and so had all his men, except that, unlike him, they had seen no combat up to now.

Their reception by the Army of the Potomac was unkind, to say the least. In addition to the usual taunts — "Why, dearest, did you leave your

earthworks behind you?" — they were greeted by the veterans, who were returning from their botched and bloody assault down the Mule Shoe, with a
gruesome demonstration of what was likely to happen to infantry in battle.
"This is what you'll catch up yonder," the wounded told them, displaying
shattered arms and other injuries Ewell's batteries had inflicted at close range.
One roadside group had a mangled corpse which they kept covered with a
blanket until one of the oversized greenhorn regiments drew abreast, and
then they would uncover it with a flourish. The heavies had been singing as
they marched, perhaps to keep their courage up, but they fell silent under the
impact of this confrontation with what was left of a man who had been where
they were headed. As it happened, the attack was suspended before they were
committed. That was yesterday, however. This was today, and they were about
to discover at first hand what combat meant.

Ewell, having found what he came looking for — or, to put the case
more critically, having blundered into what he had been in search of — would
have been glad to withdraw without bloodshed, but the bluecoats gave him no
choice except to fight, not only at a numerical disadvantage, but also without
guns to take up the challenge from the many turned against him. The resultant
two-hour struggle, which began about 5.30, might well have completed the
destruction of Lee's Second Corps if Wade Hampton had not managed to post his

*A Federal burial detail prepares temporary
graves for soldiers who died of wounds received in the
fighting in the Wilderness and at Spotsylvania.*

★

rapid-firing battery of horse artillery where it could hold the enemy off while Ewell fell back across the Ni and returned under cover of darkness to his intrenchments, minus another 900 of his men. The Federals lost a good deal more — 1535 killed or wounded or missing, most of them Tyler's — but at least they could claim a victory, having remained in control of the field and taken no less than 472 prisoners. A larger gain was the admission of the heavies to full membership in the army that had greeted them with jeers the day before. They had made up in staunchness, even veterans agreed, for what they lacked in skill. "Well, they got a little mixed and didn't fight very tactically," one of their officers replied to a question from a correspondent, "but they fought confounded plucky."

This last was good news for Grant, who was going to have to depend increasingly on such replacements in the weeks ahead. Three days ago, on May 16, with 12,000 of his cavalry away, his strength was down to 56,124 effectives — less than half the number he had mustered when he crossed the Rapidan, twelve days before. About 35,000 of the absent were battle casualties, lost in the Wilderness and here at Spotsylvania. Another 4000-odd had fallen sick and been sent to Washington hospitals to recover or to die. The rest, a substantial 14,000, were deserters or men whose enlistments had expired, members of the first of the thirty-six regiments scheduled for discharge when their time was up in May and June. There was, therefore, much encouragement for Grant in this May 19 evidence that he could count on the heavies, as well as on the newly drafted troops among them, for staunchness during the critical period in which they learned their bloody trade and became, in their turn, veterans more or less like the men who had jeered at them on their arrival but now would jeer no more.

In any case, he depended on them to lend their weight to whatever blows he decided to throw, and he did not let his heavy losses for the past two weeks, on and off the field of battle, deter him from his purpose, which was to whip the rebel army in the process of maneuvering it back on Richmond. Today's affair amounted to no more than an interruption, a twenty-four-hour delay. He would move out tomorrow night, as planned: with one exception, one revision prompted by Ewell's sortie across the Ni that afternoon, which apparently served to remind Grant just how bloody-minded Bobby Lee could be. Instead of sending Hancock well in advance of the other three corps, to be dangled as bait on the east bank of the Mattaponi, he decided to move at a much closer interval, lest the bait be gobbled before the rest of the army came up in support. Accordingly, orders were sent, not only to Hancock, but also to Warren, Wright, and Burnside, that the march to Milford Station would begin tomorrow night, May 20, and would be conducted with all possible secrecy — in the hope, once more, of stealing a march on old man Lee.

But no amount of secrecy could hide what Lee already knew as a result of Ewell's rather heavy-handed investigation of the Union dispositions in his front.

Confederate dead await burial at the Alsop farm.
More than 18,000 rebels were killed or wounded during
the Wilderness and Spotsylvania battles.

Grant had stripped his right for another shift in the opposite direction, and Lee prepared for another interception, alerting all three of his corps commanders to be ready to march at the tap of a drum. Despite such precaution, the enemy would of course move first; yet Lee had little fear that he would lose the pending race, whenever it began. He had chosen Hanover Junction as his point of concentration just beyond the North Anna, at the crossing of the two critical rail lines back to Richmond. From there he believed he would be able to parry any thrust the Federals were likely to attempt, and this time — unlike the last, in the sprint for Spotsylvania — he would have the advantage of the interior route of march, traveling the chord of the arc his adversary's movement would necessarily describe.

His confidence, in this as in much else, was based on the events of the past two weeks; especially on a comparison of losses. Though he did not know the precise figures, even for his own army, let alone Grant's — the latter had suffered a total of 36,065 casualties (17,666 in the Wilderness, 18,399 at Spotsylvania) while Lee was losing barely half as many (just under 8000 in the Wilderness, just over 10,000 at Spotsylvania) — he knew that Grant's were disproportionately heavy. No opponent, so far, had been able to sustain such losses without removal from command or frustration of his plans by Washington; nor, he hoped, would this one, despite his known tenacity and his reported unconcern for costs. Lee's confidence was in himself and in his men. "With the blessing of God, I trust we shall be able to prevent General Grant from reaching Richmond," he had told the President ten days ago, and that trust had been confirmed. Moreover, though it was true the contemplated shift to Hanover Junction would mean giving up half the region between his present position and the capital in his rear, the line of the North Anna was one of great natural strength, highly dangerous for an army attempting to cross it, as Grant's would do, in the face of determined resistance. Besides, he was presently to remind Davis, "[Grant's] difficulties will be increased as he advances, and ours diminished."

One reason for this — in addition, that is, to the advantageous lengthening and shortening of their respective lines of supply and communication, vulnerable to attack by raiders and tedious to maintain — was that Lee would be moving toward the first reinforcements he had been able to count on, or even contemplate with any real degree of hope, since the opening of Grant's triple-pronged offensive. The reason he could count on them now was that two of the Federal prongs had, in effect, been snapped off short in the course of the past week. Breckinridge, out in the Shenandoah Valley, and Beauregard, on the far side of the James, had scored tactical successes which served not only to neutralize or abolish the separate threats from those directions by Franz Sigel and Ben Butler, but also to convert at least a part of each of those two outnumbered and hard-pressed Confederate forces into reserves, available for rapid shipment by rail to the Army of Northern Virginia from the south and west; which, incidentally, was still another reason for Lee's choice of Hanover Junction, where the two lines met and crossed from Richmond and the Valley, as his point of concentration after leaving Spotsylvania.

By May 20, with the evidence getting heavier by the hour that the Federals in his immediate front were about to begin their march around his right, Lee called on both victorious commanders — Breckinridge by orders wired directly, since he was already under his command, and Beauregard by means of an urgent request to the War Department — to hasten the departure for Hanover Junction of every soldier they could spare from those two fronts.

It was well that he specified haste, for the signs of Grant's imminent departure continued to multiply all day. By nightfall Lee was so convinced that the Federals were about to march that he decided to begin his own next morning. Accordingly, he sent instructions for Ewell, whose corps would peel off from the left in order to lead the movement south, to start at daylight unless he saw an opening for a strike at the enemy rear. Old Bald Head, finding no such opportunity, stepped off at 4 a.m. May 21 — a scant six hours, events would show, after Hancock started out across the way.

★ ★ ★

★

*U*nion General Franz Sigel
set his sights on gaining control
of the single road across Massanutton Mountain whose northern
end is pictured here.

New Market;
Bermuda Hundred

Sigel's offensive, like his chief's,
was subdivided into three columns
of penetration, each with a different

1864 ★ ★ ★ ★ ★ ★

preliminary objective to be attained before all three combined for a linkup with Grant's main body in front of Richmond. His own main body, consisting of about 8000 of all arms, would march the length of the Shenandoah Valley, from Winchester to Staunton, where he would strike the Virginia Central Railroad. Crook meantime, with roughly the same number, would move west of the Valley, southward in two columns, one of about 6000 infantry under his personal direction, the other of about 2000 cavalry under Brigadier General W. W. Averell, against the Virginia & Tennessee. Crook's objective was Dublin Station and the nearby railway bridge across New River, Averell's the salt works and lead mines at Saltville and Wytheville, a day's ride west of Dublin: from which point the two would proceed east along the Virginia & Tennessee to Salem, tearing up track as they went, and then turn north, through Lexington, for a hookup with Sigel at Staunton and, subsequently, with Meade somewhere east or southeast along the Virginia Central, which was to be given the same hard-handed treatment as the reunited 16,000 moved along it to be in on the kill when Lee was brought to bay.

Crook's being the more lucrative assignment, at least in the opening stage of the campaign — salt and lead were rare necessities in the Confederacy,

★

Confederates under General Albert Jenkins were routed by a Federal brigade at Cloyd's Mountain.

and the intended double blow at Saltville and Wytheville would go far toward making them rarer — Sigel started first, on April 30, hoping to draw attention and troops away from the region beyond the Alleghenies. It worked. By the time Crook's infantry set out from Gauley Bridge on May 2, beginning the rugged trek from the Kanawha, southward up the left bank of New River to Dublin Station, a roundabout distance of more than a hundred miles, the rebel department commander was busy stripping Southwest Virginia of its few defenders in order to get them aboard trains for rapid shipment to Staunton and a fast march northward, down the turnpike, to challenge Sigel's bid for control of the wheat-rich Shenandoah Valley. Within another three days, when Averell's mounted column began its parallel march on May 5 from Logan Courthouse, fifty miles southwest of Gauley Bridge, the Confederate shift was well under way. Crook made good time, considering the nature of the terrain. At Shannon's Bridge by sunset of May 8, only seven miles from Dublin, he learned that a rebel force was lying in wait for him two miles ahead on a wooded spur of Cloyd's Mountain. A fork-bearded West Pointer, Ohio born and thirty-five years old, a veteran of Antietam and Chickamauga, he rode ahead next morning to look the position over — and found it strong. "They may whip us," he said as he lowered his binoculars, "but I guess not."

He guessed right. The Confederate force of about 3000, part militia and home guards, commanded by Brigadier General Albert Jenkins, a former Charleston lawyer in what was now called West Virginia, was routed by a charge in which one of Crook's brigade commanders, Colonel Rutherford B. Hayes, made a showing that stood him in good stead when he ran for President twelve years later. Jenkins was wounded and taken, along with two of his three guns and many rifles dropped by his green troops when they fled; Union surgeons removed his mangled arm and gave him such care as they had time for, but he died the following week, thirty-three years old and still a captive. His losses at Cloyd's Mountain numbered 538, the Federals' 643.

Crook, overcome by excitement and exhaustion — he had hurried about the contested field with his waterproof boots full of water from crossing a creek — fell to the ground in a faint as soon as he saw that the battle was won, but revived in time, attended by his staff, to order an immediate advance on Dublin and the Virginia & Tennessee Railroad, five miles ahead. Arriving before dark, he put his men to work firing and wrecking the depot installations, along with a large accumulation of military stores, and set out at first light next morning, May 10, to destroy the 400-foot wooden railway bridge across New River, eight miles east. By midday it was burning briskly, and soon afterwards it collapsed with a great hiss of steam into the river. "A fine scene it was," Hayes noted in his diary.

Having thus carried out his preliminary assignment — marching and fighting and wrecking, all three boldly and with skill — Crook now had only to wait for Averell to join him and continue the movement as planned, east along the railroad to Salem, then north through Lexington for the meeting with Sigel at Staunton. Yet he did neither. He not only declined to wait for the cavalry column, he also declined to press on eastward in accordance with his orders. Instead he decided to return at once to West Virginia: specifically to Meadow Bluff, on the Greenbrier River near Lewisburg, where he could draw supplies from Gauley Bridge, his starting point some fifty miles northwest. His reason, as he gave it two weeks later in his report, was that "I saw [at the Dublin telegraph office] dispatches from Richmond stating that General Grant had been repulsed and was retreating, which determined me to move to Lewisburg as rapidly as possible." Isolated as he was, and accepting the rebel claim at face value, he feared that Lee would send troops west by rail from Orange to cut him off and up, and under pressure of this fear he bolted for the fastness of the mountains. Not even the arrival of outriders from Averell, bringing word that the troopers had found Saltville too well guarded for attack but that the column was moving on Wytheville even now, deterred Crook from making as quick a getaway as he could manage. He simply replied that Averell was to do his best to carry out the instructions he himself had just discarded, and took off northward, well beyond New River, which he crossed upstream and down. He made good time. It was five days later, May 15, before the cavalry overtook him at Union, eight miles beyond the West Virginia line.

Averell had a harrowing tale to tell: one that was unrelieved, moreover, by any such tactical victory as Cloyd's Mountain or any such gaudy feat as the demolition of the New River bridge. He had raided in this direction before, with conspicuous success, including the burning of Salem in December, but that had been done against next to no opposition. This time there was not only a considerable force in opposition — as he was told when he reached Tazewell on May 8, just this side of the state line — it was also commanded by John Morgan, who was known to be hungry for revenge for the indignities he had suffered in the Ohio Penitentiary during the four months preceding his year-end breakout.

Now he was back in the field at last, having been rejoined by about 750 of his "terrible men," survivors of the disastrous July raid through Indiana and Ohio, and was posted at Abingdon to work with local units in defense of a department including portions of Southwest Virginia and East Tennessee. At Tazewell Averell learned that the famed Kentuckian had shifted his headquarters and his troops to Saltville when he got word that a blue column was headed that way. What his strength was Averell did not know; he estimated it at 4500, better than twice his own. Consequently, he decided to forgo the scheduled destruction of the salt works, vital though they were to the Confederacy's efforts to feed its armies, and to strike instead directly at Wytheville and the lead mines, leaving Morgan holding the bag at Saltville. He feinted in that direction on May 9, then swung east, riding hard to give the rebels the slip. He thought he had succeeded until, approaching Wytheville the following afternoon, he found Morgan drawn up to meet him at a place called Crockett's Cove.

"My men fought magnificently, driving them from hill to hill. It was certainly the greatest sight I ever witnessed to see a handful of men driving such masses before them."

— John Hunt Morgan

The position was admirably suited for defense, but that was not what Morgan had in mind. Fuming because the approach of the enemy column had delayed a projected return to his native Bluegrass, he charged and struck and kept on charging and striking the rattled Federals, who thus were afforded no chance to discover that they were not outnumbered. "My men fought magnificently, driving them from hill to hill," he wrote his wife that night. "It was certainly the greatest sight I ever witnessed to see a handful of men driving such masses before them. Averell fought his men elegantly, tried time and time again to get them to charge, but our boys gave them no time to form." This was Morgan's first engagement since the late-November jailbreak and he made the most of it until darkness ended the running fight, four miles east of Wytheville. He turned back then for Abingdon, to resume his plans for another "ride" into Kentucky, and Averell, minus 114 of his troopers, limped eastward to Dublin and beyond, where the railroad bridge had toppled hissing into New River that afternoon.

Informed by his outriders that Crook had shied off into the mountains, he forded the river and tore up another ten miles of track and culverts before turning north to overtake his chief at Union on May 15. Hungry because supplies were low, and lashed by heavy rains, the reunited column spent two days getting over the swollen Greenbrier, then trudged upstream to Meadow Bluff, May 19, on the verge of exhaustion.

Crook's infantry had been seventeen days on the march from Gauley Bridge, the last eight without a regular issue of rations, and had crossed seventeen mountain ranges, each a bit steeper, it seemed, than the one before. They had accomplished little, aside from incidental damage to the railroad and the destruction of the New River bridge, but Crook was reassured to learn at Meadow Bluff that his superior, the major general commanding the department, had accomplished even less in the Shenandoah Valley. In fact, it now developed, the wide-swinging western column had been quite right not to press on east and north to Staunton, as instructed, since Sigel had covered barely half the distance from Winchester to that point, marching deliberately up the Valley Pike, before he was obliged to turn and flee back down it, pursued by the victors of the battle that had defined the limit of his penetration.

It was Breckinridge's doing, and he did it on his own. Hearing from Lee in early May, while the Army of Northern Virginia was on its way to the confrontation with Grant in the thickets south of the Rapidan, that he was to assume "general direction of affairs" beyond the Blue Ridge, the former U.S. Vice President, electoral runner-up to Lincoln in the presidential race of 1860, continued his efforts to collect all movable troops in Southwest Virginia for a meeting with Sigel in the Valley. "I trust you will drive the enemy back," Lee had told him, and the tall, handsome Kentuckian, forty-three years old, with lustrous eyes, a ponderous brow, and the drooped mustache of a Sicilian brigand, was determined to do just that. Accordingly, he left the defense of the western reaches of his department to Jenkins and Morgan, scant though their resources would be in event of an attack, and set out for Staunton at once, by rail, with two veteran brigades of infantry totaling just under 2500 men. North of there, and hard at work observing and impeding Federal progress south of Winchester, was Brigadier General John D. Imboden, whose 1500 cavalry were all that would stand in Sigel's path until Breckinridge arrived.

The Kentuckian reached Staunton on May 12 and set off promptly down the turnpike for New Market, forty miles away, where Imboden was skirmishing with advance elements of the blue main body, still a dozen miles to the north. Including these butternut troopers, Breckinridge would go into battle with close to 5000 of all arms: a figure he attained by mustering all the militia roundabout — 750 at the most — and by summoning from Lexington the cadet corps of the Virginia Military Institute, 247 strong, all under conscription age and commanded by one of their professors, who later recalled that although Breckinridge said he hoped to keep these fifteen-, sixteen-, and seventeen-year-olds in reserve through the bloodiest part of the fighting (thus to avoid what Jefferson Davis had

★

*Virginia Military Institute cadets, called
"Katydids" by seasoned veterans, left their castle-like
barracks to fight for the South at New Market.*

referred to as "grinding the seed corn of the nation") he added in all honesty that, "should occasion require it, he would use them very freely."

Occasion was likely to require it. Pleased that he had succeeded in drawing the rebels north and east, away from the now vulnerable installations in Southwest Virginia, Sigel was intent on completing his preliminary assignment by winning control of the Shenandoah Valley before the wheat in its fields was ripe for grinding into flour to feed Lee's army. This would entail whipping the gray force gathering to meet him, and he marched south with that welcome task in mind, anticipating his first victory since Pea Ridge, out in Arkansas more than two years ago, for which he had been made a major general. All the battles he had been involved in since that time, however slightly, had been defeats — Second Bull Run and Fredericksburg were examples — with the result that his demonstrations of military competence had been limited to

★

the conduct of retreats. A book soldier, academy-trained in his native Germany, which he had fled in his mid-twenties after serving as Minister of War in the revolution of 1848, he was anxious to win the glory he had prepared for, though he did not let ambition make him rash.

Advancing from Winchester, up the turnpike that led ninety miles to Staunton, he moved with skill and proper deliberation. There were mishaps, such as the loss of 464 men in a cavalry regiment surprised and captured by Imboden while on outpost duty beyond Front Royal, May 11, but Sigel knew how to accept such incidental reverses without distraction, even though this one, combined with the need for detaching troops to guard his lengthening supply line, reduced his combat strength to roughly 6500 of all arms. Past Strasburg by then, he kept his mind on the job ahead and continued his march up the pike to Mount Jackson, terminus of the Manassas Gap Railroad, on May 14. This was only seven miles from New Market, occupation of which would give him control of the single road across Massanutton Mountain and thus secure his left flank practically all the rest of the way to Staunton. He had sent his cavalry ahead to seize the crossing of the north fork of the Shenandoah River, two miles south of Mount Jackson, and when they arrived that afternoon they were taken under fire by a rebel battery posted on a height just over a mile beyond the bridge. They settled down to a brisk artillery exchange, preparing to force a crossing, but Sigel — perhaps recalling what had happened three days ago, when nearly 500 other troopers had been gobbled up near Front Royal — sent word that he preferred to wait until the infantry came up next morning, when all arms would combine to do the thing in style.

Breckinridge was within earshot of the cannonade. Just arrived from Staunton with his two brigades, plus the VMI cadets, he was taking a late after-noon dinner with Imboden at Lacy Springs, a dozen miles to the south, and when he heard the guns begin to rumble he told the cavalryman to return at once to New Market, hold the crossing of the North Fork till dark if possible, then fall back to a position just this side of the town, where he would join him before daybreak. Imboden, with Sigel's coöperation, carried out these instruc-tions to the letter. Awakened at dawn by the arrival of the infantry — Sunday, May 15 — he assisted in getting the troops in line for what was intended to be a defensive battle. But when sunrise gave a clear view of the field, Breckinridge studied it carefully through his glasses and changed his mind. Sigel's men had crossed the river at first light to take up a position astride the turnpike north of town, and the Kentuckian apparently liked the looks of what he saw. "We can attack and whip them here," he said. "I'll do it."

And did. While the Confederates were adjusting their dispositions for attack, the guns on both sides — 28 of them Union, opposed by half as many firing north — began exchanging long-range shots across the rooftops of the town. This continued for an hour, at the end of which the gray line started forward, one brigade on the right, the other on the left, with a regiment of dismounted cavalry between them on the pike, supported by the cadets whose spruce uniforms had resulted in their being greeted with cat-calls by veterans on the march; "Katydids," they called them. Imboden struck first with a horseback charge through some woods on the right, and the infantry went forward

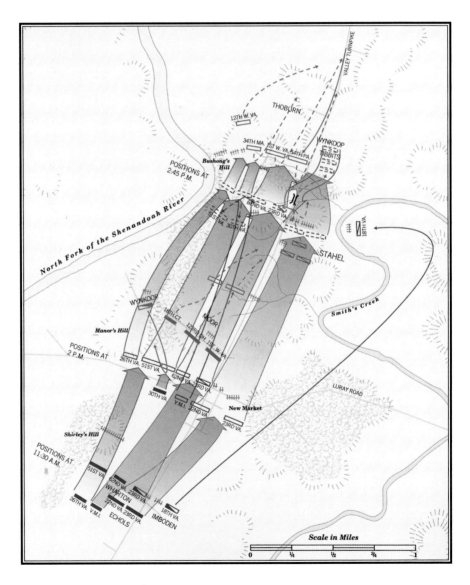

*A*t the Battle of New Market, Breckinridge's
*Confederate forces, including cadets from Virginia Military
Institute, routed the Federals under Franz Sigel.*

★

through the town, cheered by citizens who came running out to meet them. On the far side, they scattered the blue pickets, then went for the main line. Sigel disengaged skillfully and fell back half a mile, disposing his troops on high ground to the left and right of a hillock on which a six-gun battery was slamming rapid-fire shots into the ranks of the advancing rebels. Spotting this as the key to the position, Breckinridge ordered the dismounted troopers to charge and take it, supported by the cadets; which they did, though only by the hardest, not only because of heavy fire from the well-served artillery, but also because of a gully to their front, less than two hundred yards from the fuming line of guns and floored with what turned out to be calf-deep mud.

Moreover, as the movement progressed, it was the troopers who were in support. Lighter, more agile, and above all more ardent, the cadets made better time across the soft-bottomed depression, and though they were hit repeatedly with point-blank canister, they soon were among the cannoneers, having suffered better than twenty percent casualties in the charge: 8 killed and 46 wounded. Slathered with clay and stained by smoke, many of them barefoot, having lost their shoes and socks in the mud of the gully, the survivors were scarcely recognizable as yesterday's dapper Katydids. But they carried the position. "A wild yell went up," Imboden would remember, "when a cadet mounted a caisson and waved the Institute flag in triumph over it."

Sigel was in his element. Lean-faced and eager, not yet forty, his lank hair brushed dramatically back to bring out his sharp features and brief chin beard, he maintained an icy, steel-eyed posture under fire, but betrayed his inner excitement by snapping his fingers disdainfully at shellbursts as he rode about, barking orders at his staff. Unfortunately, he barked them in German, which resulted in some confusion: as, for example, when he directed that two companies of a West Virginia regiment move up to protect the six-gun battery under attack by the cadets. "To my surprise," he later protested, "there was no disposition to advance. In fact, in spite of entreaties and reproaches, the men could not be moved an inch!" And when the rest of the gray line surged forward to take advantage of the respite gained by the boy soldiers, there was nothing Sigel could do but attempt another displacement, and this he did, as skillfully as he had performed the first, though at a considerably higher cost.

By now he was back on the knoll from which the rebel horse artillery had challenged his crossing of the river yesterday, four miles north of town. He held on there, through a lull occasioned by the need for refilling the cartridge boxes of the attackers, and when they came on again he fell back across the North Fork, burning the bridge behind him. Secure from pursuit, at least for the present, he intended to stand his ground despite heavy losses (831 killed and wounded and missing, as compared to the enemy's 577) but decided a better course would be to retire to Mount Jackson, where he could rest and refit before

Cadets charge forward during the Battle of New Market in this painting by Benjamin West Clinedinst for Jackson Memorial Hall at the Virginia Military Institute.

resuming his interrupted southward march. He got there around 7 o'clock that evening, took up a stout position, and remained in it about two hours before concluding that the wisest course, after all, would be to return to Strasburg, another twenty miles back down the pike. A night march got him there the following afternoon, and after one more trifling readjustment — rearward across Cedar Creek next morning, May 17, to make camp on the heights he had left a week ago — he finished his long withdrawal from the unfortunate field of New Market and began making incisive preparations for a return.

But that was not to be; not for Sigel at any rate. Stymied at Spotsylvania, Grant was growing impatient at having heard nothing of or from his director of operations beyond the Blue Ridge. "Cannot General Sigel go up Shenandoah Valley to Staunton?" he wired Halleck, who replied that, far from advancing, Sigel was "already in full retreat. . . . If you expect anything from him you will be mistaken," Halleck added. "He will do nothing but run. He never did anything else." Grant was furious: about as much so as he was with Banks,

★

whose Red River fiasco came to an end that same week. Four days later, on May 21, Franz Sigel was relieved of his over-all command.

Lee on the other hand was delighted with his lieutenant's conduct of affairs in that direction, and was quick to express his gratitude. "I offer you the thanks of this army for the victory over General Sigel," he wired Breckinridge on the morning after the battle. "Press him down the Valley, and if practicable follow him into Maryland." This last was in line with the suggestion he had made to Stonewall Jackson, two years ago today, at the outset of the campaign that had frightened the Washington authorities into withholding troops from McClellan's drive on Richmond, and he hoped that it might have the same effect on Grant's more energetic effort. In any event, New Market had saved the wheat crop in what was called "the bread basket of Virginia," and even if Breckinridge lacked the strength to undertake a crossing of the Potomac, it at least freed a portion of his command to reinforce the army north of Richmond. Lee, in a follow-up telegram that same day, left the decision to the general on the scene. "If you can follow Sigel into Maryland, you will do more good than by joining us," he wired. "[But] if you cannot, and your command is not otherwise needed in the Valley or in your department, I desire you to prepare to join me."

Breckinridge answered next morning that he preferred the latter course. He would move, he said, with 2500 men. Anticipating the shift from Spotsylvania, Lee replied: "Proceed with infantry to Hanover Junction by railroad. Cavalry, if available, can march."

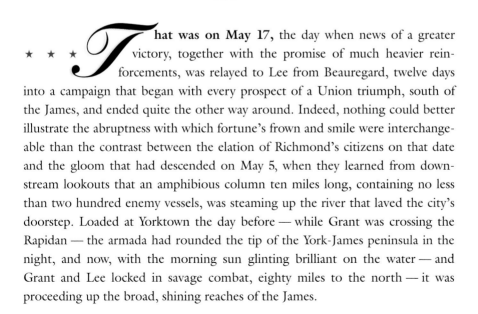

★ ★ ★ That was on May 17, the day when news of a greater victory, together with the promise of much heavier rein-forcements, was relayed to Lee from Beauregard, twelve days into a campaign that began with every prospect of a Union triumph, south of the James, and ended quite the other way around. Indeed, nothing could better illustrate the abruptness with which fortune's frown and smile were interchange-able than the contrast between the elation of Richmond's citizens on that date and the gloom that had descended on May 5, when they learned from down-stream lookouts that an amphibious column ten miles long, containing no less than two hundred enemy vessels, was steaming up the river that laved the city's doorstep. Loaded at Yorktown the day before — while Grant was crossing the Rapidan — the armada had rounded the tip of the York-James peninsula in the night, and now, with the morning sun glinting brilliant on the water — and Grant and Lee locked in savage combat, eighty miles to the north — it was proceeding up the broad, shining reaches of the James.

★

Five ironclads led the way and other warships were interspersed along the line of transports, a motley array of converted ferries, tugs and coasters, barges and canal boats, whose decks were blue with 30,000 soldiers, all proud to be playing a role in what seemed to one of them "some grand national pageant." What was more, they had a commander who knew how to supply the epitomizing gesture. Riding in the lead, Ben Butler brought his headquarters boat about, struck a pose on the hurricane deck, and steamed back down the line. As he sped past each transport, past the soldiers gaping from its rail, he swung his hat in a wide vertical arc toward the west and lurched his bulky torso in that direction, indicating their upstream goal and emphasizing his belief that nothing could stop them from reaching it in short order. Unaware that within two weeks he and they were to wind up caged — or, as his superior was to put it, "corked" — they cheered him wildly from ship after ship as he went by, then cheered again, even more wildly, as he turned and churned back up the line, still waving his hat and lunging his body toward Richmond.

After dropping one division off at City Point, within nine miles of Petersburg, the flotilla proceeded north, past the adjoining mouth of the Appomattox River, and debarked the other five divisions at Bermuda Hundred, a plantation landing eighteen crow-flight miles from the rebel capital. Ashore, as afloat, the gesticulating Butler rode with the van, and close up he was even stranger-looking than he had been when viewed across the water; "the strangest sight on a horse you ever saw," one witness thought, attempting a word portrait of the former Massachusetts senator who shared with Banks, though he was more than a year his junior at forty-five, the distinction of being the U.S. Army's ranking active major general. "With his head set immediately on a stout, shapeless body, his very squinting eyes, and a set of legs and arms that look as if made for somebody else and hastily glued to him by mistake, he presents a combination of Victor Emmanuel, Aesop, and Richard III, which is very confusing to the mind. Add to this a horse with a kind of rapid, ambling trot that shakes about the arms, legs, etc. till you don't feel quite sure whether it is a centaur or what it is, and you have a picture of this celebrated General."

Benjamin Butler landed his troops at Bermuda Hundred during the Federal push toward Richmond.

Despite the reckless, bloated look, the oddly assorted members, and the disconcerting squint of his mismatched eyes, Butler was all business here today. Mindful of Grant's injunction that he was to "use every exertion to secure footing as far up the south side of the river as you can, and as soon as you can," he landed the bulk of his army just short of the first of the half dozen looping bends or "curls" of the James, where the Confederates had heavy-caliber guns sited high on the steep bluffs to discourage efforts to approach the city by water, and next morning he began to comply with another item in his instructions: "Fortify, or rather intrench, at once, and concentrate all your troops for the field there as rapidly as you can."

Five miles west of Bermuda Hundred, between Farrar's Island and Port Walthall, the James and the Appomattox were less than four miles apart. By intrenching this line he would be safe from a frontal attack, while the rivers secured his flanks and rear. It was true, the Bermuda debarkation required a crossing of the Appomattox to reach either City Point or Petersburg, but this was better, Butler reasoned — bearing in mind Grant's double-barreled admonition "that Richmond is to be your objective point, and that there is to be coöperation between your force and the Army of the Potomac" — than having to cross it in order to reach the fattest and probably best-defended prize of all. By sundown of May 6, his first full day ashore, he not only had completed the preliminary intrenchment of the line connecting the bends of the two rivers, he also had sent a brigade of infantry another two or three miles west to look into the possibility of cutting the railroad between Petersburg and Richmond, which in turn afforded the rebel defenders their only rail connection with the Carolinas and the reinforcements they no doubt were calling for, even now, in their distress at his appearance on their doorstep.

Encouraged by a report from the brigadier who conducted the reconnaissance (he had run into spirited resistance on the turnpike, half a mile short of the railroad, but nothing that could not be brushed aside, he thought, by a more substantial force) Butler decided next morning to go for the railroad in strength, then turn southward down it to knock out Petersburg and thus assure that his rear would be unmolested when he swung north to deal with Richmond. While the others kept busy with axes and spades, improving the earthworks protecting their base from attack, four of the fourteen brigades in the two corps, each of which had three divisions, moved out to attend to this preamble to the main effort: three from Gillmore and one from Major General W. F. Smith, whose third division had debarked at City Point and was still there, despite his protest that it "might as well have been back in Fort Monroe." The march was along the spur track from Port Walthall, and their initial objective was its junction with the trunk line, three miles west.

As they approached it around midday, a spatter of fire from the skirmishers out front informed them that the junction — grandly styled Port Walthall Junction, though all it contained was a run-down depot and a couple of dilapidated shacks — was defended. The four brigades came up in turn to add their weight to the pressure being exerted, but the rebels either were there in heavy numbers or else they were determined not to yield, whatever the odds. This continued for two hours, in the course of which the Federals managed to overlap one gray flank and tear up about a quarter mile of track on the main line. But that was all. At 4 o'clock, having suffered 289 casualties, Butler decided to retire behind his fortifications and return in greater strength tomorrow; or, as it turned out, the day after.

Both good and bad news awaited him, back on Bermuda Neck. The bad was from the navy, which had sent a squadron out the day before to investigate an account by a runaway slave that the Confederates had torpedoes planted thickly in the James, especially in the vicinity of Deep Bottom, a dozen miles up the winding river from Bermuda Hundred. It was all too true: as the crew of the big double-ender *Commodore Jones* found out, about 2 o'clock that afternoon. A 2000-pound torpedo, sunk there some months ago and connected by wires to galvanic batteries on the bank, "exploded directly under the ship with terrible effect, causing her destruction instantly." So her captain later reported from a bed in the Norfolk Naval Hospital. Another witness, less disconcerted because he was less involved, being aboard another gunboat, went into more detail. "It seemed as if the bottom of the river was torn up and blown through the vessel itself," he wrote. "The *Jones* was lifted almost entirely clear of the water, and she burst in the air like an exploding firecracker. She was in small pieces when she struck the water again." For days, bodies and parts of bodies floated up and were fished out of the James; the death toll was finally put at 69.

Just now, though, the problem of how to keep the same thing from happening over and over again was solved by the capture of two men caught lurking in the brush where the batteries were cached. They had triggered the explosion, and what was more they had helped to plant other such charges up ahead. They refused to talk, however, until one of them was placed in the bow of the lead vessel and the squadron continued its upstream probe: whereupon, in the words of an interrogator, he "signified his willingness to tell all."

That more or less solved the problem of torpedoes (in any case, of the ones already planted; future sowings were of course another matter) but next day, about the time the four brigades began their skirmish down the spur track from Port Walthall, the navy was given a violent reminder that older dangers, familiar to sailors long before anyone thought of exploding powder under water, still threatened the existence of the fleet. U.S.S. *Shawneen*, a 180-ton sidewheel gunboat on patrol at Turkey Bend, dropped anchor under the loom of Malvern Hill to give her crew time out for the midday meal, only

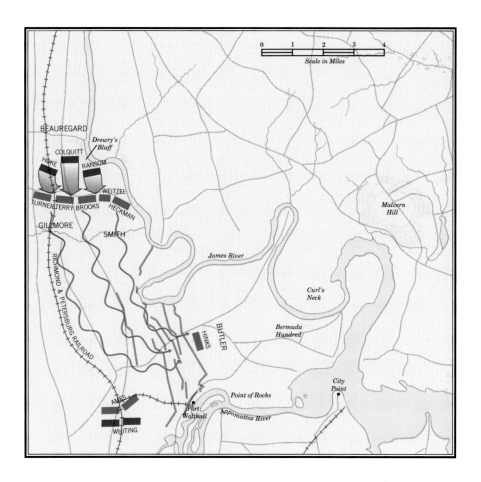

*A*t Bermuda Hundred, Butler ordered his army
to intrench and probe the enemy line for ten days before
launching the attack on the rebels at Drewry's Bluff.

to have it interrupted when a masked battery and four companies of Confederate infantry opened fire from the north bank, peppering the decks with bullets and puncturing the steam drum. While most of the crew went over the side to keep from being scalded, *Shawneen*'s captain ordered her colors struck to save the lives of the injured still aboard. Ceasing fire, the rebel colonel in command sent out a boat to remove survivors and blow the vessel up; "which was effectively done," he reported, "consigning all to the wind and waves."

Such was the bad news — bad for Butler because it meant that the navy, having lost two ships in as many days, was likely to be reluctant to give him the slam-bang close support he would want when he moved against or beyond the high-sited batteries on Chaffin's and Drewry's bluffs, fortified works

★

flanking the last tortuous upstream bend of the river below Richmond, both of them integral parts of the hard-shell outer defenses he would have to pierce if he was to put the hug on the rebel capital. The good news came from his cavalry, two brigades combined in a 3000-man division under Brigadier General August Kautz, a thirty-six-year-old German-born West Pointer. Off on his own while the rest of the army was steaming up the James, Kautz rode due west out of Suffolk on May 5 for a strike at the Petersburg & Weldon Railroad, damage to which would go far toward delaying the arrival of enemy reinforcements from the Carolinas. Encountering little opposition he did his work in a slashing style: first at Stony Creek on May 7, where he burned the hundred-foot railway bridge twenty miles south of Petersburg, and then next day at the Nottoway River, another five miles down the line, where he put the torch to a second bridge, twice as long, before turning north to rejoin the army two days later at City Point.

Encouraged by news of the first of these two burnings, which reached him on May 8, Butler spent that day in camp, secure behind his Bermuda Neck intrenchments, putting the final touches to his plans for a movement against Petersburg next morning, much heavier than the one that had taken him only as far as Port Walthall Junction the day before.

This time he got a solid half of his infantry in motion, 14,000 in all. Smith, on the left, again ran into fire as he approached the Junction and called on Gillmore, who had advanced by then to Chester Station unopposed, to come down and join the fight. Gillmore did, although regretfully, having just begun to rip up track and tear down telegraph wire along the turnpike. But when the two corps began to maneuver in accordance with a scheme for bagging the force at the Junction, the graybacks slipped from between them and scuttled south. Pursuing, the Federals found the Confederate main body dug in behind unfordable Swift Creek, three miles north of Petersburg, which in turn lay beyond the unfordable Appomattox.

When Butler came up to observe their fruitless exchange of long-range shots with the enemy on the far side of the creek, Gillmore and Smith informed him that Petersburg couldn't be taken from this direction. The thing to do, they said, was return at once to Bermuda Neck and lay a pontoon bridge across the Appomattox at Point of Rocks, which would permit an attack on Petersburg from the east. Fuming at this after-the-fact advice from the two professionals, Butler replied testily that he had no intention of building a bridge for West Pointers to retreat across as soon as things got sticky, and Smith later declared that he found this remark "of such a character as to check voluntary advice during the remainder of the campaign."

Tempers got no better overnight. Contemplating the situation next morning, with the uncrossable creek still before him, Butler decided that Petersburg was of little importance anyhow, now that Kautz had burned two bridges on the railroad in its rear. Accordingly, he ordered everyone back to Bermuda Neck, there to regroup for an advance to be made on Richmond as soon as he got his plans worked out. They returned the following day, May 11, filing in through gaps in the intrenchments around noon, and Butler retired to his tent to think things over for a while.

If he was bitter, so were his lieutenants, contrasting what had been so boldly projected with what had been so timidly and erratically performed. In Smith's opinion, based on what he had seen in the past six unprofitable days, the army commander was "as helpless as a child on the field of battle and as visionary as an opium eater in council." Butler returned the compliment in kind, including Gillmore in the indictment. Both generals, he said, "agreed upon but one thing and that was how they could thwart and interfere with me," while, to make matters worse, neither of them "really desired that the other should succeed." Feeling his reputation threatened (in the North, that is; in the South he was already known as "Beast" Butler, hanger of patriots, insulter of women) he had written to Stanton two nights ago, from the near bank of Swift Creek, reviewing his progress to date and placing it in the best possible light, even though this involved a rather ingenuous reinterpretation of his share in Grant's over-all design for the crushing of Lee and the taking of Richmond.

"We can hold out against the whole of Lee's army," he informed the Secretary, and he added for good measure: "General Grant will not be troubled with any further reinforcements to Lee from Beauregard's force."

★ ★ ★ *L*ee of course had no intention of attacking Butler, who was not even in his department, and though it was true he wanted reinforcements from any source whatever, he certainly expected none from the general opposing the southside threat, since, at the outset at least, that unfortunate commander — George Pickett, of Gettysburg fame — had practically no troops to fight with, let alone detach. He had, in all, fewer than 750 of all arms to stand in the path of the 30,000 Federals debarking at Bermuda Hundred and City Point, nine miles respectively from Drewry's Bluff and his district headquarters at Petersburg, whose garrisons were included in the total that showed him facing odds of forty-to-one or longer. Beauregard, sixty-five miles to the south at Weldon, which he had reached two weeks ago to assume command of the newly created Department of North Carolina and Southern Virginia, replied to an urgent summons from Richmond on May 5 that he was "indisposed," too ill to take the field. Three brigades were en route from his old command at Charleston; he would do his utmost to speed them northward, so long at least as the railroad stayed in operation, and would come up in person as soon as he felt well enough to travel. In the meantime, though, he left it to Pickett to improvise as best he could a defense against the host ascending the James.

Pickett himself was not even supposed to be there, having received orders the day before to proceed by rail to Hanover Junction and there await the arrival of his four brigades — two of which were now with Hoke in the movement against New Bern, down the coast, while the other two were with Major General Robert Ransom, charged with defending Richmond north of the James — for a reunion with Lee's army, then on its way eastward into the Wilderness to challenge Grant's advance. The long-haired Virginian looked forward to returning to duty under Longstreet, whose guidance he had missed these past eight months on detached service. Warned of the landings downriver today, however, he stayed to meet the threat to the near vacuum between the James and the Appomattox, although he was to regret profoundly, in the course of the next five days, that he had not caught an earlier northbound train. Those five days, May 5-10, were an unrelenting nightmare, illuminated from time to time by flashes of incredible luck which then were seen to have served perversely, not to resolve, but rather to prolong the strain on his jangled nerves.

Fortunately, two regiments from the first of the three promised brigades from Charleston reached Petersburg on the morning of May 6, and Pickett got these 600 Carolinians up the turnpike in time to delay the advance of the brigade Butler sent probing for the railroad. They managed this, though only by the hardest, and just as they were about to be overrun they were reinforced by a brigade sent down from Richmond: Tennesseans who had arrived that morning under Brigadier General Bushrod Johnson, the first of two western outfits summoned east to replace Pickett's two brigades in the capital defenses. Johnson was a heavy hitter, as he had shown by spearheading the Chickamauga breakthrough, and his attack drove the reconnoitering Federals back on the line of intrenchments constructed that day across Bermuda Neck. Pickett told Johnson to dig in along the pike, and then — reinforced by the rest of the Charleston brigade, which came up after midnight to lift his strength to about 3000 — settled down to wait, as best his tormented nerves would permit, for what tomorrow was going to bring.

What tomorrow brought was Butler's four-brigade attack, 6000 strong, and news that Kautz had burned the bridge over Stony Creek, cutting off hope for the early arrival of more troops from the south. One reinforcement Pickett did receive, however, and this was Major General D. H. Hill, famed for a ferocity in battle rivaling that of his late brother-in-law Stonewall Jackson. His caustic tongue having cost him lofty posts in both of the Confederacy's main armies — together with a promotion to lieutenant general, withdrawn when he fell out with Bragg after Chickamauga — Hill had offered his services to Beauregard as an aide-de-camp, and Beauregard sent him at once to Petersburg to see if

Pickett thought he could be of any help. Pickett did indeed think so, and put the rank-waiving North Carolinian in charge of the two brigades in position up the turnpike. Hill handled them so skillfully in the action today around Port Walthall Junction, losing 184 to inflict 289 casualties on a force twice the size of his own, that Butler pulled back, more or less baffled, and spent what was left of that day and all of the next, May 8, brooding behind his Bermuda Neck intrenchments.

Greatly relieved by this turn of events, Pickett experienced a mixed reaction to news that Hoke's projected attack on New Bern had been a failure, due to the nonarrival of the *Albemarle*, which had retired up the Roanoke River on May 5 after a three-hour fight with seven Union gunboats in the Sound from which the ironclad took her name. She had inflicted severe damage on her challengers and suffered little herself, except to her riddled stack, but the engagement had proved her so unwieldy that her skipper decided there was no hope of steaming down into Pamlico Sound to repeat at New Bern the victory she had helped to win two weeks ago at Plymouth. This meant that, without the support of the ram, Hoke's scheduled attack had to be called off: which in turn freed him and his five brigades, including the two from Pickett, for use elsewhere. Nowhere were they needed worse than at Petersburg, and Pickett was pleased to learn that they were to join him there by rail from Goldsboro — though when they would arrive was even more doubtful now than it had been the day before, word having just come in that Kautz had burned a second railway bridge, this one across the Nottoway, twice the length of the first and therefore likely to require about twice the time to replace.

Offsetting this last, there was good news from above. While Hill was making his fight for the Junction, the second western brigade reached Richmond — Alabamians under Brigadier General Archibald Gracie, another Chickamauga hero — and was sent across the James by Ransom, who not only followed in person but also brought along Pickett's other pair of brigades and posted all three in the works around Drewry's Bluff, bracing them for a stand in case the Federals turned in that direction. This addition of 4500 troops, combined with Pickett's remnant and the two brigades with Hill, increased the strength of the

August Kautz foiled the rebel's plans to bring reinforcements from the south by burning two bridges.

southside force to about 8000, roughly one third the number Butler had on Bermuda Neck. Pickett was greatly encouraged by this reduction of the odds — and so, apparently, was Beauregard, who wired from Weldon on May 8: "The water has improved my health." Whether the cause was the water or the buildup (not to mention the strangely hesitant performance by Pickett's opponent, who seemed to be groping his way piecemeal toward eventual destruction) the Louisiana general announced that he soon would be well enough to come to Petersburg and lift the awesome burden of responsibility from the district commander's shoulders.

By then Butler had ended his spell of brooding, and next morning he came on again, this time with half his army, only to pull up short on the north bank of Swift Creek, whose presence he seemed not to have suspected until now. Beauregard arrived the following day, May 10, in time to watch the baffled Army of the James — so Butler styled it — fade back once more from approximate contact and set out rearward to find sanctuary within its fortifications. Coming

---

The Hero of Sumter had specialized in providing on short notice various blueprints for total victory, simple in concept, large in scale, and characterized by daring.

---

fast behind him on the railroad were seven veteran brigades of infantry, Hoke's five from Goldsboro and two more from Charleston. All reached Petersburg by nightfall, having marched across the five-mile gap between the Nottoway and Stony Creek, where they got aboard waiting cars for the last twenty miles of their ride. Pickett's five days were up at last, and rather as if the strain had been what kept him rigid, after all, he collapsed and took to his bed with a nervous exhaustion vaguely diagnosed as "fever."

To replace him, Beauregard summoned Major General W. H. C. Whiting from Wilmington, and turned at once to the task of organizing the twelve brigades now south of the James into four divisions. Their combined strength was just under 20,000: enough, he thought, to deal with Ben Butler for once and for all by going over to the offensive, provided of course that the Beast could be lured from behind his intrenchments and out from between the two rivers protecting his flanks.

Butler complied, two days later, by moving northward against the works around Drewry's Bluff, apparently having decided to go for Richmond after all. Beauregard had anticipated this by sending Hoke with seven brigades to join Ransom, and now he prepared to follow and take command in person, leaving Whiting to hold Petersburg with the other two brigades of infantry, plus one of cavalry just come up from North Carolina. Arriving at 3 a.m. May 14, after taking a roundabout route to avoid capture, he found that the Federals had driven the defenders from some of the outworks, south and west of Drewry's, and now were consolidating their gains, obviously in preparation for an all-out assault that would open the way to Richmond. The high-spirited Creole, with his big sad bloodhound eyes and his hair brushed forward in lovelocks over his temples, did not quail before this menace; he welcomed it as a chance to catch Butler off balance and drop him with a counterpunch.

Though it came at a rather awkward time, Ransom having detached two brigades two days ago to help fend off Sheridan, whose troopers had broken through the outer defenses north of the capital, Beauregard had a plan involving Grand Strategy which he hoped would provide him with all the soldiers needed to dispose of the threat to Richmond, not only from the south, but from the north as well: not only of Butler, that is, but also of Grant. For three years now the Hero of Sumter had specialized in providing on short notice various blue-prints for total victory, simple in concept, large in scale, and characterized by daring. This one was no exception. In essence, the plan was for Lee to fall back on the capital, avoiding all but rear-guard actions in the process, then send Beauregard 10,000 of his veterans, together with Ransom's two detached brigades, as reinforcements to be used in cutting Butler off from his base and accomplishing his destruction; after which, Old Bory subsequently explained, "I would then move to attack Grant on his left flank and rear, while Lee attacked him in front." He added that he not only "felt sure of defeating Grant," but was convinced that such a stroke would "probably open the way to Washington, where we might dictate *Peace!!*"

Thus Beauregard — at 3 o'clock in the morning. Wasting no time by putting the plan on paper, he outlined it verbally for a colonel on his staff and sent him at once to Richmond with instructions to pass it on without delay to the Commander in Chief. Davis was unavailable at that hour, but Bragg was not. Having heard the proposal, he dressed and rode to Drewry's for a conference with its author. Old Bory was waiting, and launched into a fervent plea for action. "Bragg," he said, "circumstances have thrown the fate of the Confederacy in your hands and mine. Let us play our parts boldly and fearlessly. Issue those orders and I'll carry them out to the best of my ability. I'll guarantee success!" Though non-committal, the grim-faced military adviser listened to further details of the plan and returned to the capital, having promised to lay the facts before the President as soon as possible. This he did: along with his objections, which were stringent.

Not only did the scheme ignore the loss of the Shenandoah Valley and the Virginia Central Railroad, he declared, but "the retreat of General Lee, a distance of sixty miles, from the immediate front of a superior force with no less than 8000 of the enemy's cavalry between him and the Chickahominy . . . at least endangered the safety of his army if it did not involve its destruction." Moreover, he said, such a concentration of troops beyond the James was quite unnecessary; Beauregard already had a force "ample for the purpose of crushing that under Butler, if promptly and vigorously used." Davis agreed that the plan was neither practical nor requisite, and in courtesy to the Louisiana general, as well as out of concern for his touchy pride, he rode to Drewry's Bluff to tell him so in person, in the gentlest possible terms.

Beauregard's spirits drooped; but only momentarily. They rebounded at the President's assurance that Ransom's two brigades, having wound up their pursuit of Sheridan, would be ordered back across the James for a share in the attack, and Old Bory, savoring the prospect of belaboring the Beast who had tyrannized New Orleans, set to work devising a plan for assailing him, first frontally, to put him in a state of shock, and then on the flanks and rear, so that, being "thus environed by three walls of fire, [Butler] could have no resource against substantial capture or destruction, except in an attempt at partial and hazardous escape westward, away from his base, trains, or supplies."

To accomplish this consummation, his first intention was to assemble all twelve infantry brigades at Drewry's for the assault, but then he decided that, instead of waiting for the troops to arrive from Petersburg by a roundabout march to avoid the Federals on the turnpike, he would have Whiting move up to Port Walthall Junction and pitch into their rear when he heard the guns announce the opening of the attack on their front by the other ten brigades, four each

under Hoke and Ransom and two in a reserve division under Brigadier General Alfred Colquitt, who commanded one of the three brigades from Charleston. Notifying Whiting by messenger and the other three division chiefs in person, he set dawn of May 16 as the jump-off hour.

★ ★ ★ *T*hat gave them a full day to get ready, if Butler would only cooperate by remaining where he was. He did just that, though more from ineptness than by design; an attack planned for that day had to be called off when it turned out that he had provided so well for the defense of his newly won position that there were no troops left for the offensive. Butler was not greatly disturbed by this development, apparently having become inured to the fact that fumbling brought delay. For one thing, he had done well these past three days — especially by contrast with the preceding seven — and had encountered only token opposition in occupying the outworks around Drewry's. So had his cavalry, which he unleashed again when he left Bermuda Neck; Kautz had struck the Richmond & Danville two days ago, wrecking switches and culverts, and by now was astride the Southside line, tearing up sections of track. Back on the James, moreover, though the river was too shallow for the iron-clads to proceed beyond City Point, the navy had been persuaded to lend a hand by pushing a few lighter-draft gunboats up to Chaffin's for a duel with the batteries on that bluff. All this should give the rebels plenty to fret about for the next day or two, Butler reasoned; by which time he would be ready to hit them in earnest.

*T*hanks to Butler's ineptitude, the Confederates had time to bring 20,000 reinforcements to Drewry's Bluff (left) — enough to force the Federals to withdraw.

His two corps commanders, while considering themselves honor-barred from tendering any more "voluntary advice," were by no means as confident that the Confederates would be willing to abide a waiting game. Smith, in fact — called "Baldy" from his cadet days when his hair began to thin, though he protested unavailingly nowadays that he still had more of it than did many who addressed him by this unwanted sobriquet — was so disturbed by what he took to be signs of a pending assault on his position that he spent a good part of May 15, a Sunday, scavenging rebel telegraph wire along the turnpike and stringing it from stumps and bushes across his front, low to the ground to trip the unwary; "a devilish contrivance none but a Yankee could devise," Richmond papers were presently to say of this innovation which Burnside had found useful in his defense of Knoxville six months before. Smith hoped it would serve as well here on Butler's right, though he ran out of wire before he reached his flank brigade, nearest the James. He and Gillmore each had two divisions on line; his third was still at City Point, completely out of things, and one of Gillmore's was posted in reserve, back down the pike. The night was dark, soggy with intermittent rain and a heavy fog that seemed to thicken with Monday's dawn, providing a curtain through which — true to Baldy's uncommunicated prediction — the graybacks came screaming and shooting and, as it turned out, tripping over the low-strung wire across much of the Federal right front, where the blow first fell.

Along those hampered portions of the line, Smith was to say, the attackers were "slaughtered like partridges." But unfortunately, as the next phase of the fight would show, there was no wire in front of Gillmore's two divisions on the left; nor was there any in front of the brigade on the far right, where Beauregard was intent on unhinging the Union line, severing its connection with the river, and setting it up for the envelopment designed, as he said, "to separate Butler from his base and capture his whole army, if possible." Struck and scattered, the flank brigade lost five stands of colors and more than 400 prisoners, including its commander, and though the adjoining brigades and Smith's other division stood fast behind their wire, inflicting heavy casualties on Ransom, Gillmore's divisions gave ground rapidly before an advance by Hoke, also losing one of their brigade commanders, along with a good many lesser captives and five guns.

Confusion followed on both sides, due to the fog and the disjointed condition of the lines. Beauregard threw Colquitt in to plug the gap that developed between Hoke and Ransom, and Gillmore got his reserve division up in time to stiffen the resistance his troops were able to offer after falling back. By 10 o'clock, after five hours of fighting, the battle had reached the pendulous climax Old Bory intended for Whiting to resolve when he came up in the Union rear, as scheduled, to administer with his two brigades the rap that would shatter the blue mass into westward-fleeing fragments, ready to be gathered up by the brigade of saber-swinging troopers he was bringing with him, up the railroad

★

The Confederate defenses on Drewry's Bluff included gun emplacements, bomb-proofs, and a well. When Butler withdrew, he was bottled up at Bermuda Hundred.

from the Junction. Two hours ago, a lull in the fighting had allowed the sound of firing to come through from the south. It grew, then died away, which was taken to mean that Whiting had met with slight resistance and would soon be up. Since then, nothing had been heard from him, though Beauregard sent out couriers to find him somewhere down the pike, all bearing the same message: "Press on and press over everything in your front, and the day will be complete."

None of the couriers found him, for the simple yet scarcely credible reason that he was not there to be found. Not only was he not advancing, as ordered, from Port Walthall Junction; he had fallen back in a state of near collapse at the first threat of opposition, despite the protests of subordinates and Harvey Hill, who had reverted to his role of volunteer aide. A brilliant engineer, whose talent had made Wilmington's Fort Fisher the Confederacy's stoutest bastion and who had attained at West Point the highest scholastic average any cadet had ever scored, the forty-year-old Mississippian was cursed with an imagination that conjured up lurid pictures of all the bloody consequences incaution might bring on. Intelligence could be a liability when it took this form in a military man, and Chase Whiting was a case in point for the argument that a touch of stolidity, even stupidity, might be a useful component in the makeup of a field commander. In any event, wrought-up as he was from the strain of the past two lonely days at Petersburg, which he was convinced was about to be attacked by the superior blue force at City Point, he went into something resembling a trance when he encountered sporadic resistance on the turnpike beyond Swift Creek, and ordered a precipitate return to the south bank.

Dismayed, the two brigade chiefs had no choice except to obey, and

★

Hill, though he retired from Whiting's presence in disgust, later defended him from rumors that he had been drunk or under the influence of narcotics. Whiting himself had a simpler explanation, which he gave after the return to Petersburg that evening. Berated by the two brigadiers, who could not restrain their anger at having been denied a share in the battle today, he turned the command over to Hill, "deeming that harmony of action was to be preferred to any personal consideration, and feeling at the time — as, indeed, I had felt for twenty-four hours — physically unfit for action."

Up at Drewry's, the truth as to what was happening below lay well outside the realm of speculation. Expecting Whiting to appear at any moment on the far side of the field, Beauregard abstained from attempting a costly frontal assault, which might or might not be successful, to accomplish what he believed could be done at next to no cost by pressure from the rear. Jefferson Davis, who could seldom resist attending a battle whose guns were roaring within earshot, rode down from Richmond to share in the mystery and the waiting. "Ah, at last!" he said with a smile, shortly before 2 o'clock, when a burst of firing was heard from the direction of Whiting's supposed advance. It died away and did not recur, however, and Beauregard regretfully concluded that it had been produced by a cavalry skirmish, not by an infantry attack. After another two hours of fruitless waiting and increased resistance, the Creole general would report, "I reluctantly abandoned so much of my plan as contemplated more than a vigorous pursuit of Butler and driving him to his fortified base. . . . I therefore put the army in position for the night, and sent instructions to Whiting to join our right at the railroad in the morning."

As it turned out, no "driving" was needed; Butler drove himself. Badly confused by the events of the day — he had lost 4160 killed, wounded, or missing, including two brigade commanders and 1386 other prisoners, as compared to Beauregard's total of 2506 in those three categories — he ordered a nighttime withdrawal to Bermuda Neck. "The troops having been on incessant duty for five days, three of which were in a rainstorm," he informed Washington, quite as if no battle had been fought, "I retired at leisure to within my own lines." Once back there, within the sheltering arms of the two rivers, he busied himself with strengthening his three-mile line of intrenchments, followed by the victorious Confederates, who came up next morning and began digging a three-mile line of their own, studded with guns confronting those in the Union works.

Thus, after two weeks of fitful confusion, in the course of which the Federals suffered just under 6000 casualties to inflict about half as many, a stalemate was achieved; Beauregard could not get onto Bermuda Neck, but neither could Butler get off it. The Beast was caged.

Richmonders exulted in the thought of cock-eyed Butler snarling behind bars, but Grant employed a different simile to describe the outcome of his well-laid plan for obliging Lee to fall back, in haste and probable disarray, to protect the threatened capital in his rear. Angered by the news from Bermuda Hundred, which reached him hard on the heels of equally woeful accounts of what had happened to Banks and Sigel, up the Red and at New Market, he borrowed a phrase from a staff engineer whom he sent to look into the tactical situation beyond the James. Butler's army, he presently reported, "was as completely shut off from further operations directly against Richmond as if it had been in a bottle strongly corked."

As for Beauregard the corker, though he was proud of his victory and its outcome, he was by no means content. "We could and should have done more," he said. "We could and should have captured Butler's entire army." Believing that this could still be done, he returned to his former proposal that he and Lee collaborate in disposing of the enemies before them, except that this time he reversed the order of their destruction. "The crisis demands prompt and decisive action," he notified Bragg on the night of May 18, outlining a plan whereby he would detach 15,000 troops for a flank attack on Grant while Lee pulled back to the Chickahominy. Once Grant was whipped, then Lee would reinforce Beauregard for attending to Butler in much the same fashion. Admittedly the odds were long, but Old Bory considered the prize well worth the gamble, especially by contrast with what was likely to result from not trying at all. "Without such concentration," he declared, "nothing decisive can be effected, and the picture presented is one of ultimate starvation."

Davis agreed that the future seemed bleak, but he could not see that Beauregard's plan, which reached his desk the following morning, was one that would make it rosy. All the previous objections still obtained, particularly the danger to Lee in falling back before a superior blue army reported to be receiving heavy reinforcements almost daily, while he himself got none, and it was to this problem that Davis gave his attention in returning the rejected plan to Bragg. "If 15,000 men can be spared for the flank movement," he noted, "certainly 10,000 may be sent to reinforce General Lee."

This was not at all what Old Bory had had in mind, since it denied him anything more than a subservient role in Richmond's further deliverance from peril. He protested for all he was worth, and not entirely without success. Not 10,000, but 6000 were ordered detached that day, May 20, from the force that manned the intrenchments confronting and corking the bluecoats on Bermuda Neck. Pickett's four brigades, plus one of the three sent up from Charleston in the course of the past week — all five had been scheduled to do so anyhow, before Butler's appearance up the James—left next day to join or rejoin the Army of Northern Virginia.

★ ★ ★

★

A 160-foot pontoon bridge
spans the North Anna at Jericho
Mills, Virginia, where Confederates
surprised the Federal V Corps
on May 23, 1864.

T H R E E

North Anna;
Cold Harbor; Early

1864 ★ ★ ★ ★ ★ ★ *L*ee never **liked the notion** of abandoning any part of the Old Dominion to its foes, but in this case, setting out from Spotsylvania on May 21 to intercept another crablike Union sidle around his right, he not only was moving toward 8500 reinforcements, he also believed he was about to avail himself of his best chance, so far, to "end this business on the battlefield, not in a fortified place." With the two armies in motion, on more or less parallel routes, almost anything could happen, and he was exhilarated, as always, by the prospect. Best of all, though, he looked forward to the confrontation likely to follow on the line of the North Anna, a couple of miles this side of Hanover Junction, where the troops from Breckinridge and Beauregard had been told to join him in time to strengthen the attack he hoped to launch while Grant was astride the deep-banked river.

Moreover, with his army holding the inside track, there was little of the strain there had been two weeks ago in the breakneck race for Spotsylvania; Ewell, whose corps had been withdrawn across the Po at dawn, had barely 25 miles to go on the main-traveled Telegraph Road, while Hancock, whose starting point was the north bank of the Ni, had 34 roundabout miles to cover, by inferior roads and without the customary mass of rapid-firing blue troopers to clear and screen his front. This meant that Lee could avoid exhausting his men on the

★

march and still have plenty of time, at its end, for preparing the ground on which he would stand to deliver the blow he had in mind.

Ewell set off down the Telegraph Road at noon, Anderson four hours later. While Lee waited beside the Po, preparing to follow, A. P. Hill reported himself fit for duty. Despite his pallor, which seemed to deny his claim of recovery, Lee at once restored him to command, with instructions to hold his corps in position till well after nightfall unless the last of the departing Federals pulled out before that time, and sent Early ahead to resume charge of his division under Ewell. He himself left at 8 o'clock that evening. "Come, gentlemen," he told his staff, and turned Traveller's head southward in the twilight.

Two thirds of the way to Hanover Junction, having ridden past Anderson's marchers under the flooding light of a full moon, he took a two-hour rest beside Polecat Creek — which contributed its waters, but fortunately not its name, to the Mattaponi — and reached the North Anna soon after 8 o'clock next morning, about the same time the head of Ewell's column passed over and began filing into position along the south bank, covering Chesterfield Bridge, by which it had crossed, and the railroad span half a mile below, both of which were also protected by bridgeheads set up on the other side. When Anderson arrived at noon, his two divisions extended the line a mile and a half upstream to Ox Ford, the only point along this stretch of river where the right bank was higher than the left. Army headquarters was established in the southwest quadrant of the crossing of the Virginia Central and the Richmond, Fredericksburg & Potomac; Grant was reported to be marching down the latter. Breckinridge was waiting at Hanover Junction with his two brigades, as ordered, and was given a position in line between Anderson and Ewell. Pickett's division was also there (but not its ringleted commander, who was still convalescing from the strain he had been under, south of the James); Lee assigned it temporarily to Hill, who would arrive tomorrow to extend the line a couple of miles beyond Ox Ford, in case the bluecoats tried a flanking movement from that direction when they came up.

For the present, Lee required no digging to be done, partly because he did not know for sure that Grant would attempt a crossing here when he found the graybacks once more in his path, intrenched or not, and also because he wanted to give his soldiers the leisure to enjoy their first full day out of contact with the enemy since the meeting engagement in the Wilderness, seventeen bloody days ago.

Hill arrived the following morning, May 23, coming in from the west shortly before the midday appearance of the Federals from the north. His approach was by the Virginia Central, since he had crossed the North Anna near Beaver Dam by a longer westerly route to guard the wagon train, and Lee had him rest his three divisions, with Pickett's as a fourth, under cover of some woods around Anderson Station, three miles short of Hanover Junction. While

★

the last of his men were filing in to drop their packs in the shade of the trees, the first enemy columns came into sight beyond the river, heavy blue streams flowing sluggishly down the Telegraph Road and the tracks of the RF&P. Greeted by guns emplaced on high ground overlooking Ox Ford, they paused, then resumed their flow as the Union batteries took up the challenge. Short of the ford and the two bridgeheads, they stopped again and engaged the outpost rebels in the kind of long-range firefight known to veterans as a "squabble." Lee was watching with suppressed excitement, foreseeing his chance at another Fredericksburg if Grant would only continue to do as he so much hoped he would, when news arrived from the far left that another Union column was about to force a crossing beyond Jericho Mills, three or four miles above.

Hill was available to counter such an upstream threat, but Lee decided to look into it in person before disturbing Little Powell's road-worn troops. Still weary from his all-night ride two nights ago, and feeling the first twinges of an intestinal disorder, he went in a borrowed carriage to the point that was said to be menaced and studied carefully with his binoculars some bluecoats in a skirt of woods across the river. He took his time, then turned at last to a courier he had brought along. "Go back and tell A. P. Hill to leave his men in camp," he said. "This is nothing but a feint. The enemy is preparing to cross below."

He was both right and wrong in this assessment: right in a lesser, wrong in a larger sense: as he discovered when he got back to headquarters, late that afternoon, and heard the uproar of a sizeable engagement on the far left, in the upstream region he had just returned from. Warren had his whole corps there and by 4.30 had completed a crossing of the river, not at the point where Lee had reconnoitered, but at nearby Jericho Mills — which was in fact "below," as Lee had predicted, but a good deal less so than he apparently had expected. Learning that the Federals had crossed and were advancing southward through the woods in unknown strength, Hill sent Wilcox up to meet them and Heth to follow in support if needed.

Troops from the division of A. P. Hill routed the Federals crossing the North Anna at Jericho Mills.

The action opened briskly, on a promising note. Wilcox, by the luck of the draw, struck Wadsworth's depleted division, now under Brigadier General Lysander Cutler, and drove it back in panic on the other two divisions. At this point, however, things began to go badly for the attackers, who seemed to have forgotten, in the course of more than two weeks of defensive combat, how to function on the offensive. Confused by their quick success, they fought disjointedly when they moved forward to complete the Union rout. Struck in turn, they backpedaled and fell into confusion, glad to make their escape under cover of the woods and a furious rainstorm that broke over them at sundown to end the fighting before Heth arrived to join it. They had lost 642 men in the engagement, veterans who would be sorely missed in battles still to come, and had gained nothing more than the infliction of an equal number of casualties on an enemy who could far better afford the loss.

In any case, here was the first definite indication that Grant intended to attack Lee where he was, rather than continue his march downriver in search of an uncontested crossing, and presently there was another such indication, quite as definite, near the opposite end of the line. Under cover of the rainstorm that ended the Jericho Mills affair at sunset, Hancock launched a sudden two-brigade assault on the Chesterfield bridgehead, which was taken so quickly that the defenders not only had no time to fire the wooden structure in their rear, but also lost more than a hundred of their number killed or captured before they could scramble back across.

This was a small price to pay for the disclosure that the Federals were preparing to attack both Confederate wings tomorrow, above and below Ox Ford. On the off chance that it might be a ruse, employed by Grant to screen another sidle, Lee alerted Anderson to be ready for a downstream march next morning. At the same time, though — before turning in for such badly needed sleep as his cramped bowels would permit — he began devising a trap, the design for which was based on personal reconnaissance of the ground and careful study of the map, for Grant's reception if that general acted on the larger probability that he would hold to the plan whose beginnings had just been disclosed, upstream and down, for a widespread double attack on the gray army fanned out along the south bank of the river to his front.

★ ★ ★   *T*hat was just what the northern commander had in mind, and his confidence that he could bring it off, following up the double attack with a double envelopment, was shared by all around and under him, from major generals down to drummer boys and teamsters. Leaving Spotsylvania on May 21, however, after sixteen unrelenting, unavailing days of combat (waged at an average cost of 2300 casualties a day, as compared to Lee's 1100) the blue marchers had been discouraged by this second tacit admission that, despite their advantage in numbers and equipment and supplies, whenever the tactical situation was reduced to a direct confrontation, face to face, it was they and not their ragged, underfed adversaries who broke off the contest and shifted ground for another try, with the same disheartening result.

"Now what is the reason that we cannot walk straight through them with our far superior numbers?" a Michigan soldier asked, and after ruling out individual skill as a factor in the equation — "We fight as good as they" — came up with two possible answers: "They must understand the country better, or there is a screw loose somewhere in the machinery of our army."

Presently though, moving southeast, then south, and then south-southwest through a region so far untouched by war, with well-tended crops along the road and plenty of fence rails available for campfires at the end of each day's march, they perceived once more that the shift was not only sideways but forward. It was Lee, not Grant, who was yielding ground, and sooner or later — sooner, at this rate, for the march to the North Anna was better than twice the length of the one two weeks ago, out of the Wilderness — the southern commander would have none left to yield. Then would come the showdown, the last battle: which, after all, was the only one that counted in the long run, the only one they really had to win to win the war. And steadily, as this conviction grew, so did their confidence in themselves and the man who led them. A Massachusetts regiment, having crossed the Mattaponi on the morning of May 23, was slogging down the railroad, past a siding, and saw Grant, in his now tarnished uniform, perched on a flatcar gnawing a ham bone. When the New Englanders gave him a cheer he responded with a casual wave of the bone, which he then went back to. They liked that in him. It seemed to them that this singleness of purpose, this refusal to be distracted, was as characteristic of his way of fighting as it was of his way of eating. He was giving Lee the kind of attention he gave the ham bone, and it seemed to them that the result might be the same, just ahead on the North Anna — or if not there, then somewhere else this side of Richmond, where Lee would finally run out of space for backing up.

Grant believed the showdown would come here; anyhow he acted on that premise when he came within sight of the river around midday. Warren having taken the lead by turning south at Guiney Station, eight miles short of Milford, he sent him upstream to Jericho Mills and kept Hancock, who followed close behind, marching straight ahead to confront the rebels defending Chesterfield Bridge and the railroad span below. He had hoped that Lee would venture after him for an all-out scrap in the open country south and east of the Mattaponi, but since the old fox had declined the challenge there was nothing for Grant to do, as he saw it, but go for Lee where he now was. As for turning back, he had just finished making this practically impossible by closing down his Belle Plain base on the Potomac, severing all connection with that river except by sea, and opening another at nearby Port Royal on the Rappahannock. If Lee eluded him here on the North Anna he was prepared to leapfrog his base southward again when he took up the pursuit, thus keeping his supply line short and easily defended. But he did not intend to be eluded; he intended to fix the rebel army where it was by striking both of its flanks at once and moving around them to gain its rear; in which case, disadvantaged though the defenders would be, as to position as well as numbers, Lee would have no choice except to fight the showdown battle his adversary was seeking.

Soon after sunset Grant was pleased to learn that all was going well upstream and down. Warren, having crossed unmolested at Jericho Mills, had repulsed a savage attempt by A. P. Hill to drive him back across the river. He was intrenching now, as a precaution, and would press on south and east tomorrow, to strike and turn the rebel left. Hancock too was ready for full offensive action, having seized the approaches to Chesterfield Bridge by driving off or capturing the hundred or so graybacks attempting to hold it. He would cross at first light, under

On May 23, two days before this photograph was taken, Winfield Scott Hancock's Federals seized the approaches to Chesterfield Bridge, shown here.

★

instructions to serve the enemy right in much the same fashion. Burnside and Wright would be up by then, and they too would have a share in the attack, Burnside by crossing at Ox Ford to exert pressure against the center, thereby helping to fix the defenders in position, and Wright by crossing in Warren's wake to extend his right and make certain that rebel flank was overlapped and overwhelmed.

Such were the orders, and Grant turned in for a good night's sleep, with high hopes for tomorrow. These were encouraged, first thing next morning, May 24, by reports from the left and right. Hancock crossed dry-shod, unopposed, as did Wright upstream at Jericho Mills, following Warren, who encountered only token opposition when he proceeded southeast down the Virginia Central Railroad and the south bank of the river. While Burnside moved into position for a lunge across Ox Ford, good news came from Sheridan that he would be rejoining today, winding up his fifteen-day excursion down to Richmond and the James; Grant was pleased to have him back, along with his 11,000-odd troopers, presumably to undertake the welcome task of gathering up Lee's fugitives at the climax of the movement now in progress. Meantime, awaiting developments across the way, the general-in-chief attended to certain administrative and strategic details, the first of which was the incorporation of the IX Corps into the Army of the Potomac, thus ending the arrangement whereby Burnside, out of deference to his rank, had been kept awkwardly independent of Meade so far in the campaign.

Two other matters he also attended to in the course of the day, both having to do with rectifying, as best he could, the recent setbacks his diversionary efforts had suffered out in the Shenandoah Valley and down on Bermuda Neck. Sigel's successor, Major General David Hunter, was given specific instructions to accomplish all that Sigel had failed to do, and more; that is, to march up the Valley to Staunton, proceed across the Blue Ridge to Charlottesville, and continue from there southwest to Lynchburg, living off the country all the way. As for Butler, though there was no serious thought of removing him from command despite his ineptness, Grant now viewed his bottled army as a reservoir from which idle soldiers could be drawn for active service with the army still in motion under Meade. Accordingly, he was ordered to load a solid half of his infantry aboard transports — under Baldy Smith, whom Grant admired — for immediate shipment, down the James and up the York, to the Army of the Potomac. These 15,000 added reinforcements might or might not be useful, depending on what came of the maneuver now in progress across the North Anna.

Reports from there were beginning to be mixed and somewhat puzzling, not so much because of what was happening, but rather because of so much that was not. First off, finding Ox Ford covered by massed batteries frowning down from the high ground just across the way, Burnside felt obliged to state that any attempt to force a crossing at that point would result in nothing better than a bloodying of the water. Grant saw for himself that this was all too true, and accordingly changed the ruff-whiskered general's orders to avoid a profitless repulse. Leaving one division to keep up a demonstration against the ford, which in fact would serve his purpose about as well, Burnside was told to send his other two divisions — his fourth was still detached, guarding supply trains — upstream and down, to strengthen the attacks on the rebel left and right. But there was where the puzzlement came in. Neither Hancock nor Warren, who by now had been joined by Wright, had met with even a fraction of the resistance they had expected to encounter in the course of their advance. Enemy pickets did little more than fire and fall back at the slightest pressure, they reported. Except for the presence of these few graybacks, together with those in plain view on the high ground opposite Ox Ford, Lee's army might have vanished into quicksand. They found this strange, and proceeded with caution, scarcely knowing what to expect.

All Grant could do, under the circumstances, was approve the caution and advise a continuation of the advance, southeast from the right and southwest from the left. Sooner or later, he felt certain, Hancock and Warren would come upon the rebels lurking somewhere between them, over there, and grind them up as if between two millstones.

★ ★ ★   *L*ee rose early, despite a difficult night, and rode again in the borrowed carriage to visit A. P. Hill near Anderson Station. There he learned the details of yesterday's botched attack on Warren, made piecemeal by a single gray division, when a concerted blow by all the available four would have taken full advantage of the original blue confusion to wreck a solid quarter of Grant's army. Contrasting what might have been with what now was — Warren smashed, with Warren advancing southeast through the woods — Lee turned on Little Powell. "Why did you not do as Jackson would have done," he fumed: "thrown your whole force upon those people and driven them back?"

Red-bearded Little Powell had fallen out rather spectacularly, at one time or another, with every other superior he had ever had, including Longstreet and the general whose spirit was being invoked; but he held onto his temper now, rebuked though he was in the presence of his staff, and accepted from Lee, without protest, what he would never have taken from any other man. For one thing, he was aware of the justice of the charge, and for another he could see that Lee was not himself. Unaccustomed to illness, the gray commander had lost his balance under pressure of his intestinal complaint, and lashed out at Little Powell in an attempt to relieve the strain.

None of this was evident, however, when he moved on to the question of how to deal with the advancing Federals. This had to do with the preparation of the topographical trap he had devised the night before; Ewell and Anderson were already at work on their share of it on the right and in the center, down the rail-road east of Hanover Junction and along the river in the vicinity of Ox Ford.

The North Anna was no more defensible here at close range than the Rappahannock had been at Fredericksburg, for the same reason that the opposite bank, being higher, permitted the superior Union batteries to dominate the position — all, that is, but a brief stretch of the south bank overlooking Ox Ford and extending about half a mile below. Here the Confederate batteries had the advantage, and here Lee found the answer to his problem: not of how to prevent a crossing, which was practically impossible anywhere else along the line, but of how to deal with the Federals once they were on his side of the river. He would hold this stretch of high ground with half of Anderson's corps, strongly supported by artillery, and pull the other half, along with all of Ewell's, back on a line running southeast to Hanover Junction, just east of which there was swampy ground to cover this new right flank. Similarly, Hill would occupy a line extending southwest from Ox Ford to a convenient northward loop of Little River, just west of Anderson Station. Intrenched throughout its five-mile length, this inverted V, its apex to the north and both flanks securely anchored, would provide compact protection for Lee's army, either wing of which could be rein-forced at a moment's notice from the other. Best of all, though, it not only afforded superb facilities for defense; it also gave him an excellent springboard for attack. By stripping one arm of the V to a minimum needed for holding off the enemy on that side, he could mass his troops along the other arm for an attack on that isolated wing of the blue army: *which* wing did not matter, since either would have to cross the river twice in order to reinforce the other, and would therefore not be likely to arrive in time to do anything more than share in the disaster. Here was something for Grant to ponder, when and if he saw it. But the hope was that he wouldn't see it until it blew up in his face.

Leaving Hill to get started on the intrenchment of the western arm, Lee rode back to his headquarters to await developments that would determine which Union wing he would assault. Ewell and Anderson, with Breckinridge still between them, were hard at work, the former having been reinforced by the fifth of the five brigades sent up from Richmond. So skillful were the men by now at this labor, which they formerly had despised as unfit for a white man to perform, that by midday formidable earthworks, complete with slashings and abatis, had risen where none had been six hours before. This augured well for the springing of the trap, once the bluecoats came within snapping distance of its jaws. While Lee waited, however, his intestinal complaint grew worse, and though he tried to attend to administrative matters as a distraction, they only served to heighten his irascibility. The result was fairly predictable. "I have just told the old man he is not fit to command this army!" a flustered aide protested as he emerged from the tent where he had been given a dressing-down by Lee.

Before long it was obvious that the charge, though highly irreverent, was true. Even the general himself had to admit it by taking to his cot, betrayed by his entrails on the verge of the crisis he hoped to resolve by defeating, with a single well-planned attack, the foe who had maneuvered him rearward across forty miles of his beloved Virginia in the past twenty days. If Lee could not deliver the blow, then no one could. It was too late to send for Beauregard, and none of his three ranking lieutenants — one-legged Ewell, who was also nearing physical collapse, or sickly Hill, who had shown only the day before that he was in no condition for larger duties, or lackluster Anderson, who had been less than three weeks in command of anything more than a division — seemed capable of exploiting the present opportunity, which would vanish as soon as the Federals

★

*M*en of the 50th
New York Engineers
cut a road along the
south bank of the
North Anna at
Jericho Mills in this
photograph taken by
Timothy O'Sullivan.

spotted the danger and reacted, either by intrenching or by pulling back across the river for a crossing farther down, beyond reach of the trap that had been installed for their undoing. Time was passing all too fast, and the chance, once gone, might never recur. Lee on his cot broke out vehemently against this deprivation of the victory he felt slipping from his grasp.

"We must strike them a blow," he kept saying. "We must never let them pass us again. We must strike them a blow!"

Betrayed from within, he raged against fate — and rightly; for before the day was over his worst fears were realized. Hancock, nudging down from his crossing at Chesterfield Bridge, and Warren and Wright, skirmishing fitfully all the way from Jericho Mills, came at last upon what the old gray fox had devised for their destruction. Not only were the works about as formidable as the ones they had assaulted with little success at Spotsylvania, but the rebels were still at work with picks and shovels, adding traverses at critical points to avoid exposure to enfilade fire. Moreover, the blue generals were not long in perceiving that such fortifications might have an offensive as well as a defensive use.

They took a good hard look and went into a frenzy of digging, east and west, throwing up intrenchments of their own against the attack they believed might come at any moment from either arm of Lee's inverted V. And while they dug they sent headquarters word of the situation, best described years later by Evander Law, commander of one of the three Alabama brigades in the works ahead: "Grant found himself in what may be called a military dilemma. He had cut his army in two by running it upon the point of a wedge. He could not break the point, which rested upon the river, and the attempt to force it out of place by striking on its sides must of necessity be made without much concert of action between the two wings of his army, neither of which could reinforce the other without crossing the river twice; while his opponent could readily transfer his troops, as needed, from one wing to the other, across the narrow space between them."

This was no more apparent to Law, then or later, than it presently was to Grant, who quickly sent down orders canceling the attack. It was apparent, too, that as soon as a withdrawal could be effected without heavy losses, the thing to do was get back out of there. Meantime, the digging progressed and dirt continued to fly. Fortunately the graybacks seemed content with such long-range killing as their snipers and artillery could manage, but this did little to relieve the feeling on the Union side that they had once more been outgeneraled. This was their twentieth day of contact, and the showdown was no closer within their reach than at the outset. Dejection was taking its toll, along with the profitless wear and tear of the past three weeks. "The men in the ranks did not look as they did when they entered the Wilderness," one among them would recall. "Their uniforms were now torn, ragged, and stained with mud; the men had grown thin and haggard. The experience of those twenty days seemed to have added twenty years to their age."

All night they stayed there, and all next day and the following night, still digging, while Grant pondered the situation. He had never liked the notion of backing away from any predicament, most of which he had found would resolve themselves if he held on long enough for the enemy's troubles, whether he knew what they were or not, to be enlarged by time and idleness to unbearable proportions; in which case, he had also found, it was his adversary who got jumpy and pulled back, leaving the field to him. That was not likely to happen here, although Lee's headquarters had been shifted three miles down the RF&P from Hanover Junction, on his doctor's orders to provide a more restful atmosphere for the still ailing general. Fretful and regretful though he was that his well-laid trap had gone unsprung, Lee looked now to the future and the chance to devise another that would not fail. "If I can get one more pull at him," he said of Grant this morning, "I will defeat him."

But that was not likely to happen here either. On May 26, their second day of confronting the Confederates with a divided army, the Federals put on the kind of show that generally preceded a withdrawal and a shift. There were demonstrations along the river and both arms of the fortified V, together with an upstream probe by a full division of cavalry, as if for a crossing in that direction: a likely course for Grant to follow, Lee believed, since it would keep him on the direct route to Richmond and at the same time deprive Lee of the use of the Virginia Central, his only rail connection with the Shenandoah Valley, which not only provided most of the food his army ate but was also his classic route for a counteroffensive designed to frighten the Washington authorities out of their military wits, as he had done twice already to bring about the calling-off or the

Fretful and regretful though he was that his well-laid trap had gone unsprung, Lee looked now to the future and the chance to devise another that would not fail.

recall of invasions by Hooker and McClellan, last year and the year before. Though he preferred a downstream Union sidle, which he hoped would eventually put Grant in much the same position as the one that had brought Little Mac to grief two years ago, astride "the confounded Chickahominy," Lee followed his usual intelligence procedure of assuming that his adversary would do what he himself would have done in his place. For that reason, as well as the evidence of the cavalry demonstration, he thought the shift would be upstream, for a crossing beyond his left.

He was wrong: as he found out next morning, in plenty of time to rectify his error with a rapid southward march, still on the chord of the arc the Federals were traveling. Grant had pulled back under cover of darkness and set off down — not up — the North Anna, which combined with the South Anna, five miles southeast of Hanover Junction, to become the Pamunkey. The Pamunkey in turn combined with the Mattaponi to become the York, another forty miles below, but Grant marched only about one third of this distance down the left bank for a crossing at Hanovertown, which put him within fifteen miles of Richmond, ten miles closer than he had been on the North Anna. That was not his only reason for preferring to repeat his accustomed sidle to the left, around Lee's right; he would also be keeping in close touch with his supply base, leapfrogging it south once more as he moved in that direction.

As for leaving the Virginia Central in Confederate control, he counted on Hunter to conquer the Valley, now that Breckinridge had departed, and thereby deny its use to Lee even as a source of supplies, let alone as a possible avenue of invasion. Besides, he saw the outcome of this latest confrontation not as a repulse — which in fact it was, with far-reaching effects, despite its comparative bloodlessness (he had suffered only 1973 casualties, and Lee less than half that number) — but rather as conclusive proof that the opposing army had lost its fabled sting. If the rebels would not fight him there on the North Anna, with all the advantage they had secured through Lee's admitted engineering skill, they apparently were in no condition to fight him anywhere at all. Knowing nothing of Lee's debility, he assigned its results to the deterioration of the force his adversary commanded.

"Lee's army is really whipped," he informed Halleck on the day he set out down the Pamunkey. "The prisoners we now take show it, and the action of his army shows it unmistakably. A battle with them outside of intrenchments cannot be had. Our men feel that they have gained the *morale* over the enemy, and attack him with confidence. I may be mistaken," he summed up, "but I feel that our success over Lee's army is already assured."

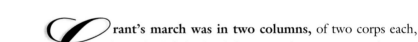

Grant's march was in two columns, of two corps each, along the left bank of the Pamunkey; Warren and Burnside crossed at Hanovertown, Wright and Hancock four miles short of there. Preceded by Sheridan's troopers, who had little to do on the way down but brush off prowling scouts, all four corps passed over on pontoon bridges between noon and midnight, May 28, and though they were delayed by a rackety seven-hour cavalry fight near Haw's Shop, three miles beyond the river, by nightfall of the following day the whole army had pushed south and west to Totopotomoy Creek, which had its beginnings above Atlee, a station on the Virginia Central about midway between the James and the South Anna, and flowed sluggishly eastward a dozen miles to join the Pamunkey just below Hanovertown. Weary from better than forty miles of marching — southeast for two days, then southwest for another — the Federals approached the marsh-fringed creek at last, within ten miles of Richmond, only to find Lee drawn up to meet them on the opposite bank, guns emplaced and all three corps arrayed for battle.

He had been there two days
waiting for Grant to make a commitment. Before sundown of May 27,
whose dawn showed the enemy gone
from the North Anna, he had covered
the eighteen miles from Hanover Junction to Atlee, where he took up a position from which he could block a variety
of approaches by the wide-ranging
bluecoats, either around the headwaters
of the Totopotomoy, which would put
them back astride the vital railroad
north of Richmond, or down across the
creek for a five-mile sprint to the Chickahominy and a quick descent on the
capital only four miles beyond.

Still obliged by his intestinal
disorder to continue using the borrowed carriage, he rode in the lead with
Ewell's corps — but not with its commander, who made the trip in an ambulance, racked by the same malady that
afflicted Lee. Ewell was so much worse
next day that he had to yield his place to
Early and accept a sick leave of indefi-
nite length; which meant that the army
now had two of its three corps, four of

*David Hunter was 62 years old
when he took command of Federal
forces in the Shenandoah Valley.*

its nine infantry divisions, and sixteen of its thirty-five original brigades under
men who had not led them at the start of the campaign.

Warned that elements of the Union host were across the Pamunkey at
Hanovertown, Lee sent Hampton and Fitzhugh Lee to Haw's Shop to discover
whether the crossing included infantry — and, if so, where it was headed. Unless
he knew that, he could not move out to meet the invaders, lest they slip around
one of his flanks for a lunge at Richmond from the north or the northeast.

The result was the largest cavalry engagement since Brandy Station,
just under a year ago. After seven hours of savage combat, mounted and dismounted, with heavy losses on both sides — especially in a green South Carolina
brigade whose troopers arrived in time for a share in a fight that converted the
survivors into veterans overnight — Fitz and Hampton were obliged to give
ground, but not before they had driven Sheridan's horsemen back on their
supports and taken prisoners from both the V and VI Corps, which gave Lee at

least half the information he was seeking. Grant's infantry was indeed over the Pamunkey, already beyond Haw's Shop, and next day it began working its way south and west along the north bank of the Totopotomoy, still without disclosing whether it intended to cross or round the creek.

Fixed in position east of Atlee until he knew the answer, the southern commander by now had received 10,000 reinforcements. This amounted to about half his losses so far in the campaign: whereas Grant had received some 40,000, roughly the number he had lost in battle. Such disproportionate attrition could have but one result, and Lee implied as much that afternoon to Jefferson Davis, who rode out from the capital to see him for the first time since the opening of the Federal offensive.

Further reinforcements would have to come from south of the James, of course, and the President was doubtful that any could be spared from there; Beauregard had been protesting all week that his force — which he had regrouped into two divisions, under Robert Hoke and Bushrod Johnson, and which he kept reminding the Commander in Chief was all that kept Butler's still-bottled army from making a sudden breakout and a dash for the back

Supply wagons of Warren's Federal V Corps cross
a pontoon bridge over the Pamunkey River at
Hanovertown, Virginia, on their way to Cold Harbor.

★

door of Richmond — had been bled down to, maybe past, the danger point. Davis made it fairly clear, before he left, that the question of detaching more troops from beyond the James would depend to a large extent on the judgment of the commander of that department.

That evening Beauregard himself appeared at Atlee for a conference, the upshot of which was that, while he sympathized with Lee in all his troubles, he could not see that they were any larger than his own. As for evidence advanced by Lee that Butler was sending men to Grant, the dapper Creole admitted that perhaps 4000 had left Bermuda Hundred aboard transports in the past few days, but he stressed the claim that a substantial 24,000 still remained to pop the cork he was trying to hold in place with only half as many troops. "My force is so small at present," he had told Davis earlier today, "that to divide it for the purpose of reinforcing Lee would jeopardize the safety of the part left to guard my lines, and would greatly endanger Richmond itself." The most he would agree to was a further study of the situation on his front, and with that he departed to return there, leaving Lee no better off, even in prospect, than he had been when the rather baffling conference began.

Next morning, May 30, Grant pressed down closer along the Totopotomoy, massing opposite Anderson in the center and overlapping Early on the right; Hill, on the left, had only cavalry in his front. That seemed to rule out the Virginia Central as the enemy objective, and presently this view was strengthened by reports that two of the four blue corps had crossed downstream and were taking up a position on the near bank, facing west. Lee believed he saw now what the Federals were up to, and also how to head them off: "After fortifying this line they will probably make another move by their left flank over toward the Chickahominy. This is just a repetition of their former movements. It can only be arrested by striking at once at that part of their force which has crossed the Totopotomoy."

These words were included in a message instructing Anderson to support Early, whose corps, being on that flank, would lead the attack designed to discourage this latest sidle around the Confederate right to gain the Old Church Road, which led down across Beaver Dam Creek to Mechanicsville, where the Seven Days had opened in flame and blood. But even if he was successful in dealing with the immediate threat to Richmond from this line, Lee saw a larger danger looming. Beyond the Chickahominy lay the James, where McClellan had found sanctuary after the holocaust of Malvern Hill. Fortunately, the Washington authorities had not seen fit to sustain him in his position on the north bank of that river, nor to approve his proposal that he cross it for a movement against Richmond from the south, astride its lines of supply from Georgia and the Carolinas. Grant was no Little Mac, however, and the high command might well have learned a lesson from what had followed its failure to sustain his predecessor. In speaking to Early, who was preparing to attack at midday, Lee did not

Lee told Jubal Early (right), the new commander of the Second Corps, to destroy Grant's army before it reached the James River in order to avoid a siege.

say, as he had said to Anderson, that the Federal threat must be "arrested"; he said, rather, that the Federals themselves must be destroyed. Otherwise the contest would come down to what he wanted to avoid, the loss of all freedom to maneuver.

"We must destroy this army of Grant's before he gets to James River," he told Early. "If he gets there it will become a siege, and then it will be a mere question of time."

Unfortunately, Early came closer to wrecking his newly inherited corps than he did to destroying even a portion of Grant's army. Repeating Hill's error at Jericho Mills, he attacked with one division and failed to bring the other two up promptly to exploit the initial success. Counterattacked from Bethesda Church, his objective on the Old Church Road, he barely managed to hold his ground, and Anderson only arrived in time for a share in the defensive action. Lee rebuked neither of them for the botched performance, in part because they were busy intrenching their new line, which at least forestalled an advance down the ridge between Beaver Dam and Totopotomoy creeks, and in part because of a report that reached him about the time it became apparent that the attack had failed — a report so alarming in its implications that it took precedence over his other dire concerns. Grant's new supply base was at White House Landing, fifteen miles down the Pamunkey from Hanovertown; Lee now received word that substantial reinforcements, identified as Smith's whole corps from Butler's army, were unloading there from transports which had left Bermuda Hundred yesterday for an overnight trip down the James and up the York.

Grievous though it was to learn that he soon would be facing still a fifth blue corps with his embattled three, the danger here was more than

★

numerical. From his debarkation point at White House, Smith was free to march due west, unhindered, to a position beyond Grant's left (to Cold Harbor, for example, a vital crossroads three miles southeast of Bethesda Church, where the Union line was anchored south of the Totopotomoy after standing firm against Early's mismanaged assault) and thus extend it beyond the reach of Lee's already thin-stretched right for a rapid swing around that flank and a leap across the Chickahominy. Convinced that this was what Grant had in mind, because it was what he would have attempted in his place, Lee first did what he could to meet the threat with what he had on hand in that direction: meaning cavalry. He sent Fitz Lee instructions to take up a position at Cold Harbor and hang on there until he was reinforced, hopefully by morning.

As things now stood, such reinforcements could not come from Hill or Anderson or Early, whose withdrawal from any part of the line would open the way for Grant to move on Atlee or Mechanicsville. They could come from only one source, beyond the James, and Lee had no time to spare for going through regular channels to procure them. Abandoning protocol he telegraphed an urgent request directly to Beauregard for every man he could spare, and when the Creole replied at sunset that the War Department would have to decide "when and what troops to order from here," Lee appealed by wire to the President in Richmond: "General Beauregard says the Department must determine what troops to send. . . . The result of this delay will be disaster. Butler's troops (Smith's corps) will be with Grant tomorrow. Hoke's division, at least, should be with me by light tomorrow."

It was unlike Lee to use the unequivocal word "disaster," and because it was unlike him it got immediate results. Davis promptly instructed Bragg to send Beauregard a peremptory order detaching Hoke's division for shipment by rail to Lee without delay, and before midnight Lee was informed that every effort was being made to get Hoke and his four brigades north of the Chickahominy by morning.

★ ★ ★   **O**nce more it was as if Lee had sat in on his adversary's councils or even paid him a visit inside his head. Dissatisfied with the Totopotomoy confrontation (as well he might be; it had cost him another 2013 killed and wounded and missing, first at Haw's Shop and then along the mazy fringes of the creek, with no gain except the infliction of about an equal number of casualties) Grant by now had decided to try another sidle: a brief one, this time, aimed at just the crossroad Lee predicted he would head for.

The choice of Cold Harbor was natural enough. It was there — well clear of the toils of the Totopotomoy, but not quite into those of the treacherous Chickahominy — that the roads from Bethesda Church and White House Landing came together, enabling him to extend his left for a meeting with Baldy Smith, whose corps was debarking fifteen miles due east. Depending more on celerity than surprise, which seemed to be unobtainable here in Virginia anyhow, Grant counted on a rapid concentration at that point for a concerted drive up the left bank of the Chickahominy, one that would strike the assembling rebels before they got set to resist it and would pen them up for capture or destruction with their backs to Powhite Creek, less than two miles west, or Beaver Dam Creek, another three miles upstream; after which he would cross the river with all five corps, either below Mechanicsville or beyond at Meadow Bridge, for a quick descent on Richmond. Accordingly, while Lee was instructing his nephew Fitz to hold Cold Harbor against all comers, Grant sent word for Sheridan to seize and hang onto that vital hub until Wright, crossing in rear of Hancock on the Totopotomoy and then in rear of Burnside and Warren at Bethesda Church, arrived for a meeting with Smith at the end of his march from White House. The result next day, May 31, was another all-out cavalry engagement.

This too was a nearly all-day fight, with no infantry involved on either side till after sunset. Beauregard's bridling reaction to Lee's request for troops had delayed Hoke's departure so effectively that his lead brigade did not unload at Meadow Bridge until near midday, and consequently did not complete its eight-mile hike down the north bank of the Chickahominy until dusk was gathering on the scene of Fitz Lee's long-drawn-out defense of the crossroad his uncle had asked him to hold. As for the Federals, there was no infantry in the attacking columns even then. Concerned with keeping his withdrawal secret in order to give him a decent head start in the shift to the southeast, Grant instructed Wright to wait for nightfall before he set out on a march that was necessarily roundabout, through Haw's Shop, since there was no direct road available down across the Totopotomoy; he would arrive tomorrow morning at the soonest.

Smith's delay was for other reasons, mostly involving slip-ups on Grant's staff. His original orders, issued when he embarked two days ago at Bermuda Hundred, called for a march from White House, up the south bank of the Pamunkey to New Castle, and from there to a position supporting the main effort on the Totopotomoy. Since then, Grant's plans had changed, but not Smith's orders, which were forgotten in all the flurry of preparation for the latest sidle. Completing his White House debarkation by midafternoon, May 31, Smith struck out northwestward, at a tangent to his intended route due west. Though he called a halt that night near Old Church, two miles short of his assigned objective, to send a wire requesting clarification from headquarters — it seemed to him he was moving into a military vacuum — the reply came back, after some delay, that his orders stood: he was to continue his march to New Castle. This he did, getting farther and farther at every step from the scene of the daylong engagement, now six miles in his left rear, which Sheridan had had to fight alone.

★

Little Phil frequently preferred it thus, so long at least as what opposed him was cavalry on its own. That was the case here, but he found it difficult to budge or even get at the graybacks, who declined to fight him in the smash-up style he favored. Instead, when he came within a mile of the crossroads about midday, with Torbert's three brigades — Torbert himself, up from his sickbed, had returned to duty the week before — he discovered Fitz Lee's two brigades dismounted and crouched behind fence-rail breastworks, which gave them the advantage of taking aim from an unjogged platform, with little exposure to the rapid-firing weapons of the horsemen galloping toward them. In their rear was Cold Harbor, a name of British derivation signifying an inn that afforded overnight lodging without hot food, adopted here because of the settlement's main feature, a frame tavern set in a triangular grove of trees at the intersection of five roads coming in from all round the compass.

Charges by Merritt and Custer were repulsed before they could be pressed home, and as the afternoon wore on it became evident that standard cavalry tactics would not serve; Sheridan had Torbert dismount his men and work them forward, troop by troop, while their fellows provided covering fire to make the defenders keep their heads down. Swarming over the dusty fields and through the brush, pumping lead from their stubby carbines, the blue troopers in their tight-fitting trousers, bobtail jackets, and short-billed kepis looked to one observer "as though they had been especially equipped for crawling through knotholes."

It was a slow and costly business, involving much risk and a good many wounds. Giving up on Baldy Smith after a patrol returned from a fruitless eastward search for some sign of his 15,000-man corps, Sheridan sent for Gregg to come down from Bethesda Church and add his two brigades to the effort being exerted, but the sun was down behind the trees along Powhite Creek by the time the courier rode off with the summons. As it turned out, such reinforcements as

Brigadier General Alfred Torbert (above) led three brigades in Phil Sheridan's Union cavalry.

reached the field before full dark were Confederate, and infantry at that.

Hard-pressed by the agile blue troopers, who were about within range for a mass charge through the gathering dusk, Fitz Lee's men looked over their shoulders and, seeing Hoke's lead brigade moving toward them up the road past the triangular grove of trees, decided the time had come to fall back on these overdue supports. They did so, only to find that the startled foot soldiers fell back too. Hot and tired from their dusty trek down the Chickahominy, and softened by two weeks of inactivity in the southside trenches, they joined what they took to be — and what now became — a general retreat, to and through Cold Harbor; which their pursuers seized and occupied, rounding up some fifty laggard graybacks in the process. Sheridan's elation over his sudden victory was modified considerably, however, when he learned from these captives that three more brigades of infantry would soon be up to join the one he had scattered. He decided, despite the arrival of Gregg's division hard on the heels of the rout, that his wisest course would be to pull back from the tavern crossroads before he was overrun. "I do not feel able to hold this place," he notified Meade as the withdrawal got under way. "With the heavy odds against me here, I do not think it prudent to hold on."

Meade thought otherwise, and so did Grant, in view of the sidle now in progress and the intended concentration there; Cold Harbor was to be reoccupied and "held at all hazards," they replied. Little Phil reversed his march, disposed his two divisions about the southwest quadrant of the crossroads, and had the dismounted troopers get to work in the darkness, throwing up temporary breastworks to provide them with cover for meeting the attack he expected would come with the dawn, if not sooner.

★ ★ ★ *I*t would come with the dawn, and the odds would be even heavier than Sheridan had feared when he pulled back, saying, "I do not think it prudent to hold on." Lee was about to go over to the offensive. What was more, in preparation for bloodier work to follow, he intended to begin with the retaking of the ground the troopers stood on.

Far from being discouraged by his nephew's report that the cross-roads had been seized by Sheridan, he saw in this development confirmation of his suspicion that Grant had another sidle in progress, that Cold Harbor was his intended point of concentration, and that so far he had nothing there but cavalry; which meant that his infantry was still in motion in that direction, strung out on roads converging from the north and east, and might therefore be defeated in detail as it came up — provided, of course, that Lee could get there first with a force substantial enough to inflict the damage he had in mind. He thought he could. Hoke's division was assembling there already, and this was only a fraction of what had become available now that Grant had tipped his hand. Formerly fixed in position east of Atlee by the danger that the Federals would round the headwaters of the Totopotomoy to turn his left, Lee was now free to draw troops from there for use on the opposite flank.

His choice was Anderson, whose strength was up to three divisions for the first time in the campaign, Pickett having rejoined him on the march from Hanover Junction. Both the Third and the Second corps had had their turns at offensive action, Hill eight days ago on the North Anna and Early here at Bethesda Church the day before, and both had failed. Now the First — Old Peter's dependables, who had rolled up the blue flank in the Wilderness and won the hairbreadth race for Spotsylvania — would have its turn. Anderson was told to pull back from his position on the Totopotomoy, leaving Little Powell to fill the gap, and make a night march down below Cold Harbor to join Hoke, who was placed under his command for the attack, first on Sheridan, to get possession of the crossroads shortly after dawn, and then on the other Union columns as they arrived from the east and north.

Though he still had not recovered sufficiently from his illness to resume direction of tactical operations, Lee advanced his headquarters to Shady Grove Church, a couple of miles southeast of Atlee Station, to be at least that much nearer the scene of tomorrow's action. Two years ago this evening, riding back from the confused field of Seven Pines — less than ten miles from where he would camp tonight — he had been informed by the President that he would replace the fallen Johnston, and next day he had assumed command of the Army of Northern Virginia. As he retired to his tent in the churchyard tonight to sleep out the final hours of this bloodiest May in American history, he had cause for hope that he would celebrate tomorrow's anniversary with an offensive victory as glorious as the one he had begun to plan on that night two years ago, when McClellan's vast blue host hovered within even easier reach of Richmond than Grant's did now.

There was no occasion for any such celebration on the hot first day of June, only a sorry repetition of the ineptness which had led Grant to believe that the fight had gone out of Lee's army. Anderson moved promptly enough, pulling Kershaw's division out of line in plenty of time for the march across Early's rear and into position on Hoke's left before daylight. His notion was to knock Sheridan back from the crossroads with a dawn attack by these two divisions, then continue the operation when the other two arrived. But a notion was all it remained. Kershaw went forward on schedule, giving his old brigade the lead, and that was when the trouble began and the offensive ended. Colonel Lawrence Keitt, a forty-year-old former congressman, had brought his green but handsomely uniformed regiment up from South Carolina the week before, and by virtue of his seniority over the other colonels took command of the brigade. Long on rank but short on combat experience, he went into his first

On June 3 at Cold Harbor, Ulysses S. Grant launched a massive head-on attack designed to drive the Confederates back to Chicka-hominy River.

attack in the gallant style of 1861, leading the way on a spirited gray charger; only to be killed by the first rattling clatter of semiautomatic fire from the two divisions of cavalry in the breastworks just ahead.

That was what had been expected by seasoned observers, who saw in Keitt's display only "inexperience and want of self control," but the reaction among his troops, recently uprooted from two years of languid garrison life in their home state, was something else. When they saw the colonel get toppled from his saddle — transformed, in the wink of an eye, from a saber-waving cynosure into a mangled corpse — they broke for the rear in what a dismayed artillerist called "the most abject rout ever committed by men in Confederate uniform." Nor was that the worst of the shame. "Some were so scared they

★

could not run, but groveled on the ground trying to burrow into the earth."

Veteran regiments on their flanks were obliged to give way too; the advance dissolved in panic, unredeemed by Hoke, who had not moved at all. First the brigade and then the division as a whole pulled out of range of the fast-firing Union carbines. Kershaw got the fallback stopped and even attempted to mount another attack, but it went no better. By the time Pickett and Field came up to form on Kershaw's left, around midmorning, so had Wright arrived with his three divisions in relief of Sheridan, who retired with pride from the defense of what he called "our little works."

They did not stay little long; Wright's men got busy with picks and shovels, deepening and extending them north and south to cover the western approaches to Cold Harbor. Smith's wandering corps slogged wearily into position alongside Wright that afternoon, reaching up to connect with Warren, whose four divisions occupied two miles of line below the Old Church Road, beyond which Burnside anchored the northern flank to the south bank of the Totopotomoy. That left only Hancock's corps and Sheridan's third division north of the creek; Grant sent word for Hancock to withdraw at nightfall for a march to the far left, where Torbert and Gregg were patrolling a boggy two-mile extension of the line down to the Chickahominy. He was instructed to come up in time to take part in a dawn assault that would be launched by all five corps.

Grant's decision to make such an attack was arrived at by a process of elimination. This was coffin corner; another sidle would involve him in the toils of the Chickahominy, and even if he cleared them intact he would find himself confronted, when he swung back west, by Richmond's permanent defenses. He would, in short, be mounting a siege, which at this stage he wanted as little as Lee did, since it represented the stalemate he had avoided from the start. His decision, then, despite the shocks and throes of the past four weeks — the stunning repulse in the green riot of the Wilderness and the unrelieved horror of Spotsylvania, which together had cost him a solid third of the infantry that crossed the Rapidan, and the close call on the North Anna, where incaution had nearly cost him the other two thirds, along with his reinforcements — was to attack the old fox where he was, or anyhow where he would be tomorrow morning. If this was coffin corner for Grant, it was something worse for Lee, whose back was to the wall of his capital and who would have neither time nor space for recovery if even a limited breakthrough could be scored. Grant kept his mind on that agreeable possibility, and when Meade suggested that something might be done with what was left of today, by way of improving tomorrow's chances, he was altogether willing.

Meade proposed a preliminary effort, restricted to the southern half of his present line, to give Wright and Smith a closer hug on the rebel works along their front and better jump-off positions from which to launch their share of the all-out dawn assault. That was how it came about that Anderson, whose four divisions were busy intrenching three miles of line, north and south of a road leading due east to Cold Harbor, was struck by a six-division attack, shortly after 5 o'clock, which not only disposed of any vestigial intention to resume his boggled offensive, but also came close to driving him from his uncompleted works. Pickett and Field held firm under pressure, but a break quickly developed between Hoke's left, where a brigade gave way in panic, and Kershaw's right. Anderson detached a brigade from Pickett to heal the breach, and by sunset the line was approximately restored. Yet the fact remained that, at a moderate price in casualties — moderate, that is, as such things went in this campaign: about 1000 for Smith, 1200 for Wright — Meade had secured the jump-off positions he wanted for tomorrow. Anderson's losses had been light, consisting mainly of stragglers captured when Hoke's left gave way, but he saw only too clearly what might come of this. "Reinforcements are necessary to enable us to hold this position," he notified Lee that night.

This message, conveying Anderson's doubts that he could hold the ground he had been ordered to advance from, put a dispiriting end to an anniversary which had dawned with high hopes that it would close with the celebration of an offensive victory. For the third time in nine days, a corps commander had shown himself incapable of mounting a sustained attack, even under favorable circumstances.

One thing common to all three attempts, in addition to failure, was that neither Lee nor his "poor Stuart" had taken part in them first hand. Jeb of course was gone for good, three weeks in his grave, and Lee was still in no condition for personal conduct of operations in the field; but that did not mean that the ailing general would not keep to his task of devising plans for the frustration of the invaders of his country and his state. Foiled in his efforts to go over to the offensive, he would continue to improvise a defensive in which, so far, he had managed to inflict casualties in ratio to the odds he faced at the opening of the campaign.

In this connection he had already moved to meet Anderson's needs before they were expressed, ordering Breckinridge to take up a position on Hoke's right tonight, and now he followed through with instructions that would add Hill's three divisions to the line tomorrow, one on the left of Early and two on the right beyond Breckinridge, tying those flanks respectively to the Totopotomoy and the Chickahominy. All this would take time, however — first for marching, then for digging — and Grant was bristling aggressively all along the seven miles of Confederate front when the sun came up on the second day of June.

Fortunately, despite the flurry, there was no attack; Lee had plenty of time to look to the extension and improvement of his line. Mounting Traveller for the first time in ten days, he rode down to Mechanicsville, where he found Breckinridge and his two brigades enjoying a leisurely breakfast, midway through their march to the far right. He got the distinguished Kentuckian back

During a six-division attack on Confederate positions at Cold Harbor, the Federal XVIII Corps advances on Joseph Kershaw's division.

on the road again and then resumed his ride, eastward past Walnut Grove Church to his new headquarters beyond Gaines Mill, a mile and a half due west of Union-held Cold Harbor and about the same distance northwest of the scene of his first victory, scored two years ago this month, when Hood and Law broke Fitz-John Porter's line on Turkey Hill, now also Union-held. Mindful of the importance of that feature of the terrain, Lee had Breckinridge go forward, about 3 o'clock that afternoon, and with the assistance of one of Hill's divisions, which had just come up, drive a brigade of bluecoats off its slopes, thus affording his artillery a position from which to dominate the Chickahominy bottoms on the right. Simultaneously on the left, Early's corps and Hill's remaining division felt out the Federal installations above Old Church Road, on toward the Totopotomoy, and after brushing aside a sizeable body of skirmishers, who yielded stubbornly, confronted the main enemy works northwest and north of Bethesda Church.

While these two adjustments were being made at opposite ends of the long line, a heavy rain began to fall, first in big individual drops, pocking the dust like buckshot scattered broadcast, and then in a steady downpour that turned the dust to mud. The discomfort was minor on both sides, compared to the relief from heat and glare and the distraction from waiting to receive or deliver the attack both knew was soon to be made, if not today then certainly tomorrow.

Rain often had a depressing effect on Lee, perhaps because it reminded him of the drenched fiasco his first campaign had been, out in western Virginia in the fall of 1861; but not now; now he valued it as a factor that would make for muddy going when the Federals moved against him. Back at his headquarters, near the ruins of Dr William Gaines's once imposing four-story gristmill on Powhite Creek — Sheridan's troopers had burned it when they passed this way two weeks ago, returning from the raid that killed Jeb Stuart — the southern commander kept to his tent, still queasy from his ten-day illness, reading the day's reports while rain drummed on the canvas overhead. He had done all he could to get all the troops he could muster into line. "Send to the field hospitals," he had told his chief lieutenants in a circular issued the last day of May, "and have every man capable of performing the duties of a soldier returned to his command." Such efforts, combined with those of Davis, who had summoned reinforcements from as far away as Florida in the course of the past two weeks, had brought his strength back up to nearly 60,000. Grant had about 110,000 across the way, but Lee feared the odds no more here than he had done elsewhere. In fact he feared them less; for, thanks to Grant's forbearance today — whatever its cause — he had had plenty of time to dispose his army as he chose. Having done so, he was content to leave the rest to God and the steady valor of his troops, whose defensive skill had by now become instinctive.

This last applied in particular to the use they made of terrain within their interlocking sectors. Whether the ground was flat or hilly, bare or wooded, firm or boggy — and it was all those things from point to various point along the line from Pole Green Church to Grapevine Bridge — they never used it more skillfully than here. Occupying their assigned positions with a view to affording themselves only so much protection as would not interfere with the delivery of a maximum of firepower, they flowed onto and into the landscape as if in response to a natural law, like water seeking its own level. The result, once they were settled in, was by no means as imposing as the fortifications they had thrown up three weeks ago at Spotsylvania or last week on the North Anna. But that too was part of the design. No such works were needed here and they knew it, having installed them with concern that they not appear so formidable as to discourage all hope of success in the minds of the Federal planners across the way. Crouched in the dripping blackness after sundown, with both flanks securely anchored on rising streams and Richmond scarcely ten miles in their rear, the defenders asked for nothing better, in the way of reward for their craftsmanship and labor, than that

---

Occupying their assigned positions . . . they flowed onto and into the landscape as if in response to a natural law, like water seeking its own level.

---

their adversaries would advance into the meshed and overlapping fields of fire they had established, unit by unit, along their seven miles of front.

They were about to get their wish. Indeed, they would have gotten it at dawn today — ten hours before they completed their concentration and were in any condition to receive it — except that Hancock's three divisions had not arrived on the Union left until about 6.30, two hours late and in no shape for fighting, tired and hungry as they were from their grueling all-night march. Grant accepted the delay as unavoidable, and rescheduled the attack for 5 o'clock that afternoon. That would do about as well, he seemed to think. But then, as the jump-off hour drew near, the rebs went into action on both flanks, seizing Turkey Hill and driving the outpost skirmishers back on their works above Bethesda Church. This called for some changes in the stand-by orders, and Grant, still unruffled, postponed the attack once more until 4.30 next morning. After all, all he wanted was a breakthrough, almost anywhere along those six or seven miles of enemy line; he could see that a hot supper and a good night's rest would add to the strength and steadiness of the men when they went forward.

Aside from a general directive that the main effort would be made by the three corps on the left, where the opposing works were close together as a result of yesterday's preliminary effort, tactics seemed to have gone by the board, at least on the upper levels of command. Neither Grant nor Meade, or for that matter any member of their two staffs, had reconnoitered any part of the Confederate position; nor had either of them organized the attack itself in any considerable detail, including the establishment of such lateral communications as might be needed to assure coöperation between units. Apparently they assumed that all such incidental problems had been covered by a sentence in Meade's circular postponing the late-afternoon attack till dawn: "Corps commanders will employ the interim in making examinations of the ground on their front and perfecting the arrangements for the assault."

New as he was to procedure in the Army of the Potomac, Baldy Smith — "aghast," he later wrote, "at the reception of such an order, which proved conclusively the utter absence of any military plan" — sent a note to Wright, who was on his left, "asking him to let me know what was to be his plan of attack, that I might conform to it, and thus have two corps acting in unison." Wright's reply was simply that he was "going to pitch in": which left Smith as much in the dark as before, and even more aghast. Grant, in short, was proceeding here at Cold Harbor as if he subscribed quite literally to the words he had written Halleck from the North Anna, a week ago today: "I feel that our success over Lee's army is already assured."

Up on the line, that was by no means the feeling prevalent among the troops who were charged with carrying out the orders contrived to bring about the result expected at headquarters. Unlike their rearward superiors, they had been uncomfortably close to the rebel works all day and knew only too well what was likely to come of any effort to assault them, let alone such a slipshod one as this. Their reaction was observed by Lieutenant Colonel Horace Porter, a young West Pointer, formerly an aide to McClellan and now serving Grant in the same capacity. Passing through the camps that rainy evening, he later wrote, "I noticed that many of the soldiers had taken off their coats and seemed to be engaged in sewing up rents in them." He thought this strange, at such a time, but when he looked closer he "found that the men were calmly writing their names and home addresses on slips of paper and pinning them on the backs of their coats, so that their bodies might be recognized and their fate made known to their families at home."

Some went even further in their gloom. A blood-stained diary, salvaged from the pocket of a dead man later picked up on the field, had this grisly final entry: "June 3. Cold Harbor. I was killed."

★ ★ ★ *T*hey came with the dawn and they came pounding, three blue corps with better than 60,000 effectives, striking for three points along the center and right center of the rebel line, which had fewer men defending its whole length than now were assaulting half of it. Advancing with a deep-throated roar — "Huzzah! Huzzah!" a

*T*roops of the 164th New York charge the Confederate
works at Cold Harbor on June 3. More than
60,000 Federals were engaged in the dawn assault.

Confederate thought they were yelling — the attackers saw black slouch hats
sprout abruptly from the empty-looking trenches up ahead, and then the works
broke into flame. A heavy bank of smoke rolled out, alive with muzzle flashes,
and the air was suddenly full of screaming lead. "It seemed more like a volcanic
blast than a battle," one Federal later said, "and was just about as destructive."

Dire as their expectations had been the night before, they perceived
now for the first time the profoundly intricate nature of the deadfall Lee had
devised for their undoing. Never before, in this or perhaps in any other war, had
so large a body of troops been exposed to such a concentration of firepower; "It
had the fury of the Wilderness musketry, with the thunders of the Gettysburg
artillery superadded," an awed cannoneer observed from his point of vantage in
the Union rear. And now, too, the committed victims saw the inadequacy of
Grant's preparation in calling for a three-pronged assault, directed against three
vague and widely spaced objectives. Smith on the right was enfiladed from his
outer flank, as was Hancock on the left, and Wright, advancing between them

with a gap on either side, found both of his flanks exposed at once to an even crueler flailing. What was worse, the closer the attackers got to the concave rebel line, the more this crossfire was intensified and the more likely an individual was to be chosen as a simultaneous target by several marksmen in the works ahead. "I could see the dust fog out of a man's clothing in two or three places where as many balls would strike him at the same moment," a defender was to say.

Under such conditions, losses tended to occur in ratio to the success of various units in closing the range. Barlow's division for example, leading Hancock's charge against Lee's right, struck a lightly defended stretch of boggy ground in Breckinridge's front and plunged on through to the main line, which buckled under sudden pressure from the cheering bluecoats. Barlow, not yet thirty — "attired in a flannel checked shirt, a threadbare pair of trousers, and an old blue kepi," he looked to a staff observer "like a highly independent mounted newsboy" — was elated to think he had scored the breakthrough Grant had called for. But his elation was short-lived. Attached to one of Hill's divisions on the adjoining slope of Turkey Hill, Joseph Finegan, who had arrived that week with two Florida battalions and been put in charge of a scratch brigade, counterattacked without waiting to be prompted and quickly restored the line, demonstrating here in Virginia the savagery he had shown at Olustee, three months ago in his home state. Barlow's men were ousted, losing heavily in the process, and it was much the same with others up the line. Though nowhere else was there a penetration, even a temporary one, wherever the range became point-blank the attack dissolved in horror; the attackers huddled together, like sheep caught in a hailstorm, and milled about distractedly in search of what little cover the terrain afforded. "They halted and began to dodge, lie down, and recoil," a watching grayback would remember, while another noted that "the dead and dying lay in front of the Confederate line in triangles, of which the apexes were the bravest men who came nearest to the breastworks under that withering, deadly fire."

The attack, now broken, had lasted just eight minutes. So brief was its duration, and so abrupt its finish, that some among the defenders had trouble crediting the fact that it had ended, while others could scarcely believe it had begun; not in earnest, at any rate. One of Hoke's brigadiers, whose troops were holding a portion of the objective assigned to Wright, square in the center of the three-corps Federal effort, afterwards testified that he "was not aware at any time of any serious assault having been given."

Part of the reason for this was the lightness of Confederate losses, especially as compared to those inflicted, although these last were not known to have been anything like as heavy as they were until the smoke began to clear. An Alabama colonel, whose regiment had three men killed and five wounded, peered out through rifts in the drifting smoke along his front, where Smith had attacked with close-packed ranks, and saw to his amazement that "the dead covered more than five acres of ground about as thickly as they could be laid." Eventually the doleful tally showed that while Lee was losing something under 1500, killed and wounded in the course of the day, Grant lost better than 7000, most of them in the course of those first eight minutes.

The attack had ended, but neither by Grant's intention nor with his consent. No sooner had the Union effort slackened than orders came for it to be renewed, and when Wright protested that he could accomplish nothing unless Hancock and Smith moved forward to protect his flanks, he was informed that they had filed the same complaint about his lack of progress in the center, which left them equally exposed. Faced with this dilemma, headquarters instructed each of the corps commanders to go forward on his own, without regard for what the others might be doing.

Up on the line, such instructions had a quality of madness, and a colonel on Wright's staff did not hesitate to say so. "To move that army farther, except by regular approaches," he declared, "was a simple and absolute impossibility, known to be such by every officer and man of the three corps engaged." Here too was a dilemma, and here too a simple answer was forthcoming. When the order to

*Seizing guns and prisoners, the 7th New York
Heavy Artillery of Francis Barlow's division overruns
the Confederate works at Cold Harbor.*

resume the attack was repeated, unit commanders responded in the same fashion by having their troops step up their rate of fire from the positions where they lay.

It went on like that all morning. Dodging shells and bullets, which continued to fall abundantly, dispatch bearers crept forward with instructions for the assault to be renewed. The firing, most of it skyward, would swell up and then subside, until another messenger arrived with another order and the process was repeated, the men lying prone and digging in, as best they could in such cramped positions, to provide themselves with a little cover between blind volleys. Finally, an order headed 1.30 came down to all three corps, eight minutes less than nine hours after it had been placed in execution: "For the present all further offensive operations will be suspended."

Over near Gaines Mill, with occasional long-range Federal projectiles landing in the clearing where his headquarters tent was pitched, Lee had spent an anxious half hour awaiting the return of couriers sent to bring him word of the outcome of the rackety assault, which opened full-voiced on the right, down near the Chickahominy, and roared quickly to a sustained climax, northward to the Totopotomoy. For all he knew, the Union infantry might get there first to announce a breakthrough half a mile east of the shell-pocked meadow overlooking the ruined mill. Mercifully, though, the wait was brief. Shortly after sunrise the couriers began returning on lathered horses, and their reports varied only in degrees of exultation. "Tell General Lee it is the same all along my front," A. P. Hill had said, pointing to where the limits of the enemy advance were marked by windrows of the dead and dying.

Confederate losses were low; incredibly low, it seemed. Hoke, as an extreme example, reported that so far, though the ground directly in front of his intrenchments was literally blue with fallen attackers, he had not lost a single man in his division. In Anderson's corps, Law was hit in the head by a stray bullet that was to take him away from his brigade for good, and Breckinridge, after ending Barlow's costly short-term penetration, was badly shaken up when his horse, struck by a solid shot, collapsed between his knees. No other high-ranking defender received so much as a scratch or a bruise throughout the length of the gray line. By midmorning, with the close-up Union effort reduced to blind volleys of musketry fired prone in response to orders for a resumption of the attack, it was clear that Lee had won what a staff colonel was to call "perhaps the easiest victory ever granted to Confederate arms by the folly of Federal commanders."

Back in Richmond, although fighting had raged even closer to the city throughout five of the Seven Days, two years ago, citizens had been jolted awake that morning by the loudest firing they had ever heard. Windows rattled with the coming of dawn and kept on rattling past midday, one apprehensive listener declared, "as if whole divisions were firing at a word of command."

No one could say, at that range, who was getting the worst and who the best of it. Before noon, as a result, distinguished visitors began arriving at Lee's headquarters in search of first-hand information. Among them was Postmaster General John H. Reagan, who brought two lawyer friends along to help find out how the battle was going. Lee told them it was going well, up to now at least, and when they wondered if the artillery wasn't unusually active here today, the general said it was, but he added, with a gesture toward the contending lines, where the drumfire of a hundred thousand rifles sounded to Reagan like the tearing of a sheet: "It is that that kills men."

What reserves did he have on hand, they asked, in case Grant managed a breakthrough at some point along his front?

"Not a regiment," Lee replied, "and that has been my condition ever since the fighting commenced on the Rappahannock. If I shorten my lines to provide a reserve, he will turn me. If I weaken my lines to provide a reserve, he will break them."

"Our loss today has been small, and our success, under the blessing of God, all that we could expect."

— Robert E. Lee

Thinking this over, the three civilians decided it was time to leave, and in the course of their ride back to the capital they met the President coming out. Today was his fifty-sixth birthday. He had spent the morning, despite the magnetic clatter of the batteries at Cold Harbor, with his three children and his wife, who was soon to be delivered of their sixth; but after lunch, unable any longer to resist the pull of guns that had been roaring for nine hours, he called for his horse and set out on the nine-mile ride to army headquarters. There he found the situation much as it had been described in a 1 o'clock dispatch ("So far every attack has been repulsed," Lee wired) except that by now the Federals had abandoned all pretense of resuming the assault. The staff atmosphere, there in the clearing above Gaines Mill, was one of elation over a victory in the making, if not in fact over one already achieved. Returning to Richmond soon after dark, Davis was pleased to read a message Seddon had just received from Lee in summary of the daylong battle, which now had ended with his army intact and Grant's considerably diminished. "Our loss today has been small," the general wrote, "and our success, under the blessing of God, all that we could expect."

Beyond the lines where Lee's men rested from their exertions, and beyond the intervening space where the dead had begun to spoil in the heat and the wounded cried for help that did not come, the repulsed survivors brooded on the outcome of a solid month of fighting. This was the thirtieth day since the two armies first made contact in the Wilderness, and Union losses were swelling toward an average of 2000 men a day. Some days it was less, some days more, and some days — this one, for example — it was far more, usually as the result of a high-level miscalculation or downright blunder. Even Grant was infected by the gloom into which his troops were plunged by today's addition to the list of headlong tactical failures. "I regret this assault more than any one I ever ordered," he told his staff that evening. Uncharacteristic as it was, the remark made for a certain awkwardness in the group, as if he had sought to relieve his anguish with a scream. "Subsequently the matter was seldom referred to in a conversation," a junior staffer was to state.

Others were less reticent. "I think Grant has had his eyes opened," Meade wrote home, not without a measure of grim satisfaction, "and is willing to admit now that Virginia and Lee's army is not Tennessee and Bragg's army."

According to some observers, such an admission was a necessity if the campaign was to continue. James Wilson, riding over for a visit, found that several members of Grant's official family, including Rawlins, "feared that the policy of direct and continuous attack, if persisted in, would ultimately so decimate and discourage the rank and file that they could not be induced to face the enemy at all. Certain it is," the cavalryman added, "that the 'smash-'em-up' policy was abandoned about that time and was never again favored at headquarters." This would indeed be welcome news, if it was true, but just now the army was in no shape to take much note of anything except its weariness and depletion. A line colonel, stunned and grimy from not having had a full night's sleep or a change of clothes since May 5, found himself in no condition to write more than a few bleak lines in a family letter. "I can only tell my wife I am alive and well," he said; "I am too stupid for any use."

In the past month the Army of the Potomac, under Grant, had lost no less than half as many men as it had lost in the previous three years under McDowell, McClellan, Pope, Burnside, Hooker, and Meade on his own. Death had become a commonplace, though learning to live with it produced a cumulative strain. High-strung Gouverneur Warren, whose four bled-down divisions had fewer troops in them by now than Wright's or Hancock's three, broke out tonight in sudden expostulation to a friend: "For thirty days it has been one funeral procession past me, and it has been too much!"

Criticism was mounting, not only against Grant, who had planned — or, strictly speaking, failed to plan — today's attack, but also against those immediately below him on the military ladder. "I am disgusted with the generalship displayed," young Emory Upton wrote his sister on the morning after the battle. "Our men have, in many cases, been foolishly and wantonly slaugh-

General George Meade, whose newly-adopted headquarters flag is shown here, wrote home that Grant "has had his eyes opened" in the Cold Harbor campaign.

tered." Next day, continuing the letter, he went further in fixing the blame. "Our loss was very heavy, and to no purpose. . . . Some of our corps commanders are not fit to be corporals. Lazy and indolent, they will not even ride along their lines; yet, without hesitancy, they will order us to attack the enemy, no matter what their position or numbers. Twenty thousand of our killed and wounded should today be in our ranks."

Horror was added to bitterness by the suffering of the wounded, still trapped between the lines, and the pervasive stench of the dead, still unburied after two sultry nights and the better part of a third day under the fierce June sun. "A deserter says Grant intends to *stink* Lee out of his position, if nothing else will suffice," a Richmond diarist noted, but a Federal staff colonel had a different explanation: "An impression prevails in the popular mind, and with some reason perhaps, that a commander who sends a flag of truce asking permission to bury his dead and bring in his wounded has lost the field of battle. Hence the resistance upon our part to ask a flag of truce."

No more willing to give that impression here in Virginia than he had been a year ago in Mississippi, following the repulse of his two assaults on the Vicksburg fortifications, the Union general held off doing anything to relieve either the stench or the drawn-out agony of his fallen soldiers until the afternoon of June 5, and even then he could not bring himself to make a forthright request for the necessary Confederate acquiescence. "It is reported to me," he then wrote Lee, "that there are wounded men, probably of both armies, now lying exposed and suffering between the lines." His suggestion was that each side be permitted to send out unarmed litter bearers to take up its casualties when no action was in progress, and he closed by saying that "any other method equally fair to both parties you may propose for meeting the end desired will be accepted by me." But Lee, who had no wounded out there, was not

105

letting his adversary off that easy. "I fear that such an arrangement will lead to misunderstanding and difficulty," he replied. "I propose therefore, instead, that when either party desires to remove their dead or wounded a flag of truce be sent, as is customary. It will always afford me pleasure to comply with such a request as far as circumstances will permit."

Thus admonished, Grant took another night to think the matter over — a night in which the cries of the injured, who now had been three days without water or relief from pain, sank to a mewling — and tried a somewhat different tack, as if he were yielding, not without magnanimity, to an urgent plea from a disadvantaged opponent. "Your communication of yesterday is received," he wrote. "I will send immediately, as you propose, to collect the dead and wounded between the lines of the two armies, and will also instruct that you be allowed to do the same." Not so, Lee answered for a second time, and after expressing "regret to find that I did not make myself understood in my communi-

Skeletal remains of Union soldiers killed at Cold Harbor await shipment to the North for reburial. Union and Confederate casualties totaled 8500 in the battle.

★

cation," proceeded to make it clear that if what Grant wanted was a cease-fire he would have to come right out and ask for it, not informally, as between two men with a common problem, but "by a flag of truce in the usual way." Grant put on as good a face as he could manage in winding up this curious exchange. "The knowledge that wounded men are now suffering from want of attention," he responded, "compels me to ask a suspension of hostilities for sufficient time to collect them in; say two hours."

By the time Lee's formal consent came back across the lines, however, the sun was down on the fourth day of exposure for the wounded and even the mewling had reached an end. Going out next morning, June 7, search parties found only two men alive out of all the Federal thousands who had fallen in the June 3 assault; the rest had either died or made it back under fire, alone or retrieved by comrades in the darkness. At the end of the truce — which had to be extended to give the burial details time to roll up the long blue carpet of festering corpses — Grant fired a parting verbal shot in concluding his white-flag skirmish with Lee: "Regretting that all my efforts for alleviating the sufferings of wounded men left upon the battlefield have been rendered nugatory, I remain, &c., U. S. Grant, Lieutenant General."

Lee made no reply to this, no doubt feeling that none was called for, and not even the northern commander's own troops were taken in by a blame-shifting pretense which did little more than show their chief at his worst. They could discount the Copperhead charge that he was a butcher, "a bull-headed Suvarov," since his methods so far had at least kept the rebels on the defensive while his own army moved forward more than sixty air-line miles. But this was something else, this sacrifice of brave men for no apparent purpose except to salve his rankled pride. Worst of all, they saw in the agony of their comrades, left to die amid the corpses on a field already lost, a preview of much agony to come, when they themselves would be left to whimper through days of pain while their leader composed notes in defense of conduct which, so far as they could see, had been indefensible from the start.

There was that, and there was the heat and thirst, the burning sun, the crowded trenches, and always the snipers, deadly at close range. "I hated sharpshooters, both Confederate and Union," a blue artillerist would recall, "and I was always glad to see them killed." Because of them, rations and ammunition had to be lugged forward along shallow parallels that followed a roundabout zigzag course and wore a man down to feeling like some unholy cross between a pack mule and a snake. "In some instances," another observer wrote, "where reg-iments whose terms of service had expired were ordered home, they had to leave the field crawling on hands and knees through trenches to the rear." That was a crowning indignity, that a man had to crouch to leave the war, at a time when he wanted to crow and shout, and that even then he might be killed on his way out.

★

Devoured by lice and redbugs, which held carnival in the filthy rags they wore for clothes and burrowed into flesh that had not been washed for more than a month, the men turned snappish, not only among themselves but toward their officers as well. Tempers flared as the conviction grew that they were doing no earthly good in their present position, yet they saw no way to change it without abandoning their drive on Richmond, a scant ten miles away. At a cost of more than 50,000 casualties, Grant had landed them in coffin corner — and it did not help to recall, as a few surviving veterans could do, that McClellan had attained more or less the same position, two years ago, at practically no cost at all.

One who could remember that was Meade, the "damned old goggle-eyed snapping turtle" who had contributed a minor miracle to the campaign by holding onto his famous hair-trigger temper through a month of tribulations and frustrations. But now, in the wake of Cold Harbor, he lost it: lost it, moreover, in much the spectacular manner which those who knew him best had been expecting all along.

Baldy Smith was the first to see it coming. Two days after the triple-pronged assault was shattered, and with thousands of his soldiers lying dead or dying in front of his works, Meade paid Smith a routine visit, in the course of which the Vermonter asked him bluntly how he "came to give such an order for battle as that of the 2d." According to Baldy, Meade's reply was "that he had worked out every plan for every move from the crossing of the Rapidan onward, that the papers were full of the doings of *Grant's* army, and that he was tired of it and was determined to let General Grant plan his own battles." The result, once Grant had been left to his own devices, was the compounded misery out there between the lines. Smith saw from this reaction what was coming of the build-up of resentment, and two days later it came.

While the burial details were at work out front at last, Meade glanced through a hometown newspaper, a five-day-old copy of the Philadelphia *Inquirer*, and his eye was caught by a paragraph that referred to him as being "entitled to great credit for the magnificent movements of the army since we left Brandy, for they have been directed by him. In battle he puts troops in action and controls their movements; in a word, he commands the army. General Grant is here only because he deems the present campaign the vital one of the war, and wishes to decide on the spot all questions that would be referred to him as general-in-chief." This was gratifying enough, but then the Pennsylvanian moved on to the following paragraph, the one that brought on the foreseen explosion. "History will record, but newspapers cannot, that on one eventful night during the present campaign Grant's presence saved the army, and the nation too; not that General Meade was on the point of committing a blunder unwittingly, but his devotion to his country made him loth to risk her last army on what he deemed a chance. Grant assumed the responsibility, and we are still on to Richmond."

Meade reacted fast. Though the piece was unsigned, he had the *Inquirer* correspondent — one Edward Crapsey — brought to his tent, confronted him with the article, and when the reporter admitted that he had written it, demanded to know the source of his remarks. Crapsey rather lamely cited "the talk of the camp," to the effect that after the second day of battle in the Wilderness, with both flanks turned and his center battered, only Grant had wanted to keep moving south. Enraged by the repetition of this "base and wicked lie," Meade placed the offender in arrest and had his adjutant draw up a general order directing that he "be put without the lines [of the army] and not permitted to return." The provost marshal was charged with the execution of the order next morning, June 8, and he carried it out in style. Wearing on his breast and back large placards lettered Libeler of the Press, Crapsey was mounted face-rearward on a mule and paraded through the camps to the accompaniment of the "Rogue's March," after which he was less ceremoniously expelled. "The commanding general trusts that this example will deter others from committing like offenses," Meade's order read, "and he takes this occasion to notify the representatives of the public press that . . . he will not hesitate to punish with the utmost rigor all [such] instances."

After the heated battle at Cold Harbor, William F. "Baldy" Smith (seated), commander of the Federal XVIII Corps, poses with his staff in camp.

★

Whatever he might have "trusted," the outcome was that Meade now had two wars on his hands, one with the rebels in his front, the other with "the representatives of the public press" in his immediate rear. Making his way to Washington, Crapsey recounted his woes to newspaper friends, who were unanimous in condemning the general for thus "wreaking his personal vengeance on an obscure friendless civilian." What was more, their publishers backed them up; Meade, one said, was "as leprous with moral cowardice as the brute that kicks a helpless cripple on the street, or beats his wife at home." By way of retaliation for what they called "this elaborate insult," they agreed that his name would never be mentioned in dispatches except in connection with a defeat, and they held to this for the next six months or more, with the result that another casualty was added to the long Cold Harbor list, a victim of journalistic strangulation.

Eleven months ago, the Gettysburg victor had been seen as a sure winner in some future presidential election; but not now. Now and for the rest of the year, a reporter noted privately, "Meade was quite as much unknown, by any correspondence from the army, as any dead hero of antiquity."

★ ★ ★ *M*eade had his woes, but so it seemed did everyone around him, high or low, in the wake of a battle whose decisive action was over in eight holocaustic minutes. Not only had it been lost, and quickly lost; it had been lost, the losers now perceived, before it began. Despite the distraction of wounds that smarted all the more from having been self-inflicted, so to speak, this made for a certain amount of bitter introspection at all levels, including the top. A colonel on Lee's staff, coupling quotes from Grant and Hamlet — admittedly an improbable combination — remarked that the Union commander's resolution "to fight it out on this line if it takes all summer" seemed, at this stage, to be "sicklied o'er with the pale cast of thought."

It was in fact, all quips aside, a time for taking stock. Beyond the knowledge that attrition was a knife that cut both ways, Grant had accepted from the outset, as a condition of the tournament, the probability that the knife would slice deeper into the ranks of the attacker; but how much deeper he hadn't known, till now. For twenty-nine days he had been losing about two men to Lee's one, and if this was hard, it was at any rate in proportion to the size of the two armies. Then came the thirtieth day, Cold Harbor, and his loss was five to one, a figure made even more doleful by the prospect that future losses were likely to be as painfully disproportionate if he tried the same thing again in this same region. Lodged as he was in coffin corner, it was no wonder if the cast of his thought was sicklied o'er, along with the thoughts of those around him, staff or line; Rawlins and Upton, for example.

Moreover, the effect of that month of losses was cumulative, like the expenses of a spender on a spree, and during the lull which now ensued the bill came due. Halleck sent him what amounted to a declaration of bankruptcy, or in any case a warning that his credit was about to be cut off. On June 7, while the burial details were at work and Meade was berating Crapsey in his tent, Old Brains served notice from Washington that the bottom of the manpower barrel was in sight: "I inclose a list of troops forwarded from this department to the Army of the Potomac since the campaign opened — 48,265 men. I shall send you a few regiments more, when all resources will be exhausted till another draft is made."

These were hard lines, coming as they did at this disappointing juncture in the campaign. Just as the addition of Smith's 15,000 from the Army of the James had not made up for the number who departed from Meade's army because their enlistments had expired or they had broken down physically under the thirty-day strain, so too was Halleck's figure, even with the inclusion of those "few regiments more," considerably short of the number who had been shot or captured in the course of the month-long drive from the Rapidan to the Chickahominy. This would make for restrictions, which in turn seemed likely to require a change in style. Up to the present, Grant had been living as it were on interest, replacing his fallen veterans with conscripts, but from now until another of Lincoln's "calls" had been responded to, and the drafted troops approximately trained for use in the field, he would be living on principal. Formerly replaceable on short notice, a man hit now would be simply one man less, a flat subtraction from the dwindling mass.

The law of diminishing utility thus obtained, and though Grant no doubt would find it cramping, if not prohibitive in its effect on his previous method of sailing headlong into whatever got in his path, it afforded in any case a gleam of hope for those around and under him. Some members of his staff had expressed the fear that any attempt to repeat the army's latest effort, here between the Totopotomoy and the Chickahominy, would render it unfit for future use. Now they could stop worrying; at least about that. Grant had no intention of provoking another Cold Harbor and they knew it, not only because they had heard him express regret that he had tried such a thing in the first place, but also because they knew that he could no longer afford it, even if he changed his mind.

One possible source of reinforcements was the remnant of Butler's army, still tightly corked in its bottle on the far side of the James and doing no earthly good except for keeping Beauregard's even smaller remnant from joining Lee. However, as a result of his casualties during the corking operation and the subsequent detachment of Smith, the cock-eyed general was down to about 10,000 men, scarcely enough to warrant the trouble of getting them on and off

★

transports and certainly not enough to make any significant change in the situation north of the Chickahominy. Besides, Grant's mind was turning now toward a use for them in the region where they were. He still thought his plan for a diversionary effort south of the James had been a good one; aside, that is, from the designation of Butler as the man to carry it out. If a real soldier, a professional rather than an all-thumbs amateur, had been in over-all command — Baldy Smith, for example — Richmond might not have fallen by now, but at least it would have been cut off from Georgia and the Carolinas by the occupation of the Petersburg rail hub, and its citizens would be tightening their belts another notch or two to relieve far greater pangs of hunger than they were feeling with their supply lines open to the south.

Grant's notion was to reinforce Butler for a breakout from Bermuda Neck, due west to Walthall Junction, or a sidle across the Appomattox for a quick descent on Petersburg. Smith's corps would go, he and his men being familiar with the southside terrain, and possibly a corps or two from Meade. In fact, the more Grant thought about it, there in the stench and dust around Cold Harbor, the more he was persuaded that the thing to do was send Meade's whole army, not only to assure the success of the operation beyond the James, but also to resolve what was fast becoming a stalemate, here on the north bank of the Chickahominy, and remove the troops from the scene of their most disheartening repulse.

Halleck was against it before he even learned the details. He preferred the slower but less risky investment of the Confederate capital from the north, which would not expose the army to the danger of being caught astride the James and would have the added virtue of covering Washington if Lee reverted to his practice of disrupting Union strategy with a strike across the Potomac. But Grant had had quite enough of maneuvering in that region.

"My idea from the start has been to beat Lee's army, if possible, north of Richmond," he admitted in a

While sealed up at Bermuda Neck, Federals could watch the enemy from their 126-foot-tall signal tower.

letter to the chief of staff on June 5, the day he opened negotiations for the burial of his dead, but he saw now that "without a greater sacrifice of human life than I am willing to make, all cannot be accomplished that I had designed." Then he told just what it was he had in mind. "I will continue to hold substantially to the ground now occupied by the Army of the Potomac, taking advantage of any favorable circumstance that may present itself, until the cavalry can be sent to destroy the Virginia Central Railroad from about Beaver Dam for some 25 or 30 miles west. When this is effected, I will move the army to the south side of James River." Cut off from supplies from the north and south, Lee would have no choice except to stay inside his capital and starve, abandon it to his foe, or come out and fight for it in the open. Grant had no doubt about the outcome if his adversary, as seemed likely from past usage, chose the third of these alternatives and tried to stage another Seven Days. "The feeling of the two armies now seems to be that the rebels can protect themselves only by strong intrenchments," he closed his letter, "while our army is not only confident of protecting itself without intrenchments, but can beat and drive the enemy whenever and wherever he can be found without this protection."

Then suddenly things began to happen fast. He learned that night that while he had been writing to Halleck, outlining his plan without committing himself to a schedule, Sigel's successor David Hunter had scored a victory out in the Shenandoah Valley that would shorten considerably the time Grant had thought he would have to devote to smashing Richmond's northwestern supply line. Disdaining the combinations his predecessor had favored — and which, it could be seen now, had contributed to the failure of that segment of the grand design for Lee's defeat — Hunter had simply notified Crook and Averell that he was heading south, up the Valley pike, and that they were to join him as soon as they could make it across the Alleghenies from their camp on the Greenbrier River. He set out from Cedar Creek on May 26, five days after taking command of the troops whipped at New Market the week before, and at the end of a ten-day hike up the turnpike, which he interrupted from time to time to demolish a gristmill, burn a barn, or drive off butternut horsemen trying to scout the column at long range, he reached the village of Piedmont, eleven miles short of Staunton, and found the rebels drawn up in his path, guns booming. Attacking forthwith he wrecked and scattered what turned out to be three scratch brigades, all that were left to defend the region after Breckinridge departed. His reward, gained at a cost of less than 500 killed and wounded, included more than 1000 prisoners, a solid fifth of the force that had opposed him; the body of Brigadier General William E. Jones, abandoned on the field by the fugitives he had commanded until he was shot; and Staunton.

Hunter occupied the town next day, his two divisions marching unopposed down streets no blue-clad troops had trod before. Two days later,

*D*rawn the evening after the June 5 battle at
Piedmont near Staunton, this sketch depicts the furious
onslaught of Federal troops under David Hunter.

on June 8, having torn up the railroad west of town as they approached, Crook
and Averell arrived from West Virginia to assist in the consumption and destruction of commissary and ordnance stores collected at Staunton for shipment to
Lee's army. With his strength thus doubled to 18,000, Hunter promptly took up
the march for Lynchburg, another important depot of supplies, located where
the Virginia & Tennessee Railroad branched east to form the Southside and the
Orange & Alexandria; after which he intended to strike northeast for Charlottesville, where he would get back astride the Virginia Central and move down
it to join Grant near Richmond, twisting rails and burning crossties as he went.

Again he was moving toward reinforcements, this time of the
doughtiest kind. Grant had no sooner learned of Hunter's coup at Piedmont
than he decided to proceed at once with the opening phase of the plan he had
outlined that day for Halleck. He sent for Sheridan and gave him orders to take
off at dawn of June 7, westward around Lee's north flank, for a link-up with
Hunter near Charlottesville; he was to lend the help of his hard-handed troopers
in wrecking the Virginia Central on his way back and, if necessary, fight off any

★

graybacks, mounted or dismounted, who might try to interfere. In this connection Grant conferred next day with Meade, explaining the ticklish necessity of keeping enough pressure on Lee to discourage him from sending any part of his army against Sheridan or Hunter, yet not so much pressure that Lee would fall back to the permanent fortifications in his rear, whose strength might also permit such a detachment of troops for the protection of the vital rail supply route from the Shenandoah Valley. (This was also why Grant, in addition to his habitual disinclination in such matters, had not wanted to risk encouraging his opponent by making a forthright request for permission to bury his dead and bring in the wounded suffering in his front.) At the same time, Meade was instructed to start work on a second line of intrenchments, just in rear of his present works, stout enough to be held by a skeleton force if Lee attacked while the army was in the early stages of its withdrawal across the Chickahominy, down beyond White Oak Swamp, to and across the James.

One thing more Grant did while Sheridan was preparing to take off next morning, and that was to call in two of his aides, Horace Porter and another young lieutenant colonel, Cyrus Comstock, who was also a West Pointer and a trained engineer. Both were familiar with the region to be traversed, having served under McClellan in the course of that general's "change of base" two years ago, and Grant had a double mission for them: one as carriers of instructions for Butler at Bermuda Hundred, the other as selectors of a site for what promised to be the longest pontoon bridge in American military history. "Explain the contemplated movement fully to General Butler," he told them, "and see that the necessary precautions are made by him to render his position secure against any attack from Lee's forces while the Army of the Potomac is making its movement." That was their first assignment, and the second, involving engineering skill, followed close behind. "You will then select the best point on the river for the crossing."

They left, and the following day — with Sheridan's troopers gone before dawn, the burial squads at their grisly task out front, and Meade in a snit over Crapsey's piece in the *Inquirer* — Grant got to work, while awaiting the outcome of his preliminary arrangements, on logistic details of the projected shift. He did so, however, over the continuing objections of the chief of staff. Halleck had been against a southside campaign two years ago, when McClellan pled so fervently for permission to undertake what Grant was about to do, and he still was as much opposed as ever, believing that such a maneuver was practically an invitation for Lee to cross the Potomac. The old fox had already crossed it twice without success, it was true, but the third time might prove to be the charm that won him Washington, especially now that Grant, having stripped its forts of soldiers, proposed to leave it strategically uncovered.

Old Brains continued thus to take counsel of his fears; but not

Grant, whose mind was quite made up. "We can defend Washington best," he informed Halleck, putting an end to discussion of the matter, "by keeping Lee so occupied that he cannot detach enough troops to capture it. I shall prepare at once to move across James River."

★ ★ ★ *G*rant being Grant, and Halleck having long since lost the veto, that was that. The Union commander was soon to find, however, that his effort to keep Lee so occupied with the close-up defense of Richmond that he would not feel able to send any considerable part of his outnumbered force against Hunter or Sheridan had failed.

Learning on June 6 of Jones's defeat at Piedmont and Hunter's rapid occupation of Staunton, Lee sent at once for Breckinridge and informed him that he and his two brigades would be leaving next morning for Lynchburg to prevent the capture of that important railroad junction by the bluecoats they had whipped three weeks ago under Sigel, a hundred miles to the north. Instructed to combine his 2100 veterans with the Piedmont fugitives for this purpose, the Kentuckian left on schedule, determined to repeat his New Market triumph, although he would be facing longer odds and was personally in a near-invalid condition as a result of having his horse collapse on him four days ago.

With Grant likely to resume his hammering at any moment, here at Cold Harbor or elsewhere along a semicircular arc from Atlee Station down to Chaffin's Bluff — all within ten miles of Capitol Square — even so minor a reduction in strength as this detachment of two brigades was a risky business for Lee, no matter how urgent the need. Yet before the day was over he was warned of another threat which called for a second detachment, larger and more critical than the first. Sheridan, he learned from outpost scouts, had taken off before dawn with two of his divisions, about the same time Breckinridge left Richmond, headed west by rail for Lynchburg. The bandy-legged cavalryman's march was north, across the Pamunkey; he made camp that night on the near bank of the Mattaponi, and next morning — June 8 — he was reported moving west. Lee reasoned that the blue horsemen intended to effect a junction with Hunter on this or the far side of the Blue Ridge, somewhere along the Virginia Central, which they would obstruct while waiting for him to join them for the return march. If Sheridan was to be thwarted it would have to be done by a force as mobile as his own, and though Lee found it hard to deprive himself of a single trooper at a time when his adversary was no doubt contemplating another sidle, he sent Hampton orders to set out next morning, with his own and Fitzhugh Lee's divisions, to intercept the raiders before they reached either Hunter or the railroad.

Yet this too, as it turned out, was a day that brought unwelcome news of the need for still another reduction of the outnumbered army in its

★

trenches near Cold Harbor. Crook and Averell, Lee was informed, had joined Hunter that morning in Staunton, doubling his strength beyond anything Breckinridge, with less than a third as many troops — including the Piedmont fugitives, once he managed to round them up — could be expected to confront, much less defeat. Obviously he would have to be reinforced; but how? Then came the notion Halleck was even now warning Grant that his proposed maneuver would invite from Lee, who had a way of making a virtue of necessity. Hunter's strength was put at 20,000, and it was clear that if he was to be stopped it would have to be done by two or three divisions, available only — if at all — from the Confederate main body.

Such a decrease in the force confronting Grant, merely for the sake of blocking Hunter, seemed little short of suicidal. But how would it be if a sizeable detachment could be used offensively, as a means not only of reclaiming the Shenandoah Valley and covering the supply lines leading to it, but also of threatening Washington by crossing the Potomac? Twice before, a dispersion of force, made in the face of odds as long or longer, had relieved the pressure on Richmond by playing on the fears of the Union high command. McClellan and Hooker had been recalled to protect the menaced capital in their rear; so might Grant be summoned back to meet a similar threat. Impossible though it seemed

Ulysses S. Grant (left), with Theodore Bowers (standing) and John Rawlins, studies a map at his headquarters in June 1864. His objective was Richmond.

at this fitful juncture, such a maneuver was never really out of Lee's mind, and it was especially attractive now that rumors had begun to fly that Grant was designing a shift to the James, perhaps for a link-up with Butler on the other side. "If he gets there it will become a siege," Lee had told Early the week before, "and then it will be a mere question of time."

Hampton had no sooner taken off next morning, riding the chord of Sheridan's arc to intercept him, than an alarm from beyond the James lent credence to the rumor that the Federals were preparing a new effort in that direction, or in any case an improved resumption of the old one. Butler, crossing a portion of his command from Bermuda Neck by a pontoon bridge he had thrown across the Appomattox near Port Walthall, launched a dawn attack on the Petersburg intrenchments, four miles south. Beauregard, down to fewer than 8000 troops by now, managed to contain and repulse this cavalry-infantry assault because of the strength of the works and the valiance of the men who occupied them, mostly under- and over-aged members of a militia battalion, reinforced for the crisis by volunteers from the city hospital and the county jail. In the resultant "Battle of the Patients and the Penitents," as it came to be called, these inexperienced defenders — inspired by a local Negro band whose vigorous playing gave the attackers the impression that the works were heavily manned — held their own long enough for grayjacket cavalry to arrive from the main line, beyond the Appomattox, and drive the bluecoats off. It was over by midafternoon, a near thing at best, and Beauregard, though proud of what had been achieved, warned that he could not be expected to repeat the performance unless the troops he had sent Lee were restored to him. Moreover, he told the War Department, they had better be returned at once, since in his opinion today's attack presaged a much larger one soon to come.

"This movement must be a reconnaissance connected with Grant's future operations," he wired Bragg while the fight was still in progress, and presently he added, by way of emphasizing the risk: "Without the troops sent to General Lee I will have to elect between abandoning lines on Bermuda Neck and those of Petersburg. Please give me the views of the Government on the subject."

Presented thus with a choice between losing Richmond to assault or by starvation, Bragg could only reply that the mercurial Creole was to do what he could to hold both positions, while he himself conferred with Davis, who authorized the return of Gracie's brigade from the capital defenses, and with Lee, who agreed to alert Hoke's division for a crossing at Drewry's in case another southside attack developed. Mainly, though, the Virginian saw this abortive maneuver of Butler's as a feint, designed to distract his attention from more serious threats presented by more dependable Union commanders on the north side of the James: by Meade, who might even now be bracing his army for another

★

*N*ear Cold Harbor, Federal cavalry horses stand outside the
Old Church Hotel, Philip Sheridan's headquarters
before he began his raid on the Virginia Central Railroad.

all-out lunge, here at Cold Harbor or elsewhere along the Richmond-hugging arc: by Hunter, who was evidently about to resume his march from Staunton, with either Lynchburg or Charlottesville as his intermediate goal, preparatory to a combination with Meade: or by Sheridan, who was in motion between the other two, probably with the intention of descending on the Virginia Central before linking up with Hunter for a return march that would complete the destruction of that vital supply line. Despite a rather superfluous warning from the President, who added his voice to Bragg's — "The indications are that Grant, despairing of a direct attack, is now seeking to embarrass you by flank movements" — Lee could not see that the thing to do, at this critical juncture, was weaken his army below the present danger point for the sake of relieving Beauregard's fears as to what Butler might or might not be up to, down on the far side of the James. Until Grant's intentions became clearer, and until he could see what came of the two detachments already made — Breckinridge, two days ago, and Hampton just this morning — Lee preferred to hold what he had, and hope that others, elsewhere, would measure up to his expectations.

★

Wade Hampton, whose assignment to lead the two-division column in pursuit of Sheridan was the nearest Lee had come to designating a successor to the fallen Stuart, was intent on fulfilling his share of the army commander's hopes, not so much because of a desire for fame or an ache for glory — "I pray for peace," he would presently say in a letter to his sister, having won the coveted post by demonstrating his fitness for it in the current operation; "I would not give peace for all the military glory of Bonaparte" — as because of a habitual determination to accomplish what was required of him, in this as in other phases of a life of privileged responsibility. He wore no plume, no red-lined cape, and a minimum of braid, preferring a flat-brimmed brown felt hat and a plain gray jacket of civilian cut. His manner, while friendly, was grave, and though he was perhaps the richest man in the South, his spurs were brass, not gold. A Virginia trooper noted another difference between the Carolinian and his predecessor as chief of cavalry, which was that, whereas Jeb had "sometimes seemed to have a delight in trying to discharge his mission with the smallest possible number of men, Hampton believed in superiority of force and exerted himself to concentrate all the men he could at the point of contact."

Superiority of force would not be possible short of the point of contact in this case; for though both mounted columns were composed of two divisions containing a total of five brigades, Sheridan had 8000 troopers, compared to Hampton's 5000, and four batteries of horse artillery opposing three. One advantage the gray riders had, however, and this was that they traveled lighter, with fewer impediments to slow them down. The Federals had a train of 125 supply wagons and ambulances, as well as a herd of beef to butcher on the march, while all the Confederates had was an issue of three-day rations, consisting of half a pound of bacon and a pound and a half of hardtack, carried on the person, along with a sack of horse corn slung from the pommel of each saddle.

Another advantage, although no one could be sure of it beforehand, was that Lee had been right about Sheridan's objective; Hampton had a much shorter distance to travel, northwest from Atlee, across the South Anna, in order to get there first. This he did, despite the blue column's two-day head start in setting out on its roundabout route from Cold Harbor, first north across the Pamunkey, then west through Chilesburg, up the left bank of the North Anna for a crossing short of Gordonsville and a quick descent, as ordered, on the Virginia Central between that place and Louisa Court House, a dozen miles down the track. Shortly after sunrise, June 11, within about three miles of his objective at the outset of his fifth day on the go, Sheridan ran into fire from rebel skirmishers, who, he now found, had arrived the previous evening and had rested from their two-day ride within earshot of the bugles that called his troopers to horse this morning.

Hampton was not only there, he was attacking in accordance with plans made the night before, after learning that he had won the race for the stretch of railroad Sheridan had in mind to wreck. His own division, with three brigades, was to advance northeast from Trevilian Station, eight miles short of Gordonsville and half that distance above Louisa, where Fitz Lee, having bivouacked his two brigades nearby, was to set out north at daybreak for a convergence upon Sheridan's camp, five miles away. Each division had a convenient road to move on, and Hampton at least was unhindered on the approach march. Hearing firing off to the east, which he took to be Fitz brushing pickets from his path, he sent his lead brigade forward, dismounted, and made contact with the Federals, driving them rapidly back on their supports, who resisted stubbornly even when hit by a second brigade. Hampton withheld full commitment, waiting for Lee to come up and strike the defenders flank and rear.

At this point, however, a sudden clatter from the south informed him that his own rear had been struck. By what, and how, he did not wait to learn. Disengaging with all possible speed, and pursued now by the enemy he had driven, he withdrew to find a host of blue marauders laying claim to his headquarters and the 800 horses left behind when he dismounted his lead brigade for the sunrise attack. He attacked again, this time rearward, and what had been a battle became a melee.

Wade Hampton's Confederate horsemen clash with a Federal cavalry brigade led by George A. Custer at Trevilian Station near Gordonsville on June 11.

★

The marauders were members of Custer's brigade, one of Torbert's three. While the other two were holding fast under pressure from Hampton, Gregg's division had got the jump on Fitz and driven him back toward Louisa, enabling the Michiganders to slip between the converging gray columns for a penetration deep into Hampton's rear, near Trevilian. Yet they had no sooner begun to gather the fruits of their boldness — the 800 riderless horses, several ordnance wagons, and a couple of guns being held there in reserve — than they were hit, simultaneously from the north and east, by three hornet-mad rebel brigades, two of them Hampton's and one Lee's. Custer not only had to abandon what he had won; he also lost much that he brought with him, including a considerable number of troopers shot or captured, his headquarters wagon containing all his records and spare clothes, and his Negro cook Eliza, known to the soldiers as "the Queen of Sheba" because she usually rode in a dilapidated family carriage the yellow-haired general had commandeered for her professional use and comfort. Shaken, he fell back to the station and held on grimly against the odds, while Torbert fought his way down with the other two brigades and Gregg continued to slug it out with Fitz. The result was about as bewildering to one side as to the other, and was to be even more confusing to future students attempting to reconcile conflicting reports of the action. The Confederates at last pulled back, Hampton toward Gordonsville and Lee in the opposite direction. Sheridan did not pursue, west or east, but contented himself with holding the four miles of track between Trevilian and Louisa. It was a gloomy night for the Federals, especially those in Custer's brigade, which had lost heavily today; but their dejection was relieved, just before sunup, by the reappearance of the Queen of Sheba, grinning broadly and lugging along the gaudy young general's personal valise, which she had managed to bring with her when she stole out of the rebel lines and into her own.

Sheridan was far from pleased with the development of events. After a night of fitful sleep, with graybacks hovering east and west — about to be joined, for all he knew, by reinforcements from both directions, infantry by rail and cavalry on horseback — he put Gregg to work with sledges and crowbars on the four-mile stretch of track and prepared to enlarge his present limits of destruction, first by driving Hampton back on Gordonsville, eight miles northwest, and then by thrusting him aside to clear the way for the scheduled meeting with Hunter, another twenty miles up the line at Charlottesville.

It was past noon, however, before he got Torbert deployed for action; by which time Fitz Lee had joined Hampton, coming roundabout from Louisa, and the two divisions were dug in just above Trevilian, blocking both the Virginia Central and the turnpike leading west. Repeated and costly dismounted assaults failed to budge the rebels, snug in their works, and after nightfall, Gregg having done all the damage he could to the railroad within

★

*P*hilip Sheridan
(reclining far
right) confers with
commanders of his
Federal cavalry
corps during a
break in the raid
on the Virginia
Central Railroad.

the cramped limits of the Federal occupation, Sheridan decided to abandon both his position and his mission.

Under cover of darkness he withdrew across the North Anna and took up the return march, retracing the route that had brought him to the unhappy confrontation at Trevilian. He pulled back, he said, because his supplies and munitions were low and there was no word from Hunter, either at Charlottesville or elsewhere, as to their intended combination. In any case, having spent four days on the march out, he took nine to make it back to White House Landing, his ambulances overloaded with wounded and his horses distressed at being reduced to a diet of bearded wheat.

Meantime, the limited damage Gregg had done the railroad was repaired so promptly by work gangs that Virginia Central trains were back on schedule before Sheridan reached the Pamunkey and recrossed it under the protection of gunboats whose heavy-caliber frown kept the still-hovering butternut cavalry at bay. Hampton had lost nearly 1100 men in the course of the raid; Sheridan reckoned his own loss at about 800, though a more accurate revision put the figure at 1516, considerably better than twice the number he had lost on the Richmond raid the month before.

R. E. Lee of course was pleased to learn that Little Phil had been disposed of as a threat to his main supply route from the Shenandoah Valley: so pleased, indeed, that he at last named Hampton, rather than his nephew Fitz, as his new chief of cavalry. But word of Sheridan's repulse came in the wake of news of a fateful development, out beyond the Blue Ridge, which not only

★

presented a more substantial menace to the newly delivered supply line, but also served notice that, even if the railroad escaped seizure, there would be little in the way of supplies available for shipment from the region, either to Richmond or to any other point in the shrinking Confederacy.

The news was that David Hunter, his strength doubled by the arrival of Crook two days before, had resumed his march up the Valley on June 10. Leaving Breckinridge holding the bag at Rockfish Gap, where the Virginia Central passed through the mountains east of Staunton — the Kentuckian had shifted there from Lynchburg to block the western approach to Charlottesville, which he thought was next on the Union list — Hunter struck out south, not east, and by noon of the day the cavalry battle opened near Trevilian Station, eighty air-line miles away, reached Lexington and took under fire, from across North River, the crenelated turrets and ramparts of V.M.I., whose cadets had shared in the defeat of his predecessor four weeks ago. Marching in, flags flying, he completed his work of destruction, next day and the day after, by putting the torch to what was left of the Institute and turning his soldiers loose on the town to plunder a number of private homes and the library of Washington College. For good measure, after a visit to Stonewall Jackson's grave — perhaps to make certain the famed rebel had not come bursting out of it in his wrath — Hunter ordered the residence of Former Governor John Letcher burned, as he later reported, in retaliation for its absent owner's having issued "a violent and inflammatory proclamation . . . inciting the population of the country to rise and wage guerrilla warfare on my troops."

Such hard-handedness toward civilians was remindful of John Pope, of whom Lee had said: "He ought to be suppressed," and then had proceeded to do just that by dividing his army, confronted near Richmond by a superior force, and sending part of it north and west, under the one-time V.M.I. professor now buried in outraged Lexington, against the fire-breathing secondary invader attempting a descent on his left flank and rear. Close though the resemblance was between the situations then and now, there were also differences, none of them advantageous from the Confederate point of view. One was that Jackson, Lee's right arm, was no longer available to carry out the suppression, and another was the present depleted condition of the Army of Northern Virginia, which had lost in the past forty days a solid forty percent of the strength it had enjoyed at the beginning of the campaign.

Its casualties totaled about 27,000, and though it had inflicted a precisely tabulated 54,929 — a number greater than all its original infantry and artillery combined — the forty percent figure, unlike Grant's forty-five percent, applied at the higher levels of rank as well as at the lower. Of the 58 general officers in command of troops on the eve of conflict, back in early May, no less than 23 had fallen in battle, eight of them killed, thirteen gravely wounded, and two

★

captured. Nor was the distribution of these casualties, high and low, by any means even throughout the three corps. Hardest hit of all was the Second: just the one Lee had in mind to detach, since it contained, as a nucleus, the survivors of Jackson's old Army of the Valley and was therefore more familiar than the others with the region Hunter was laying waste. Not only had the corps commander been replaced, but so had the leaders of two of the three divisions, while of the twelve original brigade commanders only one remained at his post, two having been promoted and the other nine shot or captured. At Spotsylvania the corps had lost the equivalent of a full division, and this contributed largely to the reduction, by half, of its outset strength of just over 17,000. There now were barely 8000 infantry in its ranks, distributed through three divisions with only three brigades in each, all but one under leaders new to their responsibilities.

These were drawbacks not to be ignored in reaching a decision; but neither was the need for dealing promptly with Hunter to be passed over. From his current position at Lexington he would no doubt cross the Blue Ridge, marching southeast against Lynchburg or northeast against Charlottesville. One would be about as bad as the other, so far as Richmond was concerned, and there was also the possibility that the wide-ranging Hunter might move against them both, in that order. At Lynchburg, just under a hundred miles due west of the capital, he would be in a position to wreck not only the Southside Railroad

After torching the barracks of the Virginia Military Institute (above), Federal troops plundered homes and burned the residence of a former Virginia governor.

but also the James River Canal, both vital to the subsistence of Richmond's citizens and its armies, while at Charlottesville he would be back astride the Virginia Central, which he would destroy, with or without Sheridan's help, on the march to join Grant or come down on Lee's flank. Reduced to those terms, the problem solved itself, insofar at least as they applied to reaching a decision. Like Pope, Hunter would have to be "suppressed," or anyhow stopped and, if possible, driven back. Lee's mind was quite made up.

Moreover, there was the persuasive chance that in moving against the despoilers of Lexington he would be killing two birds with one stone. If, after disposing of the bluecoats out in the Valley, the gray column then moved down it, to and across the Potomac to threaten Washington from the rear, still larger benefits might accrue. There was small chance, at this late stage, that Grant's whole force would be recalled — as McClellan's had been — from the gates of Richmond, but it was altogether possible that he would be required to detach part of it for the close-up defense of his capital; or else, in desperation to avoid that, he might be provoked into launching another ill-considered Cold Harbor assault, there or elsewhere, in an attempt to settle the issue overnight. In either event, Lee reasoned, his adversary would be reduced enough for the Army of Northern Virginia to launch an all-out assault of its own: hopefully one that would be as productive as the Seven Days offensive, but in any case one that would be conducted with all the fighting skill his soldiers had acquired in their many victories since that grim beginning under his command.

His decision reached — June 12, a Sunday; the horseback fight was into its second day at Trevilian Station, and Hunter was putting the torch to Governor Letcher's house in Lexington — Lee sent for Jubal Early to talk over with him the nature of his mission. Tall despite an arthritic stoop, a bachelor at forty-seven, dour of face, with a scraggly beard and a habit of profanity, this fellow Virginian and West Pointer was admittedly no Stonewall; but who was? No other corps commander since the fall of Longstreet had done any better on the offensive, and though this was surely the faintest of praise — since, conversely, it could also be said that none had done any worse — the only really black mark against him was his failure, in conjunction with Ewell on the second day in the Wilderness, to take prompt advantage of Gordon's report that Sedgwick's flank was open to attack. No such opportunities must be missed if he was to succeed against the odds that lay before him, first in the Valley and then beyond the Potomac. Tactful as always, Lee made this clear in giving Early verbal instructions for setting out next morning, before daylight, with all three of his divisions and two battalions of artillery.

Following as it did the detachment of Breckinridge, with whom he would combine to cover Charlottesville and Lynchburg, Early's departure would deprive Lee of nearly a fourth of his infantry; yet, even with the inclusion

★

of the Piedmont fugitives, the gray force would not be up to Hunter's present strength. Victory would have to be won by superior generalship, by celerity, stealth, and an absolute dedication to the offensive: in short, by the application of principles dear to the commander of the erstwhile Army of the Valley, which was now to be resurrected under Early.

In written orders, sent that night while the Second Corps veterans were preparing feverishly and happily to be gone with the dawn, these hopes were repeated, together with specific instructions for the march. It would be northwest, like Hampton's four days earlier, for a link-up with Breckinridge near Rockfish Gap and a quick descent on Hunter before he reached Lynchburg. After that, if all went well, would come the northward march against a new old adversary, Abraham Lincoln — and, through Lincoln and his fears, against U. S. Grant, who presumably would still be knocking at the gates of Richmond, a hundred miles away.

★ ★ ★ *G*rant might still be knocking when the time came, but if so it would be at the back gate, not the front. Under cover of the darkness that would obscure Early's departure, north and west, the Army of the Potomac had begun its withdrawal, east and south, from its works around Cold Harbor for the crossing of the James. Moreover, if all went as intended, here and elsewhere, the issue would have been settled — so far, at least, as Richmond was concerned — well before any rebel detachment, of whatever size, had time to reach the Potomac, much less cross it to threaten Washington. With Sheridan astride the Virginia Central and Hunter about to wreck both the Southside Railroad and the James River Canal at Lynchburg (Grant did not know that Sheridan was being driven off that evening, any more than he knew that Lee was sending Early next morning to do the same to Hunter) Federal seizure of the Petersburg rail hub would cut all but one of the gray capital's major supply lines, the Richmond & Danville, which had only been extended down to Greensboro, North Carolina, the month before. No single route, let alone one as limited as this, could supply the city's needs, including subsistence for its defenders; Lee, more than ever, would be obliged to evacuate his capital or come out from behind his intrenchments for a fight in the open, and Grant did not believe that the Confederacy could survive what would follow the adoption of either course.

He had bided his time, anticipating solutions, and when they came he moved swiftly. When the two aides, Porter and Comstock, returned from their reconnaissance that Sunday morning to report that they had found a good site for the pontoon bridge across the James, ten miles downriver from City Point and just beyond Charles City Court House, he evidenced some measure of the strain he had been under this past week. "While listening to our report," Porter

would recall, "Grant showed the only nervousness he ever manifested in my presence. After smoking his cigar vigorously for some minutes, he removed it from his mouth, put it on the table, and allowed it to go out; then relighted it, gave a few puffs, and laid it aside again. We could hardly get the words out of our mouths fast enough to suit him, and the numerous questions he asked were uttered with much greater rapidity than usual." This was a different Grant from the stolid, twig-whittling commander of the past six weeks. It was, as the next few days would show, the Grant of the Vicksburg campaign, fast on the march, sudden in striking, and above all quick to improvise amid rapidly developing events. "At the close of the interview," Porter wrote, still amazed years later at the transformation in his chief, "he informed us that he would begin the movement that night."

It began, in point of fact, that afternoon, when Grant and Meade and their two staffs proceeded down the north bank of the Chickahominy, past Dispatch Station on the defunct York River Railroad, to make camp for the night beside a clump of catalpa trees in the yard of a farmhouse near Long Bridge, where two of the five corps were to cross the river, ten miles downstream from the present Union left. The bridge was out, but Wilson's cavalry splashed across the shallows, just after sundown, and got to work throwing a pontoon span to be used by Warren, who began his march in the twilight and was over the river by midnight. Hancock and Wright meantime fell back to the newly dug second

This painting by Edward Henry depicts the Federal supply base at City Point, at the confluence of the James and Appomattox rivers near Petersburg, Virginia.

line, under orders to hold it at all costs, in case Lee got wind of the withdrawal and launched a night attack. Smith and Burnside simultaneously marched rearward from their positions on the right, the latter turning south beyond the railroad for a crossing of the Chickahominy at Jones Bridge, five miles below Long Bridge, and Smith continuing east to White House Landing, where transports were waiting to give his troops a fast, restful trip down the York and up the James to Bermuda Hundred.

Satisfied that Lee had no overnight interference in mind, Hancock and Wright pulled out after midnight to follow Warren and Burnside, respectively, over Long and Jones bridges. Once across, three of the four corps would march hard for Charles City and the James, but Warren was instructed to turn west and take up a defensive position near Riddell's Shop in support of Wilson's troopers, who would patrol the region between White Oak Swamp and Malvern Hill in case Lee, having missed his chance tonight, tried to strike tomorrow at the blue army in motion across his front. Like Wright and Hancock earlier, once he was convinced that Lee had been outfoxed, Warren would take up the march for Charles City and the crossing of the James.

Intricate as these various interdependent movements were, they had been worked out in accordance with the required logistics of allotted time and road space. All went smoothly. Despite the heat of the night and the choking

★

dust stirred up by more than a hundred thousand pairs of shoes, the men stepped out smartly in the darkness, glad to be leaving a dismal field where they had buried so many comrades after so much purposeless suffering. Occupied as they had been with improving their intrenchments, right up to the hour they got orders to withdraw, they took it as an excellent sign that their departure had been preceded by no rumor that a shift was being considered, since what came as a surprise to them was likely to be even more of one to the johnnies across the way, including Old Man Lee. "It was not now the custom," one veteran observed approvingly, "to inform the rank and file, and the newspapers and the enemy, of intended movements."

He and others like him in those several widespread dusty columns could remember another nighttime withdrawal from that same field, just two weeks short of two full years ago, and though Cold Harbor was in itself an even more horrendous experience than Gaines Mill, the feeling now was different, and altogether better. Now as then the march was south, away from the scene of a defeat; but they felt now — as they had not done then, while trudging some of these same James-bound roads — that they were moving toward a victory, even Victory itself.

Grant thought so, too, and on sounder ground, knowing, as they did not, what he had devised for the undoing of the rebels on the far side of the river. Smith, whose corps was familiar with the terrain down there, would arrive first, being steam-propelled, and after going ashore at Bermuda Hundred would repeat the maneuver Butler had rehearsed four days ago, across the Appomattox, when his Petersburg reconnaissance-in-strength was stalled by green militia, convicts, convalescents, and Negro bandsmen. That was not likely to happen this time, for three reasons.

One was that Baldy would be in charge of the advance, not the non-professional Butler, and Grant had already explained to his fellow West Pointer the importance of striking hard and fast. Another was that this attack would not only be made in much greater strength than the other, but would also be launched with the advantage of knowing the layout of the Petersburg defenses. The third reason was that, if there was any delay in the quick reduction of the place, Hancock — whose three divisions, in the lead on the march from Cold Harbor, would be ferried across the James to save time while the 2100-foot pontoon bridge was being assembled — would soon be down to add the weight of the hardest-hitting corps in Meade's army to the pressure Smith was exerting. As for the others, Burnside, Warren, and Wright would be arriving in that order behind Hancock and could be used as then seemed best: probably for a breakout westward from Bermuda Neck, dislodging Beauregard's cork, and a turning movement against Drewry's Bluff, which would block the path of any reinforcements Lee might try to send to Petersburg when he found what Grant had been up to all this time.

★

Members of the two staffs — Grant's and Meade's — shared the sanguine expectations of their chiefs, at least to the extent that they were privy to the plan, and their confidence grew as the day wore on and they rode south, doubling the columns of guns and men on the dusty roads. All the signs were that the army had indeed stolen a march on Lee, whose cavalry, unable to penetrate Wilson's screen below the Chickahominy, could give him no inkling of what was in progress east of Riddell's Shop, near which Warren's four divisions remained in position without firing a shot all afternoon, so effectively did the blue troopers perform, and then resumed their roundabout hike for the James. By that time the head of Hancock's column had come within sight of the broad, shining river, its choppy little waves as bright as polished hatchets in the sunlight.

Transports and gunboats were riding at anchor, all with steam up for the crossing, and army engineers were at work assembling their pontoons for the nearly half-mile span by which the other three corps would cross, tomorrow and the next day. An officer on Meade's staff observed Hancock's troops slogging down to Wilcox Landing just before sunset, hot and tired from their thirty-mile overnight march, their faded, sweat-splotched uniforms in tatters from forty days of combat, and was struck by the thought that, so far as these hard-bitten veterans were concerned, "the more they serve, the less they look

Photographed from atop a supply wagon, Federal troops cross the James River on a 2100-foot pontoon bridge installed by engineers on June 14.

★

like soldiers and the more they resemble day laborers who have bought second-hand military clothes." Then he watched them react with suspicion and puzzled dislike, much as he himself had done earlier, to their first sight of the neatly turned-out sailors and the engineers in uniforms of dark unweathered blue, until at last they saw, as he had seen, what it was that was so wrong about these strangers. They were clean — clean as visitors from some dirtless planet — and Grant's men, after six weeks on the go, shooting and being shot at, with neither the water nor the time for bathing, had become mistrustful of anyone not as grimy as themselves.

Yet despite the grime and the suspicion that went with it, despite the added weariness and the fret that over the past six weeks they had suffered three separate 18,000-man subtractions from their ranks — first in the Wilderness, then at Spotsylvania, and last on the North Anna, Totopotomoy Creek, and the Chickahominy — their spirits were even higher near the end of the Jamesward trek

---

"The picture presented is one of ultimate starvation."

— Pierre G. T. Beauregard

---

than at the outset: not only from being on the move again, away from the stench and snipers at Cold Harbor, but also because they could see what had begun to come of this latest sidle. Though they knew nothing of what lay ahead, on the far side of the shining river, they trusted Grant to make the most of the fact that they had given Lee the slip the night before and stolen a march on him today.

They had indeed done both those things, and were now in a position to do more. The first Lee had known of their departure was at sunup — two hours after Early withdrew his three divisions and set out for the Shenandoah Valley — when messengers reached headquarters, back near Gaines Mill, with reports that the Yankees were gone from their works around Cold Harbor. Advancing scouts uncovered a second line of intrenchments, newly dug and intricately fashioned as if for permanent occupation, but these too were deserted, as were the woods and fields a mile and more beyond. June 13, which was to have been the fortieth day of contact for the two armies, turned out to be a day of practically no contact at all; Grant was gone, vanished with his blue-clad throng, perhaps toward the lower stretches of the Chickahominy, more likely to a new base on the James from which to mount a new advance on Richmond, either by crossing the river for a back-door attack or else by moving up its near bank for an all-out assault on the capital fortifications.

★

Whichever it was, Lee warned the government of this latest threat and moved to meet it, shifting south to put what was left of his army in position below White Oak Swamp, where he would block the eastern approaches to the city and also be closer to Drewry's for a crossing in case the blow was aimed at Beauregard. While his son's two thin-spread cavalry brigades — all that were left since Hampton and Fitz Lee took out after Sheridan four days ago — probed unsuccessfully at rapid-firing masses of Federal horsemen coming down the Long Bridge Road toward Riddell's Shop, he posted Hill's corps in their support, athwart the field of the Seven Days fight at Glendale, and Anderson's off to the right, reaching down to Malvern Hill, which the cavalry then occupied as a post of observation, although nothing of much interest could be seen from there except a good deal of apparently purposeless activity by Union gunboats at Deep Bottom, down below.

Lee's ranks were so gravely thinned by Early's departure that he might have been expected to recall him while there still was time; but when the President inquired that afternoon whether this might not be the wisest course, Lee replied, rather laconically, that he did not think so. At the end of the Forty Days, as at the beginning, he remained the gambler he had always been, the believer that the weaker force must take the longer chances.

"I do not know that the necessity for his presence today is greater than it was yesterday," he said of Early. "His troops would make us more secure here, but success in the Valley would relieve our difficulties that at present press heavily upon us."

Those first four words, "I do not know," were the crux of the matter. All the prisoners taken so far today had been cavalry, which left him with nothing but guesses as to the whereabouts of the Union infantry and artillery, all hundred thousand of them. Most likely they were in motion for the James, but whether Grant intended for them to cross it or advance up the north bank Lee could not tell; nor could he act, for fear of being decoyed out of position, until he secured more or less definite information as to which course his adversary had taken or would take. Either way, the defense of Richmond had come down to a siege, the thing he had tried hardest to avoid.

"This army cannot stand a siege," he had told Little Powell a month ago, just as Beauregard, one week later, had warned Bragg: "The picture presented is one of ultimate starvation."

★   ★   ★

*Heading toward Atlanta,
Sherman abandoned the railroad
on May 20 to avoid this narrow
pass at Allatoona, defended by a
rebel fort on the hilltop at left.*

F O U R

Dalton to Pine Mountain

1864 ★ ★ ★ ★ ★ ★

A ir-line, the hundred-mile distance from **Chattanooga** to Atlanta was the same as that from Washington to Richmond, and so were the respective sizes of the armies, which in each paired case gave the Union commander a roughly two-to-one numerical advantage. But there for the most part the resemblance stopped. Meade and Sherman (or for that matter Grant and Sherman, since that was what it came to) were as different from each other as were Lee and Johnston, two very different men indeed, and so too — despite the fact that down in Georgia, as in Virginia, the rivers mainly ran athwart the projected lines of advance and retreat — was the terrain, flat or gently rolling in the East, but mountainous in the West and therefore eminently defensible, at any rate in theory, although few of the place-names strewn about the map had been connected with much bloodshed since the era when settlers ousted the aborigines.

In point of fact, harking back to those massacre days, Sherman had something similar in mind for the Confederates to his front, military and civilian. "If the North design to conquer the South," he had written home two years ago, "we must begin at Kentucky and reconquer the country from there as we did from the Indians."

Now that he faced completion of that massive undertaking, he was in

★

what he liked to call "high feather." Instructed by Grant "to move against Johnston's army, break it up, and get into the interior of the enemy's country as far as you can, inflicting all the damage you can against their war resources," the red-haired Ohioan, by way of showing how well he understood his task, replied in paraphrase: "I am to knock Jos. Johnston, and to do as much damage to the resources of the enemy as possible."

By way of help in carrying out this project he would have an advantage, a man-made facility available neither to his flintlock-carrying predecessors nor to his cohorts in the East: namely, a rapid-transit all-weather supply line in the form of a railroad, the Western & Atlantic, running all the way to Atlanta — provided, of course, he could put and keep it in shape while nudging Johnston backward; for the rebels would surely wreck it in their wake, and almost as surely would strike at it with cavalry in his rear as he advanced. With this in mind, he made the training of rail repair gangs an integral part of his preparations, including

---

"I am to knock Jos. Johnston, and to do as much damage to the resources of the enemy as possible."

— William Tecumseh Sherman

---

daily workouts as rigorous and precise as the drill required of gun crews, and elevated gandy dancers to a combat status as high as that of riflemen or cannoneers. The same precaution was taken with regard to the much longer line extending rearward from Chattanooga, up through Middle Tennessee and across Kentucky to Louisville, his main supply base on the Ohio. Practically all of this more than three hundred miles of highly frangible track was subject to strikes by grayback troopers from adjoining departments, hard-handed horsemen schooled in destruction by John Morgan and Bedford Forrest, and though Sherman planned to keep these slashers occupied by making adjunctive trouble for them in their own back yards, he also hoped to forestall or reduce the delays that were likely to attend such depredations, in case the raiders broke out anyhow, by turning Nashville into what an amazed staff brigadier presently described as "one vast storehouse — warehouses covering city blocks, one a quarter of a mile long; stables by the ten and twenty acres, repair shops by the fieldful." Also of help in reducing the supply problem would be a certain amount of belt-tightening by the troops, whose divisional trains, in accordance with Sherman's orders, would carry only "five days' bacon, twenty days' bread, and thirty days' salt, sugar, and coffee; nothing else but arms and ammunition."

The main thing, as the commanding general saw it, was to keep moving: and this applied as much to rearward personnel as it did to the men up front. "I'm going to move on Joe Johnston the day Grant telegraphs me he is going to hit Bobby Lee," he told a quartermaster officer. "And if you don't have my army supplied, and keep it supplied, we'll eat your mules up, sir; eat your mules up!" Having passed before through un-fought-over regions of the South — recently, for example, on a march across the midriff of Mississippi, from Vicksburg to Meridian and back — he was aware of another resource which he did not intend to neglect. "Georgia has a million of inhabitants," he wrote Grant. "If they can live, we should not starve."

Thus Sherman; a violent-talking man whose bite at times measured up to his bark, and whose commitment was to total war. "I believe in fighting in a double sense," he said this spring, "first to gain physical results and next to inspire respect on which to build up our nation's power." Tecumseh or "Cump" to his family, he was Uncle Billy to his soldiers, one of whom called him "the most American-looking man I ever saw; tall and lank, not very erect, with hair like thatch, which he rubs up with his hands, a rusty beard trimmed close, a wrinkled face, sharp, prominent red nose, small, bright eyes, coarse red hands; black felt hat slouched over the eyes, dirty dickey with the points wilted down, black old-fashioned stock, brown field officer's coat with high collar and no shoulder straps, muddy trowsers and one spur. He carries his hands in his pockets, is very awkward in his gait and motions, talks continually and with immense rapidity." Such intensity often brought on a reaction in observers, including this one. "At his departure I felt it a relief, and experienced almost an exhaustion after the excitement of his vigorous presence."

All this, moreover, was by way of diversion, a spare-time release of superabundant energy from an organism described by another associate as "boiling over with ideas, crammed full of feeling, discussing every subject and pronouncing on all." His main concern for the past two months, as Grant's western heir, had been how to get at or around Johnston's army, posted thirty miles southeast of Chattanooga for the past five months, in occupation of Dalton and the wide, hilly valley of the Oostanaula, which extended southward forty-odd miles to the Etowah and southwestward about the same distance to Rome, where the two rivers combined to form the Coosa. The immediate tactical problem was Rocky Face Ridge, a steep, knife-edge bastion twenty miles long, rimming the upper valley on the west to cover Dalton and the railroad, which after piercing the ridge at Mill Creek Gap, one third of the way down, ran south and east for another hundred miles, through Resaca and Kingston, Allatoona and Marietta, on across the Chattahoochee to Atlanta, Johnston's base and Sherman's goal in the campaign about to open, here in North Georgia, in conjunction with Meade's plunge across the Rapidan, six hundred crow-flight miles to the northeast.

★

*On May 8, Sherman made a feint down this road
into the heavily defended Mill Creek Gap, then flanked
the rebels to the south of their stronghold at Dalton.*

Unlike Meade — thanks to Banks, holed up by now in Alexandria after his defeat at Sabine Crossroads — Sherman would not have the supposed advantage of diversionary attacks on the enemy flank or rear by troops from other departments, such as Sigel and Butler had been told to make. Whatever was going to be accomplished in the way of driving or maneuvering Johnston from his position along that ridge would have to be done by the men on hand. And though it was true that at present the Federals enjoyed a better than two-to-one numerical advantage (Johnston had just under 45,000 of all arms, with 138 guns, while Sherman had just over 110,000, with 254) the prospect was anything but pleasing. For one thing — thanks again to Banks, who was in no position to discourage, let alone interfere with, anything the Confederates might take it in mind to do on this side of the Mississippi River — Johnston had another 19,000 effectives and 50 guns, down in Alabama under Polk, presumably ready to join him at the first sign of danger, whereas Sherman could only look forward

★

to receiving about 10,000 due back next month from reënlistment furloughs. That still would leave him roughly a two-to-one advantage, but this by no means assured victory in assailing a position such as the one the rebels occupied, just ahead on Rocky Face Ridge.

Johnston, while successfully resisting Richmond's efforts to nudge him forward across the Tennessee, had spent the past four months preparing to resist the pending Union effort to prod him backward across the Chatta-hoochee. His two infantry corps, commanded by Lieutenant Generals William J. Hardee and John Bell Hood, each with about 20,000 men, were disposed along the northern half of the ridge, charged with giving particular attention to defending Mill Creek Gap, four miles northwest of Dalton, and Dug Gap, a second notch in the knife edge, five miles south. From the north end of this fortified position, Major General Joseph Wheeler's 5000 cavalry extended the line eastward to give warning in case the Federals tried to descend on Dalton by rounding the upper end of the ridge for a southward strike down the Oostanaula valley, where the ground was far less rugged and less easy to defend.

Sherman had no intention of moving in that direction, however, since to do so would uncover his base at Chattanooga: which brought him, regrettably, back to the dilemma of having to challenge the rebs in their apparently unassailable position, dead ahead on Rocky Face Ridge, securely intrenched and with high-sited guns ready-laid to blast the life out of whatever moved against them, in whatever strength. Moreover, as if nature had not done enough for him already, Johnston's engineers had lengthened the odds against the attackers by clogging the culverts of the railway ramp on the near side of the ridge, thus converting Mill Creek into an artificial lake across the rear of the gap that bore its name. Natives had a grislier designation; Buzzard Roost, they called the desolate notch through which the railroad wound its way. But Sherman, when at last he got a look at the rocky, high-walled gorge, catching glints of sunlight on the guns emplaced for its defense, pronounced it nothing less than "the terrible door of death," a term which would apply about as well to Dug Gap, just below.

George Thomas, who had felt out the gray defenses back in February, as a diversion intended to discourage Johnston from sending reinforcements to Polk while Sherman marched on Meridian, came up with the suggestion that, while McPherson and Schofield took over the position he now held in front of Ringgold, confronting the Rocky Face intrenchments, he take his four-corps Army of the Cumberland down the west side of the ridge to its far end, then press on eastward through unguarded Snake Creek Gap for a descent on the railroad near Resaca, fifteen miles in Johnston's rear. At best, this would expose the Confederates to a mauling when they fell back to protect their life line, as they would be obliged to do; while at worst, even if they somehow managed to avoid encirclement, it would turn them out of their all-but-impregnable position

★

between Chattanooga and Dalton and thus convert the present stalemate, which favored the defenders, into a war of maneuver, which would favor the side with the greater number of troops and guns.

Sherman, though the result his lieutenant promised was all he hoped for, rejected the proposal for two reasons. Thomas's command, twice the size of McPherson's and Schofield's combined, comprised a solid two thirds of the Federal total; secrecy would surely be lost in withdrawing so large a force and moving it such a distance, first across the enemy's front, then round his flank — and without secrecy, Sherman was convinced, it would be dangerous in the extreme to divide his army in the presence of so wily an adversary as the distinguished Virginian he faced. That was the first reason. The second was Thomas himself, the plodding, imperturbable Rock of Chickamauga. His specialty was staunchness, not celerity, the quality most needed in the movement he proposed.

But then, having dismissed the project as impractical when examined from that angle, Sherman shifted his point of view and experienced a surge of joy not unlike that of a poet revising the rejected draft of a poem he now perceives

The men of the 154th New York, General John Geary's vanguard, make a futile charge on the clearly unassailable Confederate position at Rocky Face Ridge.

will become the jewel of his collection. Celerity, presumed to be lacking in Thomas, was McPherson's hallmark, and the size of his command — just under 25,000, as compared to Thomas's more than 70,000 — seemed about right for the job. Moreover, there would be no need for a withdrawal from the immediate presence of a vigilant opponent; McPherson's two corps, not yet on line, could march south from Chattanooga, under cover of Taylor's Ridge, then swing east through Ship's Gap and Villanow to make a sudden descent on Resaca, by way of Snake Creek Gap, for the cutting of Johnston's life line before the Virginian even knew he was threatened from that direction, his attention having been focused all the while on Thomas, active in his front, and on Schofield, who would feint with his 13,000-man Army of the Ohio against the opposite flank, which lay in the path of his march down the railroad from Knoxville.

Thus Sherman set the pattern for the campaign about to open in North Georgia, a pattern that would utilize Thomas's outsized command — which contained more infantry and cavalry than all of Johnston's army, including the troops in Alabama under Polk — as the holding force, fixing the enemy in place, while McPherson and Schofield probed or rounded his flank or flanks to prise or chevy him out of position and expose him to being assailed on the march, or in any case to being struck before he had time to do much digging, anywhere between Dalton and Atlanta.

Sherman was delighted at the prospect, now that it loomed, and he also took a chauvinistic pleasure in the fact that such an arrangement gave the stellar role to McPherson, his favorite as well as Grant's, and the Army of the Tennessee, which had been his own and, up till Vicksburg, Grant's. Grant would approve, he knew when he wrote him of the plan, and as soon as that approval came down he passed the word to his three lieutenants. They would be in position no later than May 3, troops alerted for the jump-off next day, coincidental with Meade's crossing of the Rapidan.

And so it was. Detraining on schedule at Cleveland, where the East Tennessee & Georgia, coming down from Knoxville, branched to connect with Chattanooga and Dalton, both just under thirty miles away, Schofield prepared to march his army — in reality a corps, with three divisions of infantry and one of cavalry — southward along the left fork of the railroad to Red Clay, the state-line hamlet from which he was to launch his disconcerting strike at Johnston's right, down the valley east of Rocky Face. Thomas was poised beyond Ringgold, prepared to confront the defenders on the ridge and hold them in position there by pressing hard against Buzzard Roost and Dug Gap, threatening a breakthrough at both places. McPherson meantime had moved down to Lee & Gordon's Mills, at the south end of Chickamauga battlefield, which gave him a twelve-mile leg on the roundabout march to Resaca and the Oostanaula crossing. On May 4, in accordance with orders, all three began their separate movements designed to "knock Jos. Johnston." Sherman rode with Thomas in the center, but his hopes were with McPherson; "my whiplash," he called the Army of the Tennessee.

Despite the setbacks the rebels had suffered East and West in the past year, hard fighting lay ahead and Sherman knew it. "No amount of poverty or adversity seems to shake their faith," he marveled; "niggers gone, wealth and luxury gone, money worthless, starvation in view . . . yet I see no sign of let up — some few deserters, plenty tired of war, but the masses determined to fight it out." What they needed was more violent persuasion, he believed, and he was prepared to give it in full measure. "All that has gone before is mere skirmishing," he wrote his wife on setting forth.

Mere skirmishing was all it came to in the course of the next two days — the horrendous span of the Wilderness conflict, up in Virginia, where Lee and Meade lost better than 25,000 men between them — while Thomas felt his way forward along the Western & Atlantic and Schofield trudged down the other railroad to Red Clay, which took its name from the salmon-colored soil, powdery in dry weather and a torment to the nostrils of men on the march, but quick to turn as slippery as grease, newcomers would soon discover, under the influence of even the briefest shower.

There was no hurry at this stage of the game, both commanders having been told to give McPherson plenty of time on his roundabout march. On the third day out, the Cumberlanders ran into their first substantial opposition at Tunnel Hill, where the railroad went underground before emerging for its plunge through the gap in the ridge, two miles beyond. The rebs had set up a fortified outpost here, and Thomas had to attack with a whole corps next day, May 7, in order to drive them back on their main line, dug in along the steep west slope of Rocky Face Ridge, above Buzzard Roost and below it down to Dug Gap, five miles south. While this success — so complete, indeed, that the Confederate rear guard had no time to damage the tunnel before retreating — was being followed up, preparatory to coming to grips in earnest with the defenders on their ridge, Schofield crossed the Georgia line and pressed on for Varnell Station, his initial objective, a little less than midway between Red Clay and Dalton. Harassed by small bodies of gray horsemen, he moved slowly, that day and the next, and then on May 9 detached a brigade of cavalry to brush these gadflies from his path. It was a mistake. Wheeler's troopers, fading back, drew the blue riders out of contact with the main body, then turned and, with a sudden, unexpected slash, killed or captured some 150 of them, including the colonel in command, and drove the remainder headlong from the field.

Sherman was no more upset by this than he was by Thomas's lack of progress on the near side of the intervening ridge. Three full-scale assaults the day before, and another five today — mainly against Mill Creek Gap, but also against

*U*nion troops swarm a slope near Dug Gap in
one of the strong feints by which Sherman kept
the rebels locked in their defense at Rocky Face Ridge.

Dug Gap, down the line — had met with failure in varying degrees. Two of the uphill attacks, in fact, had managed to put blue troops on the actual crest, within clear sight of Dalton, but they stayed there no longer than it took the defenders to counterattack and drive them back downhill. If anything, this was better than he had expected them to do: especially after his first hard look at what he described as "the terrible door of death that Johnston had prepared for them in the Buzzard Roost." Thomas and Schofield were charged with attracting and holding the attention of the rebels in their respective fronts, and this they had surely done. Sherman's main concern and hopes were still with McPherson, far off beyond the mountains to the south. What one observer called his "electric alertness," while following the progress of the fighting down the railroad below Ringgold, was probably due more to anxiety about his protégé, from whom he had heard nothing in the past three days, than it was to any expectation of victory in Thomas's contest on Rocky Face or Schofield's around Varnell Station, half a dozen miles across the way. Believing strongly in McPherson's military judgment and acumen, he had given him full discretion in conducting the movement designed to outfox Johnston; but he knew only too well that in war few things were certain, least of all the safety of a column deep in the enemy rear, no matter how capably led.

Then all, or nearly all, his worries vanished, giving way to jubilation and high feather. Taking an early supper near Tunnel Hill late that afternoon, May 9, he was delighted to receive a courier bearing McPherson's first dispatch, written that morning when he emerged from Snake Creek Gap after rounding the far end of Rocky Face Ridge. He was within five miles of Resaca, he reported, and pressing on, with nothing to contest his progress but a scattered handful of butternut horsemen flushed out of the brush on the west side of the gap. Sherman boiled over with elation at the news, for it meant that by now McPherson's guns most likely had destroyed the bridges across the Oostanaula, thereby cutting the Confederates at Dalton off from all supplies and reinforcements south of that critical point; in which case they would have no choice except to turn and flee, and when they did he would come down hard and heavy on their rear, while McPherson stood firm in their front, astride the railroad.

An engraving from an Alfred Waud sketch depicts the Federal advance — yet another of Sherman's strong feints — into Mill Creek Gap on May 8, 1864.

★

Exultant, he banged the table so emphatically with his fist that the supper dishes did a rattling dance. "I've got Joe Johnston dead!" he cried.

★ ★ ★ **He very nearly did; very nearly;** except that Johnston, taking alarm at the first sign of his advance, had moved to forestall him without even suspecting what he was up to, out there beyond the screening ridges to the west and south. The bluecoats had no sooner stirred from their camps, May 4, than the southern commander renewed his plea to Richmond for reinforcements from Polk, even if they amounted to no more than a single division. "I urge you to send [these troops] at once to Rome, and put them at my disposal till the enemy can be met," he wired Bragg. Bragg replied, promptly for once, with orders for Polk to do as Johnston asked. Moreover, Jefferson Davis (in still another instance of that "presidential interference" with which his critics often charged him) enlarged the order by telegraphing instructions for his friend the bishop-general to go along in person and take with him not only the one requested division, but also "any other available force at your command."

Polk had three divisions of infantry and one of cavalry, a total of 19,000 men. His decision was to hold none of them back except a garrison of about 2000 for Selma. After getting the first division on the road to Rome, where boxcars were being collected to speed this advance contingent down the branch line, east to Kingston, then northward up the Western & Atlantic to join Johnston around Dalton, he prepared to follow with the rest next day for a share in the task of keeping the Yankees out of Atlanta and the heartland.

That was how it came about that Sherman's "whiplash" lost its sting. For while Polk was en route from Demopolis — first by rail, through Selma and Talladega, to Blue Mountain, the end of the line, and then on foot the rest of the way, seventy rugged miles cross-country to Rome — a brigade of about 2000 men under Brigadier General James Cantey was summoned from Mobile to join him there and thus complete what would constitute a third corps for the Army of Tennessee, roughly equal in strength to each of the other two. Traveling all the way by rail, through Montgomery and Atlanta, Cantey reached Rome on May 5, but was shifted two days later to Resaca, clearing the way for Polk's arrival, placing him closer to Dalton in case he was needed sooner, and incidentally doubling the strength of the small garrison in the intrenchments Johnston had had constructed there to cover the critical Oostanaula crossing.

Two mornings later, on May 9, after pausing only long enough to send the message that would cause Sherman to set the supper dishes dancing, McPherson pressed on across Sugar Valley, still driving the handful of butter-nut cavalry before him, and at midday, within a mile of Resaca, came under heavy infantry fire from a line of intrenchments, anchored on the south to the

Oostanaula and curving west and north of the town.

There were only about 4000 Confederates in the works; but McPherson did not know that, and in any case this was about 4000 more than he expected. He felt out the defenses, found them stout, and decided that under the circumstances, unsupported as he was, deep in the rear of an enemy twice his size, his wisest course was to exercise the discretion his orders afforded him and return to Snake Creek Gap, where his 25,000 would be safe from attack by whatever forces Johnston had sent or was sending to meet this no-longer-secret threat to the rebel life line. He was back in the gap by nightfall, and there, with both flanks covered, his front intrenched, and his rear out of reach of the enemy east of the ridge, he lay coiled in compact security — like a snake, ready to strike, or a whip laid away in a cubbyhole, unused.

When Johnston learned that evening of the sudden appearance of bluecoats in his rear he reacted by ordering Hood to move at once with three divisions, one from his own and two from Hardee's corps, to help Cantey meet any renewal of the threat. Hood did so, but when he reconnoitered west of Resaca next afternoon and reported McPherson still immured in Snake Creek Gap, Johnston interpreted the movement as a feint designed to draw his attention away from the main Union effort to turn or overrun the northern half of Rocky Face Ridge. Accordingly, he told Hood to come back to his former position but to drop Hardee's two divisions off at Tilton, a station on the railroad between Dalton and Resaca, from which they could move swiftly to meet a crisis in either direction.

Hardee, stripped of half his corps, had been puzzled by the relative inactivity of Thomas, who, after three days of obstinate hammering, had finally slackened his effort to break through the two gaps. "I am only uneasy about my right," the Georgia-born West Pointer said, "and won't be uneasy about that when Hood returns." All the same, finding himself "unable to decide what the Yankees are endeavoring to accomplish," he began to suspect that they were up to something not in Johnston's calculations.

And so, by now, did Johnston himself. Polk had reached Rome today with his lead division and was sending it on to Resaca ahead of the others, which were close behind. This gave Johnston considerably more security at both places, but still he wondered at the easing of the pressure against one end of the ridge while McPherson took up a position off the other end. He began to suspect that Sherman might be moving more than McPherson, perhaps in the same direction and even farther, for a crossing of the river deep in his rear. Next morning, May 11, he gave Wheeler orders to send some horsemen around the north end of Rocky Face, if possible, for a probe at the flank of the Federals in position there. "Try to ascertain where their left rests," he told him, "and whether they are in motion toward the Oostanaula."

★

These Confederate earthworks, overlooking the small town of Resaca (left background), came under heavy fire from the Union infantry on the morning of May 9.

Altogether aware of Sherman's advantage, that with close to twice the number of troops he could apply immobilizing pressure in front while rounding or striking one or both Confederate flanks, Johnston had to count on luck as well as skill in maneuvering his opponent into committing some tactical gaffe that would expose the superior blue army, or anyhow some vital portion of it, to destruction. Such an opportunity, if it came, could scarcely occur except while that army was in motion, and for this reason — plus the fact that it had always been his style, his inclination, even back in the Old Dominion, around Manassas or down on the York-James peninsula — the Virginian was prepared from the outset to relinquish almost any position, no matter how strong, if by so doing he could encourage his adversary, on taking up the pursuit, to commit the blunder that might lead to his undoing. The odds against this were long, he knew, but so were the odds he faced. Moreover, he would be falling back toward reinforcements, even if they amounted to no more than Governor Brown's kid-glove militia, and would be shortening his supply line while the enemy's grew longer and more vulnerable.

He also took encouragement from the belief that Sherman — who, after all, had been relieved of duty, back in the first year of the war, under suspicion

★

of insanity — was high-strung, erratic in the extreme, and reported to be enamored of long-chance experiments, both tactical and strategic. These were qualities much to be desired in an opponent at this juncture. The trouble was that Johnston himself, with far less margin for error, had to rely on subordinates quite as erratic and a good deal more temperamental. "If I were President," he confided to a friend soon after taking over the faction-riddled Army of Tennessee, which had just been driven from Missionary Ridge after eighteen months under Braxton Bragg, "I'd distribute the generals of this army over the Confederacy."

In point of fact, that was precisely what R. E. Lee had been doing with some of those subordinates who failed or displeased or failed to please him in the course of the past two years; but Johnston, less in harmony with the authorities in Richmond, mainly had to make do with what he had. Fortunately, this wholesale condemnation did not include the leaders immediately below him on the military ladder. Highly dependable if not brilliant in the discharge of their duties, Polk and Hardee had been corps commanders ever since Shiloh, and Hood, though young and new to both his post and the army — he was thirty-two and had been made a lieutenant general at the time of his transfer from Longstreet, just three months ago, whereas Polk and Hardee, fifty-eight and thirty-eight respectively, had held that rank ever since it was created in the fall of '62 — was a fighter any chief would be glad to have at his disposal when victory swung in the balance and an extra measure of savagery was called for.

While he thus was counting his blessings and woes — and incidentally, such was the diminution of blue pressure against the gaps, admonishing some impetuous artillerists on Rocky Face Ridge for firing at targets not worth their ammunition — he sent word for Polk to proceed at once from Rome to Resaca, where he would assume command "and make the proper dispositions to defend the passage of the river and our communications." Johnston also took the occasion to suggest "the immediate movement of Forrest [who had been left behind for the defense of North Mississippi] into Middle Tennessee." Quite as desirous of cutting Sherman's life line as Sherman was of cutting his, he added that he was "fully persuaded" that Forrest, rested by now from his raid on Paducah and the reduction of Fort Pillow, "would meet no force there that could resist him."

What might come of this he did not know; such a decision, involving the abandonment of a portion of the President's home state to Yankee depredations, was up to Richmond. But as evidence accumulated in Dalton that some kind of movement was in progress on the other side of Rocky Face, Johnston took the precaution of shifting another of Hardee's divisions south of Dug Gap, to a position with a road in its rear leading down into Sugar Valley. Late in the day Wheeler returned from his probe of the Union left with confirmation of the wisdom of such precautions. Beyond the ridge, the Federals were "moving everything" to their right, though whether they were massing near Dug Gap for a renewal of their try for a breakthrough there, or were heading for Snake Creek Gap to join McPherson for an attack on Resaca, or had it in mind to slog on past both gateways for a crossing of the Oostanaula farther down, no one could say. In any case Johnston saw that if it turned out to be either of the last two choices he could not long remain where he now was; he would certainly have to fall back no later than tomorrow. The question was whether he would end his withdrawal on this or the far side of the river fifteen miles in his rear.

That evening he was encouraged by a visit and some welcome news from Polk, who had encountered Hood at Resaca and returned with him to

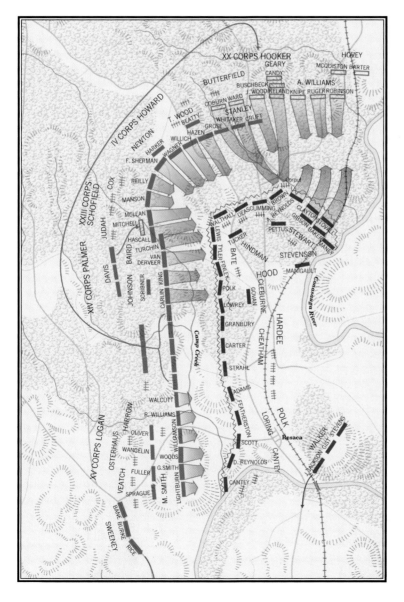

Weathering two days of furious Union assaults, Johnston abandoned his defenses on a commanding ridge above Resaca when Federals threatened his line of retreat.

Dalton for a conference with their chief. The good news was that his second division had reached Rome today, was already on its way by rail to join the first in the Resaca intrenchments, and would soon be followed by the other two, expected at Rome tomorrow. Johnston shook his old friend warmly by the hand; they had been cadets together at West Point thirty-five years ago. "How can I thank you?" he said with feeling. "I asked for a division, but you have come yourself and brought me your army."

Polk flushed with pleasure at the praise, and after the council of war had ended, around midnight, took part in another exchange which gave him even greater pleasure than the first. On the train ride up to Dalton, Hood had confided that he wished to be baptized and received into the Church, and now that army business was out of the way the churchman was glad to oblige. Episcopal Bishop of Louisiana for twenty years before the war, he often remarked that he looked forward to returning to his priestly calling as soon as the fighting was over and independence had been won. Meantime he seldom neglected a chance, such as this, to work for the salvation of any soul. The two repaired to the young general's quarters, accompanied by members of their staffs, and there by candlelight Polk performed the baptismal rites, using a tin washpan for a font. Then came the confirmation. Because of the mutilations Hood had suffered at Chickamauga and Gettysburg, where he had lost a leg and the use of one arm, the bishop absolved the candidate from kneeling, as was customary, suggesting instead that he remain seated for the ceremony. But Hood would have none of this. If he could not kneel, and he could not, he would stand. And thus it was that, leaning on his crutches, the big tawny-bearded Kentuckian was received into the fold. "Defend, O Lord, this thy child with thy heavenly grace," the bishop intoned, his hand upon the bowed head before him, "that he may continue thine forever, and daily increase in thy Holy Spirit more and more, until he come unto thy everlasting kingdom."

Despite the lateness of the hour, Polk returned that night to Resaca, charged with holding the place on his own until such time as the rest of the now three-corps army joined him. He was unlikely to be alone for long, however; Johnston's mind was about made up. Next morning, as evidence of a full-scale Union sidle continued to mount, he decided to evacuate Dalton — or, more accurately, to complete the evacuation, since nearly half of his army, exclusive of Polk, was already south of the town in any case — as soon as the night was dark enough to mask his withdrawal from the covering ridge.

He would do so, what was more, with small regret. "The position had little to recommend it," he afterwards explained. "At Dalton the Federal army, even if beaten, would have had a secure place of refuge at Chattanooga, while our only place of safety was Atlanta, a hundred miles off with three rivers intervening. . . . I therefore decided to remain on the defensive." His mind, it

★

would seem from this subsequent outline of his strategic intentions, was already on the third of those three rivers. "Fighting under cover," he went on, "we would have trifling losses compared with those inflicted. Moreover, due to its lengthening lines the numerical superiority of the Federal army would be reduced daily so that we might hope to cope with it on equal terms beyond the Chattahoochee, where defeat would be its destruction."

This did not mean that he did not hope to inflict a defeat on the enemy in the course of his hundred-mile withdrawal. He did hope for it, despite the odds, either as the result of breaking the railroad deep in Sherman's rear, which would oblige the blue host to retire, or else as the result of catching his adversary in a tactical blunder that would expose him to piecemeal destruction somewhere down the line: maybe even within the next couple of days near Resaca, Johnston's intended first stop, on the near bank of the Oostanaula, first of the three rivers in his rear.

That was his destination now, and by sunrise next morning — Friday the 13th — not a Confederate was left on the northern half of Rocky Face Ridge or in Dalton itself. Johnston was off on what an opposing general called "one of his clean retreats."

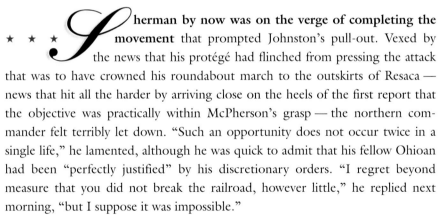

★ ★ ★ ***S**herman by now was on the verge of completing the movement* that prompted Johnston's pull-out. Vexed by the news that his protégé had flinched from pressing the attack that was to have crowned his roundabout march to the outskirts of Resaca — news that hit all the harder by arriving close on the heels of the first report that the objective was practically within McPherson's grasp — the northern commander felt terribly let down. "Such an opportunity does not occur twice in a single life," he lamented, although he was quick to admit that his fellow Ohioan had been "perfectly justified" by his discretionary orders. "I regret beyond measure that you did not break the railroad, however little," he replied next morning, "but I suppose it was impossible."

He rather suspected that he should have used a larger force on the flanking operation, as Thomas originally suggested, and he planned to follow through by doing so now, all out. Leaving one corps of infantry and a cavalry division to continue the demonstration in front of "the terrible door of death," thereby covering Chattanooga and holding the Confederate main body in position around Dalton, he would march the rest of Thomas's army and all of Schofield's down the valley west of Rocky Face Ridge, on around its lower end, to join McPherson for a massive lunge at Resaca, the railroad that

★

*On the Federal left at Resaca, the 5th Indiana
Battery, supported by a brigade of Union infantry, fires
on Hood's Confederate line in the distance.*

ran through it, and the vital river-crossing in its rear. Johnston then would be
cut off from his base, with no choice except to scatter or give battle: which in
either case, as Sherman saw it, would result in his defeat. There was of course
an outside chance that Johnston, who would have the advantage of moving a
shorter distance over superior roads, might fall rapidly back on Resaca, while
the rest of the blue army was en route, and turn on the force holed up in Snake
Creek Gap; but that had been considered and taken care of, more or less,
beforehand. "Should he attack you," Sherman told McPherson at the close of
the dispatch informing him of his measureless regret and his new plan, "fight
him to the last and I will get to you."

      This was a good deal easier said, and planned, than done. Close to
70,000 troops had to be disengaged from contact with an enemy mainly on high
ground, which made secrecy all the more difficult to maintain, and put in motion
on narrow, meandering roads. A day was needed to get ready, then better than
two more for the march. It was late afternoon of the fourth day, Friday the 13th,
before the three commands were consolidated and put into attack formations,
west of Resaca, for the contemplated lunge. By then the sun was too far down
for anything more than a bit of preliminary skirmishing, including a crossroads
cavalry clash in which Judson Kilpatrick and Joe Wheeler — West Pointers

★

both, the former four months into and the latter four months short of his twenty-eighth year — took each other's measure. Kilpatrick was unhorsed by a stray bullet on this unlucky day, and though friendly troopers managed to lug him off the field before the graybacks could get at him, he would be out of action for some weeks.

Regrettable as this was, the loss of time on the cramped approach march down the valley was even more so. McPherson, Thomas, and Schofield were on hand and in line of battle by sundown, within gun range of the rebel works, but Johnston was there ahead of them with all three of his corps, Hood and Hardee having completed their retrograde movement from Dalton before noon. Increased in strength by nearly one third with the addition of Polk's corps to their army, they occupied skillfully laid-out intrenchments that ran in a long convex line from the Oostanaula, downstream from Resaca on their left, to the near bank of a tributary river, the Connasauga, on their right beyond the railroad north of town.

Sherman was neither daunted nor discouraged by his loss of the race for Resaca; Johnston was there, inviting attack with his back to the river, and the redhead planned to oblige him. "I will press him all that is possible," he wired Halleck. "Weather fine and troops in fine order. All is working well." Informed that Grant had emerged from the Wilderness and now was mauling Lee at Spotsylvania, he added, still in the pep-talk vein: "Let us keep the ball rolling."

It rolled, but only a short distance in the course of the day-long fight; Johnston's engineers had given him all he asked in the way of protection for his men. McPherson, on the right — goaded no doubt by Sherman's reproach when they met in Snake Creek Gap the day before: "Well, Mac, you missed the opportunity of your life" — scored what little gain there was by driving Polk's forward elements from some high ground west of the town. Elsewhere along the four-mile curve of the rebel works, the ball either stopped or rebounded. Thomas made no headway in the center, and Schofield took a beating on the left, beyond the railroad, when the Confederates in his front launched a sudden attack that drove him back nearly half a mile as the day ended. This came about as the result of Johnston's calculation that McPherson's success against his left, down near the Oostanaula, must mean that Sherman was concentrating most of his strength in that direction. Accordingly, while Bishop Polk, informally clad in an old hunting shirt and a slouch hat, stiffened his resistance to limit the enemy gains in his front, and Hardee continued to stand fast in the center, wearing by contrast a new dove-gray uniform with fire-gilt buttons and a white cravat, Johnston sent word for Hood to test the Union left for the weakness he suspected. This Hood did, with good results which might have been much better if darkness had not put an end to his pursuit. Johnston, highly pleased, ordered a renewal of the attack at first light next morning.

★

He had been in excellent spirits all that day, riding from point to point along the line, at his jaunty best "in a light or mole colored hat, with a black feather in it." A Tennessee private, seeing him thus, recalled the scene years later. A small man, neatly turned out and genial in manner, fluffy white side-whiskers framing the wedge-shaped face with its trim mustache and grizzled chin beard — "like the pictures you see hung upon the walls," the veteran was to write — Johnston sat his horse, head cocked to catch the swell of gunfire, left and right and center, where Polk and Hood and Hardee were defending the works his foresight had provided. Scattered whoops of recognition prompted the rest of the troops in the passing column of Tennesseans, "and the very ground seems to shake with cheers. Old Joe smiles as blandly as a modest maid, raises his hat in acknowledgement, makes a polite bow, and rides toward the firing."

This brightened outlook persisted into the night, but darkened progressively in reaction to the arrival, in all too rapid sequence, of three unwelcome intelligence reports. While visiting Hood on the right he learned that the Union corps left at Dalton had completed its march down the railroad this evening to reinforce Schofield, and riding westward to confer with Polk he found McPherson had brought artillery onto the high ground lost today, with the result that long-range shells were able to reach both the railway and turnpike bridges close in his rear. Endangering as it did his line of retreat, this gave him pause indeed. He instructed his staff engineer to throw a pontoon bridge a mile above the permanent spans, beyond reach of the Yankee guns, and start at once to build a road leading down to it on the near bank and away from it on the other. Sensitive as always to such threats to his flanks or rear, he countermanded Hood's instructions for tomorrow and told him to return instead to the position from which he had launched his attack this afternoon. Presently, with the arrival of the third unwelcome bit of news, he had cause for greater alarm and even greater caution. Cavalry scouts reported that enemy units of considerable strength had crossed the Oostanaula several miles downstream, where a deep eastward bend of the river brought them within easy reach of the Western & Atlantic.

Johnston reacted swiftly to this threat to the railroad and his line of retreat by ordering the immediate detachment of Major General W. H. T. Walker's division from Hardee for a night march to the reported point of crossing, there to contest any further advance by the Federals while the rest of the army prepared for a quick withdrawal across the river, either to reinforce Walker or outstrip the blue column which by then might have overwhelmed him.

Morning brought a renewal of Federal pressure all along the line, quite as if there had been no reduction for a sidle. Johnston held his ground, awaiting developments, and shortly after noon received a dispatch from Walker informing him that the report of a downstream crossing was untrue. By then the pressure against Resaca had somewhat diminished, and Johnston decided to go

*W*aud accurately depicts Resaca's terrain, but Hindman's
rebels were not likely, as shown here, to have stepped
outside their earthworks even to lay down a deadly fire.

back to his plan for a renewal of the attack by Hood, who promptly returned
to the position he had won the day before. A battery, pushed well to the front to
support the jump-off, opened prematurely and was replied to so effectively, by
infantry and counterbattery fire, that the cannoneers had to abandon all four
guns, left mute and unattended between the lines. This did not augur well for
the success of Hood's assault, but as he was about to go forward in all-out
earnest, a message came from the army commander, once more canceling the
attack and instructing the three lieutenant generals to attend a council of war
that evening at his headquarters.

There they learned the reason for this second change of plans. A
follow-up dispatch from Walker reported the bluecoats over the downstream
Oostanaula after all, and Johnston had decided to give up Resaca. The council
had not been called for a discussion of his decision, but rather for the assignment
of routes on the march to meet this threat to the army's life line; Polk and

Hardee would use the turnpike and railway spans, despite the danger of long-range interdictory fire, and Hood the new-laid pontoon bridge.

All went as planned, or nearly so, including heavy volleys of musketry by front-line units at midnight to cover the withdrawal of iron-tired artillery and supply vehicles. Rear guards took up the pontoons and loaded them onto wagons for use in crossing other rivers, farther south, and the railroad bridge was set afire to burn till it fell hissing into the Oostanaula. Through some administrative oversight — not unlike the one at Tunnel Hill a week ago, which left the railway tunnel unobstructed — in the last-minute confusion, as dawn was breaking, the turnpike bridge was overlooked and left standing, fit for use by the pursuers. All that was really lost in the way of army property, however, was the four-gun Confederate battery abandoned between Hood's and Schofield's lines that afternoon. This came hard for the young Kentucky-born West Pointer, who had a great deal of pride in such matters (in time he would take it even harder, since they turned out to be the only guns Johnston lost in the whole course of the campaign) but who consoled himself, as best he could, by pointing out "that they were four old iron pieces, not worth the sacrifice of the life of even one man."

Sherman pressed on after the retiring Confederates, hoping to catch up with them before they had time to develop still another stout position in which to receive him, and continued simultaneously two flanking operations he had set in motion two days ago, both involving only cavalry at the outset. Kilpatrick's division, minus its wounded leader, had been sent five miles downriver on May 14 to install a pair of pontoon bridges at Lay's Ferry, and Sherman had followed this up yesterday by detaching Brigadier General Thomas Sweeny's infantry division from McPherson to march down and cross the river at that point, along with Kilpatrick's troopers, in order to menace Johnston's rear; which Sweeny had done with such success that the graybacks were now in full retreat.

At the same time, a wider, deeper, and potentially even more profitable thrust was launched by sending another of Thomas's mounted divisions, under Brigadier General Kenner Garrard, far down the right bank of the Oostanaula to threaten and if possible enter Rome, wrecking its factories and iron works and taking over the branch-line railroad leading east along the north bank of the Etowah to Kingston, on the Western & Atlantic, better than twenty miles below Resaca. Now that Johnston was falling back, Sherman decided to beef up this deeper probe by sending Brigadier General Jefferson C. Davis's division of Cumberlanders to follow the cavalry and take part in the raid on Rome and the eastward strike at Kingston.

The red-haired commander was leaving no card unplayed in his eagerness to come to grips with his skittish opponent, and he scoffed at the notion, advanced by several members of his staff, that Johnston was falling back quite willingly, in accordance with a plan to draw his pursuers southward to their destruction. "Had he remained in Dalton another hour, it would have been his total defeat," Sherman insisted, "and he only evacuated Resaca because his safety demanded it." As for the disappointment some critics expressed at his failure, so far, to bring the wily Virginian to all-or-nothing battle — particularly before Polk arrived from Alabama, in the interim between Dalton and Resaca, to shorten the long numerical odds — he countered that, while he shared the regret that he had not managed to do this, he also saw a clear advantage in the way the campaign had developed up to now. "Of course I was disappointed not to have crippled his army more at that particular stage of the game," he later wrote; "but, as it resulted, these rapid successes gave us the initiative, and the usual impulse of a conquering army."

Determined to make the most of that conquering impulse, he devised a pursuit combining speed with other tactical advantages. While Thomas struck out down the railroad, hard in the wake of the fleeing enemy, McPherson was instructed to proceed at once to Lay's Ferry for a crossing that would place him well to the right on the march south, in position to make another rapid flanking

*Attacking rebels face savage artillery fire near
Lay's Ferry in a belated attempt to dislodge Thomas Sweeny
from his Federal bridgehead on the Oostanaula.*

★

movement as soon as the rebels called a halt or were brought to one by pressure against their rear, and Schofield was told to do the same in the opposite direction, crossing upstream from Resaca at Field's Ferry for a march well to the east, in case it developed that the enemy right was the flank that should be turned. This not only increased the celerity of the pursuit by not funneling all the Federal troops down one crowded road; it also assured that when the time came for fighting, all three component armies would be ready for action in their accustomed roles, Thomas's as the holding force and McPherson's and Schofield's as flankers. Moreover, to bring all three into better numerical balance and lessen the traffic on the turnpike, Sherman detached Hooker's three divisions from Thomas and sent them off to the left with Schofield, whose strength thus was raised to more than 30,000 while Thomas's was reduced to about 40,000, three other divisions, including two of cavalry, having already been detached for the raid on Rome, still in progress down the Oostanaula, and the preliminary crossing at Lay's Ferry, where Sweeny's division rejoined McPherson, together with Kilpatrick's troopers, who fanned out frontward to provide a screen for the column west of the railroad.

    The first day's march, May 16, ended at Calhoun, where Sherman thought it likely that Johnston would make a stand, six miles down the track from Resaca, but before he could call in either of the lateral columns, which were also over the river by then, the Confederate rear guard pulled out southward in the darkness, headed apparently for Adairsville, ten miles down the line. There was heavier skirmishing there next day near sundown, but dawn of May 18 showed the graybacks gone again. Schofield by now was in the vicinity of Sallacoa and McPherson at McGuire, hamlets respectively half a dozen miles east and west of Adairsville; Sherman, riding with Thomas in the center, held to this spread-eagle formation as he took up the march for Kingston, another ten miles down the Western & Atlantic. He felt certain that Johnston would dig in there, on the near bank of the Etowah, and he wanted to get at him before he had much chance to get set for the shock.

    Spirits were high in all three columns of pursuit, not only because the rebs were on the run, having been turned out of two practically impregnable positions in less than two weeks, but also because well-drilled rail repair gangs — helped considerably, it was true, by the enemy's rattled negligence in failing to obstruct the tunnel short of Buzzard Roost — had functioned with such efficiency that even the troops out front, in the process of covering better than half the distance from Chattanooga to Atlanta, had scarcely missed a meal along the way. "The rapidity with which the badly broken railroad was repaired seemed miraculous," Major General O. O. Howard, one of Thomas's corps commanders, later noted. "We had hardly left Dalton before trains with ammunition and other supplies arrived. While our skirmishing was going on at Calhoun, the locomotive

*On May 15, Hooker's troops haul a Napoleon
cannon from a captured Georgia battery as the Union
infantry duels with the enemy in the background.*

whistle sounded in Resaca. The telegraphers were nearly as rapid: the lines were
in order to Adairsville on the morning of the 18th. While we were breaking up
the state arsenal at Adairsville, caring for the wounded, and bringing in Confederate
prisoners, word was telegraphed from Resaca that bacon, hard bread, and coffee
were already there at our service."

All this had been accomplished, moreover, at a cost of fewer than
4000 casualties, and not only was this figure much lower than had been anticipated, it was also — despite the supposed high price entailed in attacking prepared
defenses — not much larger than the enemy total, which included a number of
lightly wounded men who had to be left behind and thus became permanent
losses, as captives, whereas a Union soldier, left behind under similar circumstances, could be patched up and returned to duty, sometimes overnight. It was
no wonder then, with success achieved at so low a cost and without the sacrifice

of creature comforts, that spirits were high and the outcome of the expected Kingston confrontation seemed foregone. What was more, as the three main widespread columns prepared for a convergence at that point — forty air-line miles from Tunnel Hill, scene of the opening clash eleven days ago — word came that a prize even more valuable than the state arsenal at Adairsville had fallen into the hands of the invaders. That same morning, May 18, Rome fell undefended to Davis and Garrard, who soon would be working their way east along the branch-line railroad to rejoin the Army of the Cumberland.

Rome with its factories and iron works, so important to the rebel cause, was a strategic plum worth giving thanks for, but tactically the railroad was a prize worth even more, since practically all of Johnston's reinforcements had reached him by that route. Now it was closed, except to Federal use, and Sherman — still with Thomas, who was engaged in what Howard called "a running skirmish" down the Western & Atlantic with troops from Hardee's corps, which apparently had been given the rear-guard post of honor on the Confederate retreat — had 100,000 effectives converging as fast as their legs could carry them toward Kingston, where reports indicated that Johnston had at last been brought to bay with his back to the Etowah River.

★ ★ ★ *F*or once, by dint of hard marching on rural roads and steady pressure on the rebel rear, execution matched conception; the convergence would be effected by midday tomorrow, May 19, on schedule and with each of the three component armies in its assigned position for the final thrust, Schofield left, McPherson right, and Thomas center. The trouble was that Sherman, for all the speed and precision of his approach, was converging on a vacuum. Johnston was not at Kingston; he was at Cassville, five miles east, preparing to spring an ambush that would eliminate, or at any rate badly mangle, a solid third of the blue force whose commander had at last afforded him the opportunity he had been awaiting ever since the campaign opened, two weeks and better than forty miles ago.

Leaving Resaca, two days back, he had intended to make a stand at Calhoun, provided he could find a suitable position — athwart a rather narrow valley, say, which would afford protection for his flanks and thus oblige the Federals to come at him head-on, their numerical advantage canceled by the limited width of front — but when reconnaissance revealed none he moved on that night, hoping to find what he was seeking near Adairsville the following day, May 17. He did not. He did, however, receive a telegraphic dispatch and some cavalry reports which together had the double effect of lifting his spirits and enabling him to arrive at a plan for stopping the blue army in its tracks. Stephen Lee, left in charge of the adjoining department when Polk departed for Georgia, responded to Johnston's week-old request by announcing that Forrest, with

3500 picked horsemen and two batteries of artillery, would set out within three days for an attack on Sherman's lines of supply and communication up in Middle Tennessee. This was welcome news, indeed, and Johnston called a council of war that evening to pass it on to his corps commanders, along with their respective assignments for carrying out his table-turning plan.

Intelligence reports from Wheeler made it clear that Sherman's pursuit was in three columns, widely spaced, and now that Johnston had decided to continue his march toward the Etowah, he saw in this a rare opportunity to deal with one of those isolated segments before it could call on either of the other two for help. From Adairsville, railroad and turnpike ran due south to Kingston; Hardee would continue on that route, skirmishing as he went, to draw Thomas after him and encourage the impression that he was guarding the rear of the other two corps as they moved ahead of him, down the tracks and pike, for a stand at Kingston. But that was by no means to be the case. Polk and Hood would march instead by a road leading east of south to Cassville, a village about two miles on this side of the Western & Atlantic, which swung due east at Kingston, five miles west.

The advantage was that Schofield, reinforced to 30,000, would pass near there on his way to the convergence Sherman would surely order when he became convinced that the graybacks intended to call a halt at Kingston. With Thomas five miles off, McPherson perhaps ten, and Hardee in position to delay their eastward advance along the railroad, Hood and Polk should have ample time to dispose of Schofield before the other two could reach him. With any luck, all three gray corps could then combine to take on Thomas and strike at McPherson when he came up in turn. Dealt with piecemeal, all three Union armies might be destroyed in short order, or anyhow crippled and brought to a stumbling halt; which would serve about as well, since they soon would get the news that Forrest had severed their life line, up in Tennessee. That would leave them no choice except starvation or retreat. Either way, the campaign would be over and the world once more would stand amazed at still another Confederate triumph against overwhelming odds.

Eager though they were to take up their divergent marches, which were to end with a long-deferred return to the offensive, all three corps commanders went with their chief to his tent, where Polk donned his surplice and stood in front of an improvised altar, preparing to fulfill a request Mrs Johnston had made in a letter written two days ago. She wanted the bishop to do for her husband what he had done for Hood the week before; "lead my soldier nearer to God. General Johnston has never been baptised. It is the dearest wish of my heart that he should be, and that you should perform the ceremony." Once more with candlelight glinting on the brass and gold lace of the uniforms of candidate and witnesses, the rite of baptism was performed, after which the group dispersed to prepare for the execution of the plan designed to reverse the tide of war in North Georgia.

Hardee took up his march, southward down the railroad, and with the dawn resumed his "running skirmish" with Thomas, who continued to press hard upon his rear. Meantime the other two corps set out on the road for Cassville, Hood in front with orders to occupy a position tonight from which to strike at the left of Schofield's column next morning, while Polk attacked the front; Hardee would join them from Kingston, later in the day, so that all three could then turn on Thomas and McPherson, simultaneously or in sequence, when they came up in response to Schofield's cries for help.

Unwelcome news from Stephen Lee reached Johnston in the course of the approach march, to the effect that a heavy enemy movement out of Memphis had obliged him to postpone Forrest's raid on Sherman's life line. Offsetting this somewhat, however, there was a report from Richmond that the Federals had acknowledged the so-far loss of 45,000 men in Virginia, thirty-one of them generals, and this gave rise to the airing of a theory by some members of Johnston's staff that Sherman's intention was to maneuver his adversary south of the Etowah, then call a halt and hurry reinforcements to the bled-down Army of the Potomac. Johnston put no stock in such talk; he remained intent on the prospect of giving Sherman so much trouble, on this side of the Etowah, that he soon would be seeking assistance, not sending it either to Meade or to Banks, whose fight at Yellow Bayou today was the last on his costly, disheartened retreat down Red River.

Nightfall found the divided Confederate army in position: Hardee at Kingston, prepared to turn east, and Hood and Polk at Cassville, their ambush laid. Johnston's spirits were as high as Sherman's across the way, and on far sounder grounds. Some measure of the Virginian's confidence and martial elation came through in a general order he composed that night and had read at the head of each regiment next morning, May 19:

> Soldiers of the Army of Tennessee:
>
> You have displayed the highest qualities of the soldier
> — firmness in combat, patience under toil. By your
> courage and skill you have repulsed every assault of the
> enemy. By marches by day and marches by night you
> have defeated every attempt upon your communications.
> Your communications are secured. You will now turn and

★

march to meet his advancing columns. Fully confiding in

the conduct of the officers, the courage of the soldiers,

I lead you to battle. We may confidently trust that the

Almighty Father will still reward the patriots' toils and

the patriots' banners. Cheered by the success of our

brothers in Virginia and beyond the Mississippi, our

efforts will equal theirs. Strengthened by His support,

these efforts will be crowned with the like glories.

J. E. Johnston,

General.

Despite the weariness resulting from three days and four nights of marches broken only by rearward skirmishes and fitful snatches of roadside sleep — not to mention the cumulative depression that went with having abandoned better than forty miles of highly defensible terrain without so much as a single fight that attained the dignity of a full-scale battle — the reaction on all levels to the reading of this order, from regimental commanders down to drummer boys, was quite as ecstatic as even its author could have wished.

Among those officers who were better informed on current events, mainly through having read such newspapers as were available in camp and on the march, there lately had been growing an anxiety that the good effect of the news from Louisiana and Virginia, which had raised the price of gold on the New York market to 210, would be impaired by the apparently irreversible retreat of the Confederates in North Georgia. Now though, with the word that they were going over to the offensive, their anxiety was relieved and their hope soared, anticipating a still greater drop in the pocketbook barometer that best measured northern greed and fears. As for the men in the ranks, though their faith in Old Joe had never wavered, their spirits took an even higher bounce as they stood and heard the order read to them this morning.

"I never saw troops happier or more certain of success," one private would recall. "A sort of grand halo illuminated every soldier's face. . . . We were going to whip and rout the Yankees."

Johnston apparently shared this conviction that the Yankees would be whipped and routed: especially as it applied to Schofield, who was reported to be advancing heedlessly into the trap about to be sprung northwest of Cassville. At 10.20, hearing from Hardee that Thomas was moving in strength

on Kingston and soon would be too heavily committed to effect a rapid disen-
gagement, he sent his chief of staff, Brigadier General W. W. Mackall — who
had served Bragg, his West Point classmate, in the same capacity — to tell Polk
and Hood "to make quick work" of their combined lunge at Schofield, so that
they would be ready to turn without delay on Thomas, when he came up in
Hardee's wake, for the second phase of the Confederate offensive. With accustomed caution, Johnston added to Hood's instructions a warning that, in
launching his flank attack, he was not to undertake "too wide a movement,"
lest he lose contact with Polk on his left, which not only might leave Schofield
an escape hatch, but also would delay the consolidation of all three corps for
the follow-up strike at Thomas and McPherson.

Such a warning was altogether superfluous, the staffer found when he
encountered Hood near Cassville. Not only had the Kentuckian moved out before
Mackall got there; by now he was moving back again, feverishly preparing to take
up a defensive position in which to resist attack by a blue column reported to be
advancing on a road in his right rear, skirmishers deployed and guns booming.

Mackall sent word of this surprise development to Johnston, who
flatly declined to credit the report. "It can't be," he said. He did not believe
the Federals were there because none of Polk's cavalry had encountered them
this morning while reconnoitering in that direction. (In point of fact, they had
not been there earlier this morning, and it was entirely accidental that they
were there at all. A nomadic fragment from Major General Daniel Butterfield's
division, Hooker's corps, they had missed a turning, lost their way, and wound
up deep in Hood's right rear, some five miles east of their comrades trudging
south on the far side of Cassville.) All the same, though Johnston did not believe
in their existence — then, any more than he did ten years later, when he declared: "The report upon which General Hood acted was manifestly untrue"
— he took no chances. Having rejected the evidence, he proceeded to act upon
it. "If that's so," he said, examining the situation on a map, "General Hood
will have to fall back at once."

Accordingly, when Mackall presently returned, he sent him riding
again to Polk and Hood with orders canceling their attack. Once more, as had
been its custom for the past two weeks, the army would take up a stout defensive
position and there await developments: meaning Sherman.

Johnston quickly found what he was seeking along a wooded ridge
immediately southeast of Cassville, overlooking the town and the "broad, open,
elevated valley" in which it lay. Hood and Polk fell back to there, followed
prudently by Schofield, who by now had notified Sherman of the snare he had
so narrowly avoided, and Hardee came up that afternoon to take position on
their left, closely pursued by Thomas and McPherson, the latter having closed
the gap between him and the Cumberlanders in the course of the daylong skirmish,

★

*In this J. F. E. Hillen sketch, Federal troops perched on
boxcars arrive at Kingston, Georgia, several
miles above the Confederate stronghold at Allatoona Pass.*

first north, then east of Kingston. Before sundown the guns of both armies were banging away at each other, arching their shots above the hill-cradled streets and rooftops of the village. Despite the dismay of the townspeople at this harrowing turn of events ("Consternation of citizens," a staff lieutenant jotted in his diary; "many flee, leaving all; some take away few effects, some remain between hostile fires") Johnston was greatly pleased with his new position, later referring to it as "the best I saw occupied during the war."

Polk and Hood did not agree with this assessment, and they said as much that evening when they came to headquarters for the council of war to which they had been summoned. Protesting that Union batteries enfiladed that portion of the ridge where their lines joined, they liked the position so little, in fact, that both wanted to leave it at the earliest possible moment. The army had no choice, they said, except to schedule a dawn attack, on the chance of beating Sherman to the punch, or else to fall back tonight across the Etowah. Johnston did not want to do either: certainly not attack the reunited Federals with no better promise of success than the tactical situation seemed to him to afford. Hardee, who arrived at this point in the discussion, sided altogether with his chief, hoping

★

like him that Sherman would oblige them tomorrow by exposing his superior numbers to severe and sudden curtailment by advancing them head-on across that broad, open valley to challenge the defenders on the wooded ridge.

Johnston ended by deciding to retreat. He did so, he explained later, not because he agreed with Hood and Polk that the position had its drawbacks, but "in the belief that the confidence of the commanders of two of the three corps of the army, of their inability to resist the enemy, would inevitably be communicated to their troops, and produce that inability."

The fall-back to the Etowah that night, though Sherman made no attempt to interfere, was by far the most disruptive of the campaign. "All hurried off without regard to order," the young staff diarist recorded. "Reach Cartersville before day, troops come in after day. General Johnston comes up — all hurried over bridges; great confusion caused by mixing trains and by trains which crossed first parking at river's edge and others winding around wrong roads."

> *The fall-back to the Etowah that night, though Sherman made no attempt to interfere, was by far the most disruptive of the campaign.*

Much of the mixup was a manifestation of the army's chagrin at the two-step disappointment it had suffered, first in the cancellation of the attack, which came hard on the heels of the reading of Old Joe's "I lead you to battle" address — "I could not restrain my tears when I found we could not strike," Mackall confessed in a home letter — and then in the directive, which came down that night, for a resumption of the southward march. "Change of line not understood but thought all right," the diarist put it, "but night retreat after issuing general order impaired confidence; great alarm in country round. Troops think no stand to be made north of Chattahoochee, where supply train is sent." Civilians north and immediately south of the Etowah reacted to their abandonment much as the people of Cassville had done the day before, milling about like ants in an upset ant hill. Johnston put the blame, or anyhow most of it, on Hood, and so did members of his staff, including the diarist, who wrote: "One lieutenant general talks about attack and not giving ground, publicly, and quietly urges retreat."

By way of consolation for its woes, the disgruntled army could see for itself the strength of its new position near Allatoona, four miles down the Western & Atlantic from the river. Here, beginning the day of their arrival, May 20, Johnston had his soldiers throw up breastworks commanding the deep, narrow gorge through which the railroad snaked its way, his flanks protected, left and right, by Pumpkin Vine and Allatoona creeks. Fifteen miles to the south, his new supply base was Marietta, just beyond Kennesaw Mountain, about midway between the Etowah and the Chattahoochee, last of the three main rivers between Chattanooga and Atlanta.

Allatoona Pass, as the gorge through this spur of the Appalachians was called, was a still more "terrible door of death" than Buzzard Roost had been, some sixty miles to the north. Paradoxically, though, it was precisely in this abundance of natural strength that the strategic weakness of the position lay. Sherman would be even less apt to call for a main effort here than he had been at Rocky Face Ridge. His solution, now as then, would most likely be to try another sidle — and there was always the danger that, sooner or later, one or another of these complicated flank maneuvers would succeed in accomplishing its purpose of placing the superior blue army squarely between the Confederates and Atlanta; in which case Johnston would have no choice except to attack the Federals where they were, intrenched and waiting, or scatter into the surrounding hills. Either course would mean the loss not only of the campaign (meaning Atlanta) but also of the army, whether by destruction or disintegration, the difference being that one would be somewhat less sudden than the other. All Johnston could do, in the way of attempting to forestall such a calamity, was alert Wheeler to be on the lookout for the first sign of another sidle, up or down the Etowah. He felt sure that one was pending, but he could not move to thwart it until he knew its direction, right or left.

One other thing he could attempt, however, and that was to protect himself from his detractors, in some measure at least, by putting his performance in the best possible light for his Richmond superiors, with emphasis on his desire for coming to grips with his pursuer. Since this latest retreat had no doubt set his critics' teeth on edge, he no sooner crossed the Etowah than he got off a wire to the President explaining the cancellation of the "general attack" he had ordered yesterday: "While the officer charged with the lead was advancing he was deceived by a false report that a heavy column of the enemy had turned our right and was close upon him, and took a defensive position. When the mistake was discovered it was too late to resume the movement." Despite this disappointment, which had obliged him to continue the withdrawal, he pointed out that he had "kept near [Sherman] to prevent his detaching to Virginia, as you directed, and have repulsed every attack he has made."

Next day, May 21, the army having spent the night improving its position near Allatoona, still with no sign of what the Federals were up to, he followed through with another message along similar lines. "In the last six days the enemy has pressed us back to this point, thirty-two miles," he conceded, but he assured Davis that, all this time, "I have earnestly sought an opportunity to strike." The trouble was that Sherman, by constantly extending his right as he moved down the railroad, had obliged the defenders to give ground no less constantly, and then, "by fortifying the moment he halted," had also "made an assault upon his superior forces too hazardous." Without committing himself to anything specific — as, indeed, he could scarcely be expected to do, under the circumstances outlined here — Johnston wanted the Commander in Chief to know that he was in full agreement as to the need for going over to the offensive at the earliest possible moment. Meantime, despite the discouragements generally involved in making a lengthy retrograde movement, he was pleased to report that the slightness of his losses from straggling or desertion showed that the army was in good shape for such exertions as he might presently require.

The answer came not from Davis — not just yet — but from Bragg, who combined good news with bad and wound up with a flourish that seemed to indicate that the Georgia commander perhaps had oversold his case. Another brigade of infantry from Mobile and a regiment of South Carolina cavalry were on their way to join him, but these were the last the government would be sending.

"From the high condition in which your army is reported," the message ended, "we confidently rely on a brilliant success."

★ ★ ★ Johnston's concern, lest the very strength of his Alla-toona position deprive him of the quick defensive victory he felt certain he would score if his adversary could only be persuaded to attack him there, was better founded than he knew. Two decades back, as a young artillery lieutenant on detached duty at Marietta with the inspector general, Sherman "rode or walked, exploring creeks, valleys, hills" in the surrounding region, while his less energetic comrades "spent their leisure Sundays reading novels, card-playing, or sleeping." Now this seemingly useless pastime stood him in good stead. "Twenty years later the thing that helped me to win battles in Georgia was my perfect knowledge of the country. I knew more of Georgia than the rebels did." In the course of his rambles, sketch pad in hand, he had spent several days investigating some Indian mounds on the south bank of the Etowah, just north of the gorge where Johnston was in-trenched, and "I therefore knew that the Allatoona Pass was very strong, would be hard to force, and resolved not even to attempt it, but to turn the position."

First, though, he would call a halt, a brief time-out from war; the combat troops would take a welcome three-day rest ("to replenish and fit up," he explained to Halleck) while Colonel W. W. Wright and his 2000 nimble rail repairmen, having rebuilt the Resaca bridge in jig time, put the Western & Atlantic back in operation down to Kingston. "The dead were buried, the sick

★

and wounded were made more comfortable, and everybody got his mail and wrote letters," one appreciative officer would recall. Then on May 23, with twenty days' rations in his wagons, Sherman was ready to cut loose from the railroad and strike out cross-country with everything he had.

His preliminary objective on this all-out flanking operation was Dallas, a road-hub settlement just under twenty miles west of Marietta and about the same distance southwest of Allatoona, where Johnston would be left holding the bag unless he pulled back in time to meet this massive threat to his new supply base, fifteen miles down the track in his rear. As usual, Thomas would take the direct central route, south from Kingston through Euharlee and Stilesboro, while Schofield marched on his left, by way of Burnt Hickory, and McPherson swung well to the right, through Van Wert, to approach Dallas from the west.

The march would be a rigorous one, Sherman knew from previous exploration, "as the country was very obscure, mostly in a state of nature, densely wooded and with few roads." It might take longer than he planned: in which case, he told Halleck, his twenty-day rations could be stretched to thirty. But he was not inclined to worry much as he set out from Kingston, riding with Thomas across the Etowah; "the Rubicon of Georgia," he called that river in a dispatch sent just after he gave the jump-off signal. "We are now all in motion like a vast hive of bees," he declared, fairly buzzing with pleasure at being once more on the go, "and expect to swarm along the Chattahoochee in five days."

So he said. But when Schofield captured a lone gray rider at Burnt Hickory next day and found on him a dispatch which showed Johnston already reacting to this latest turning movement, Sherman not only knew that secrecy had gone by the board, along with all hope for a substantial head start in the projected five-day sprint for the Chattahoochee; he also perceived that "it accordingly became necessary to use great caution, lest some of the minor columns should fall into ambush," as Schofield had so nearly done, four days ago, near Cassville.

Caution was indeed called for, he found out the following morning, May 25, when Thomas pressed down in advance of the other two armies for a crossing of Pumpkin Vine Creek. Hooker had the lead, driving butternut cavalry pickets over a bridge which they set on fire just as the first of his three divisions came in sight. He doused the flames, double-timed across, and continued his pursuit of the skittery horsemen. Four miles northeast of Dallas, near a Methodist meeting-house called New Hope Church, he came under fire from a mass of rebel infantry whose march he had apparently interrupted. With soldierly instinct, and as if determined to justify his nom de guerre, Fighting Joe shook out a line of skirmishers and attacked with his lead division, commanded by Brigadier General John W. Geary, a six-foot six-inch Pennsylvanian who had been San Francisco's first mayor and a territorial governor of Kansas. A colonel in the Mexican War before he was thirty, he now was forty-four and had seen much

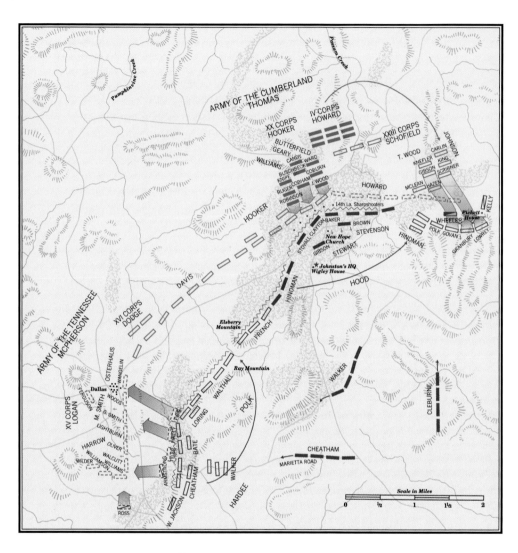

After rebels shifted west to block a Union flanking movement, both sides locked into a week of fighting around New Hope Church, Pickett's Mill, and Dallas.

fighting, East and West, including Chancellorsville and Gettysburg, Wauhatchie and Chattanooga, but in none of these had he and his men found harder work than was required of them in the next three hours around New Hope Church, which the attackers ever afterwards referred to as the "Hell Hole."

What Geary struck, and promptly rebounded from, was Hood. His corps had been last of the three to leave Allatoona the day before, when Johnston, warned by Wheeler that Sherman was off on another sidle, marched southwest up the near bank of Pumpkin Vine Creek to intercept him around Dallas. Hardee was there now, with Polk in position on his right to connect with Hood near New Hope Church; so that what Hooker had encountered was not a mere segment of Johnston's army on the march, as he first thought, but the entire right wing of that army, already beginning to scratch out intrenchments in expectation of his arrival hard on the heels of the cavalry pickets fading back before him through what Sherman called "the obscurity of the ambushed country."

Undaunted by the truth, which he began to suspect as soon as Geary was flung back, Hooker brought up his other two divisions, led by Butterfield and Brigadier General Alpheus Williams, massed them on a front no wider than Geary had spanned alone, and sent them forward, closely packed, against the rebel center.

As a result, Major General Alexander P. Stewart's division caught the brunt of the all-out blue attack, some 20,000 strong. Known to his soldiers as "Old Straight," the nickname he had acquired while teaching mathematics at West Point and at Cumberland University in his home state of Tennessee, Stewart was forty-two and a veteran of all the army's battles, a strict disciplinarian much admired by his men, who gave him today all he asked of them, and more: especially the artillerists, whose guns were advantageously sited to exact a heavy toll from the charging bluecoats. Hooker's three divisions could make no headway against this one, despite two hours of trying without pause. Hood's other two divisions, under Major Generals Thomas Hindman and Carter Stevenson, had little to do on the left and right of the sector being assaulted, but when Johnston himself, alarmed by the desperate nature of the struggle, sent to ask Stewart if he needed reinforcements, the Tennessean replied calmly: "My own troops will hold the position."

Still another hour of such fighting remained, and it was this third hour, even more than the previous two, that prompted the Hell Hole description of the scene. Thunder rumbled and lightning crackled from a huge black cloud that gathered above the crossroad, dwarfing the boom of guns and the flicker of muzzle flashes, then loosed its torrential burden with all the abruptness of a water-filled bag split open, drenching men already wet with sweat from heat and exertion, whether prone behind log barricades or scrambling through bullet- and rain-whipped brush. "No more persistent attack or determined resistance was anywhere made," Stewart was to report with impartial praise.

Thunderstorm and fighting came to a simultaneous end as the cloud blew off and the sun went down in a glory of red and purple beyond Dallas and the mountains to the west. Hooker put his casualties at 1665 killed or wounded, but the Confederates, knowing his reputation for understating his own losses while overestimating those of his opponent, were convinced the figure was much too low, since they themselves, fighting mostly behind cover, had lost nearly half that many in the course of the three-hour contest.

Darkness made the going hard for the rest of Thomas's army, coming up in the center, as well as for the other two, closing in on the left and right. "All was hurry and confusion," a Kentucky Federal recorded in his diary, "nearly everyone swearing at the top of his voice." Sherman would later recall that he "slept on the ground, without cover, alongside of a log, [and] got little sleep," but Schofield had worse luck. Swept off his horse by a low-hanging branch while combing the moonless woods in search of Sherman's bivouac, he was hurt by the fall and would be out of action for several days; leadership of his Army of the Ohio passed temporarily to Brigadier General Jacob Cox, the senior division commander. McPherson made it nearly to Dallas by daylight, coming in from the west to find Hardee securely intrenched there, as were Polk and Hood to the northeast.

Sherman probed cautiously at the five-mile rebel line, all that day and part of the next, but found no weakness he considered would justify attack. Accordingly, by midmorning of the second day of unproductive probing, May 27, he decided to turn Johnston's right with a strike at Pickett's Mill, two miles beyond the Hell Hole Hooker had failed to take two days ago. This time Howard drew the assignment, and presently all three of his divisions were in position, massed for assault in case there was serious opposition.

There was indeed, and "serious" was by no means too strong a description of what he was about to encounter in the way of resistance. Suspecting that the Federals would attempt some such maneuver, Johnston the day before had instructed Hardee to shift one of his divisions from the far left to a position beyond Hood's right: specifically, to Pickett's Mill. It was Howard's ill fortune — as it had been Sherman's, on Missionary Ridge six months ago, and Hooker's, two days later at Ringgold Gap — that the division posted in his path was Major General Patrick Cleburne's, by common agreement the best in Johnston's army. Before emigrating to become a lawyer in Helena, Arkansas, Irish-born Cleburne had done a three-year hitch in Her Majesty's 41st Regiment of Foot, an experience that stood the former corporal in good stead when it came to training his division of Arkansans, Texans, Mississippians, and Tennesseans. Except under specific orders, which sometimes had to be repeated, he and his men had never given up a piece of ground assigned to their defense; nor did they do so here today at Pickett's Mill.

One-armed Howard gave the lead to his fellow West Pointer, Brigadier General Thomas Wood — whose abrupt, inadvertent withdrawal under orders at Chickamauga had created the "chasm" through which Longstreet plunged to defeat Rosecrans. Wood had his division in place by early afternoon, formed six ranks deep for an end-on strike at the rebel flank, wherever it might be. He moved out, floundered about for a couple of hours in the heavy brush, then paused for some badly needed rest, having sighted the newly turned earth of fresh intrenchments through the trees. It was 4.30 by the time he got his

A Waud engraving, based on a photograph of the New Hope Church battlefield, depicts the misery of combat in a furious thunderstorm at the "Hell Hole."

three brigades in motion again, still in a compact formation of two lines each, and what turned out to be a three-hour fight, with an equally horrendous night-time epilogue added for good measure, began almost at once.

His repulse was as complete as it was sudden. Ahead through the trees, as the close-packed blue infantry came on, the head-logs of the newly dug rebel intrenchments seemed to burst into flame, and a long, low cloud of smoke boiled up and out, billowing as it grew, lighted from within by the pinkish yellow blink and stab of muzzle flashes; Cleburne's emphasis on rapid-fire marksmanship in training produced a clatter as continuous as the uproar in a 5000-man boiler factory and an incidence of casualties that matched the stepped-up rate of fire. Wood's division fell apart, transformed abruptly from a compact mass into huddled clusters groping for cover in such low ground as the field afforded. "Under these circumstances," Howard reported, "it became evident that the assault had failed." He brought up reinforcements from Major General John M. Palmer's

★

adjoining corps, as well as from Schofield's army, which was posted in reserve here on the Union left, and did what he could "to bring off the wounded and to prevent a successful sally of the enemy from his works."

Darkness helped in both these efforts, but not much. At 10 o'clock, in a rare night action, Cleburne threw Brigadier General Hiram Granbury's Texas brigade into a charge that swept through a ravine where a number of fugitives from the attack had taken refuge, capturing all that were left alive when it was over. Howard's losses in Wood's division alone were 1457 killed, wounded, or captured. Cleburne's were 448, although Howard thought them higher in advancing a claim that "the enemy suffered immensely in the action, and regarded it as the severest attack made during this eventful campaign."

Now it was Johnston's turn to try his hand at what Sherman had been attempting all along. Reasoning that if his adversary was thus extending his left he might also have weakened his right, the Virginian told Hardee to test the Federal defenses around Dallas next morning. Hardee did, passing the word for Major General William Bate to make a probing attack with his division. Bate's repulse, though not as bloody, was as complete as Wood's had been the day before, at the far end of the line. He lost close to 400 men, half of them from the dwindling "Orphan" brigade of Kentuckians under Brigadier General Joseph Lewis, successor to Mrs Lincoln's brother-in-law, Ben Hardin Helm, who had fallen at Chickamauga.

All Bate got for his pains was the knowledge that McPherson was still around Dallas, apparently in undiminished strength — although the fact was he had been under orders to pull out for a march beyond New Hope Church and was about to leave when the rebel attack exploded against his works. Having fought it off, with fewer than half the casualties he inflicted, he notified Sherman and held his ground, awaiting instructions.

Meantime Johnston convened a council of war, at which Hood proposed that his corps be shifted eastward, beyond Cleburne, for an attack on the Union left, to be taken up in sequence by the other two corps with strikes at the right and center. Johnston liked the plan and issued the necessary orders, stipulating that Polk and Hardee would go forward when they heard Hood's artillery begin to roar. They waited past dawn and through sunup, May 29, poised for assault, heads cocked to catch the boom of guns that did not come.

What came instead, around midmorning, was a note from Hood informing Johnston that he had found a newly arrived blue division intrenched in his path, perpendicular to the line he had scouted the day before. Finding it "inexpedient" to advance under these conditions, he had halted and now awaited new instructions. Johnston promptly canceled the offensive, directing instead that the army give all its attention to improving its defenses.

McPherson, Thomas, and Schofield were doing the same across the way, each on his own initiative, with the result that both lines grew more formidable than any seen so far in the campaign. Quick to improvise intrenchments — "The rebs must carry their breastworks with them," Federals were saying, marveling at the speed with which their adversaries could establish field fortifications, while the Confederates returned the compliment by remarking that "Sherman's men march with a rifle in one hand and a spade in the other" — blue and gray alike had become adept at the art of making any position well-nigh impregnable within a couple of days. While some troops hastily scratched and scooped out a ditch with bayonets and wooden shovels, canteen halves and fingers, others felled trees to provide timber for the dirt-and-log revetment, atop which a head log would rest on poles extending rearward across the trench to keep it from falling on the defenders in case it was struck by a shell while they were firing through the slit along its bottom between the skid poles. Other trees out front were cut so that their tops fell toward the enemy, their interlaced branches providing an entanglement to discourage assault, and if

---

Blue and gray alike had become adept at the art of making any position well-nigh impregnable within a couple of days.

---

there was time for more methodical work, sharpened stakes were set in holes bored in logs and these too were placed to delay or impale attackers; *chevaux-de-frise* was the engineers' term for these spiky devices, which Westerners on both sides called "sheep racks." Whatever their name, they were cruelly effective and contributed largely to the invulnerability of the occupants of the trenches, taking it easy under the shade of blankets laid over the works to shield them from the sun. Taking it easy, that is, in a relative sense; for the snipers were sharp-eyed, quick to shoot from dawn to dusk, and the pickets on both sides were fearfully trigger-happy from dusk to dawn; Thomas alone was expending 200,000 rounds of small-arms ammunition daily.

May now ended, and as June came in, two days after Bate's repulse by McPherson helped to offset the subtractions Hooker and Howard had undergone in their assaults on Stewart and Cleburne, both commanders could take a backward look at what the four-week "running skirmish," uninterrupted by anything approaching either the dignity or the carnage of a full-scale battle, had cost them. Sherman's loss throughout the month of May was 9299, including nearly two thousand killed and missing; Johnston's, less precisely tabulated, was about 8500, three thousand of them captured or otherwise missing, left behind

*This view of the field at New Hope Church after the
battle on May 25 shows Confederate breastworks
fashioned of dirt packed around a frame of timbers.*

on his retrograde movement from Dalton to Dallas. Not even the larger of the
two was a shudder-provoking figure at this stage of the war — particularly in
comparison with the one being registered simultaneously in Virginia, where
Meade was losing men at the rate of 2000 a day and would lose three times that
many tomorrow, within less than twenty minutes, at Cold Harbor — but Sherman
was getting edgy, all the same, over his inability to come to grips with his opponent
on any terms except those that would clearly involve self-slaughter.

This he declined, around New Hope Church, as he had done before,
wherever the Confederates called a halt to invite attack on their intrenchments. Instead, he continued to extend his left flank eastward toward the
Western & Atlantic, obliging Johnston to conform by extending his right to
keep him from slipping past it.

He was eager to get back astride the railroad, since two of his
mounted divisions — Garrard's, which had rejoined from Rome, and another
led by Major General George Stoneman, former chief of cavalry in the Army of

the Potomac, under Hooker, now filling that position in Schofield's Army of the Ohio — had seized lightly held Allatoona Pass that morning, June 1, clearing the way for Sherman's rail repair gangs to extend his all-weather supply line across the Etowah, down to Acworth and beyond.

Though Acworth was within ten miles of New Hope Church, the going would be rough, not only because of the rugged nature of the terrain and the probable interference of the rebels, but also because on the day Allatoona fell the rain began to fall as well: no brief tumultuous spring thunderstorm, such as had drenched the Hell Hole fighters, stopping about as abruptly as it started, but rather the slow, steady, apparently endless downpour of a dripping Georgia June. "Rain! Rain!! Rain!!!" an entry in a soggy diary read a few days later. This was as much of a strain on the spirits of men as it was on the backs and legs of mules who lugged ration and ammunition wagons through soupy troughs of wet red clay that once had passed for roads. "These were the hardest times the army experienced," Howard was to say, looking back. "It rained continuously for seventeen days; the roads, becoming as broad as the fields, were a series of quagmires."

Mosquitoes stung and thrived, along with something new that bit and burrowed: redbugs, *Eutrombicula alfreddugesi* — chiggers. "Chigres are big, and red as blood," an Illinois private wrote. "They will crawl through any cloth and bite worse than fleas, and poison the flesh very badly. Many of the boys anoint their bodies with bacon rines which chigres can't go. Salt water bathing would cure them but salt is too scarce to use on human flesh."

Salt was not the only scarcity. Cut loose from their bountiful rail supply line, and with little chance to forage on their own, the troops had to live mainly on hardtack and bacon. Men began to come down with the symptoms of scurvy, "black-mouthed, loose-toothed fellows" who went on the roam in search of wild onions or anything green and fit to eat, though with small success in this barren, up-and-down backwoods region, miles off the main track. It was, as Howard said, a difficult time for everyone concerned, including Sherman.

Then on the night of June 4, the sounds of withdrawal muffled by the drumming of the rain, Johnston gave him the slip again. Morning showed the Confederates gone, and though some of his soldiers cheered "the nocturnal departure of the rebellious gentlemen," Sherman himself was far from pleased: especially when he received reports of their new position, which seemed, on the face of it, about as strong as any they had occupied in the past four weeks. Hardee held the left, on Lost Mountain and at Gilgal Church, Polk the center, from Pine Mountain to the Western & Atlantic, six miles below Acworth, and Hood the right, across the railroad, along the base of Brush Mountain. Cavalry covered and extended the flanks, Wheeler eastward, beyond Hood, and Brigadier General William H. Jackson's division, which had come with Polk from Alabama, westward beyond Hardee. Kennesaw Mountain, a commanding height, was two miles in the rear, handy in case another fall-back was required, and Marietta about the same distance beyond its crest, which was less than twenty air-line miles from the heart of Atlanta.

By the following day, June 6, the three Union armies were again in confrontation with their foe, Thomas in the center, Schofield on the right, and McPherson on the left, astride the railroad at Big Shanty, a little more than midway between Allatoona and Marietta. Three days later Major General Francis P. Blair, Junior — brother of Lincoln's Postmaster General and a close friend of Sherman's — rejoined McPherson, bringing the 10,000 men of his corps back from their reënlistment furloughs and, incidentally, more than making up for the combat losses in all three armies up to now. By June 11 the hard-working railroad crews had the track repaired all the way to Big Shanty, and the troops, back on full rations and fairly well rested from their recent excursion through the wilds, felt much better.

"If we get to Atlanta in a week, all right," one veteran wrote home. "If it takes two months you won't hear this army grumbling."

Sherman was inclined to be less patient at this point. Though he was pleased that his latest sidle had accomplished its main purpose by obliging the rebels to give up impregnable Allatoona Pass, he was disappointed that it had not taken him all the way to the Chattahoochee (as he had predicted it would do, within five days) instead of fifteen rugged miles short of that river, with Johnston dug in across his front and able to look down his throat, so to speak, from the high ground up ahead.

Obviously, if the graybacks were to be dislodged at something less than an altogether grievous price in casualties, this called for another sidle. Yet Sherman did not much like the notion of setting out on still another round-about march away from the railroad: mainly, no doubt, because the last one had cost him more than he had planned for, both in morale and blood. In fact, before he crossed the Etowah and started his swing around Dallas, his losses had actually been lower than his adversary's, but now, as a result of the repulses he had suffered at New Hope Church and Pickett's Mill, they were nearly a thousand higher. Moreover, it seemed to him that his practice of avoiding pitched battle, wherever the terrain appeared unfavorable, had tended to make his soldiers unaggressive, timid in the face of possible ambush, and flinchy when confronted by intrenchments. Schofield, recovered by now from his horseback fall the week before, accounted for the reaction somewhat differently, seeing the nonprofessional volunteers and draftees as men who brought to army life, and to war itself, the practicality they had learned as civilians with the need for earning a living in the peacetime world outside. "The veteran American soldier fights very much as he has been accustomed to work his farm or run his sawmill," the young West Pointer declared. "He wants to see a fair prospect that it is going to pay."

That might be; Sherman yielded to no man in his admiration for and his understanding of the western volunteer. Still it seemed to him that all three armies were in danger of losing their fighting edge, if indeed they had not already lost it, and he put most of the blame on their commanders. Even McPherson, protégé or not, had begun to receive tart messages complaining of his slowness on the march. As for Schofield, he had come a long way from measuring up to

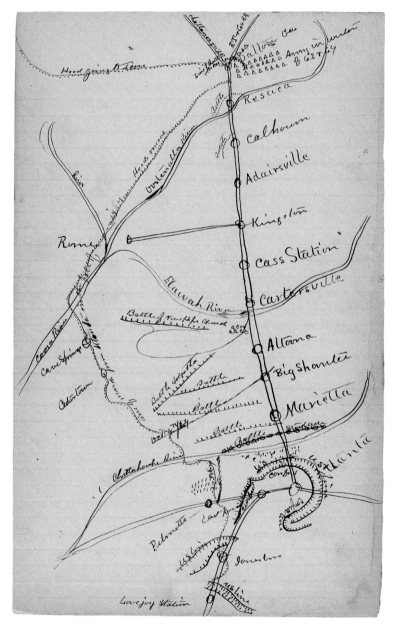

This sketch from the diary of a Texas cavalryman, who was fighting as part of the Confederate infantry, tracks Sherman's advance from Dalton to Atlanta.

expectations, and Sherman did not hesitate to say so. But Thomas, who had direct charge of two thirds of all the Federals in North Georgia, was the main object of the redhead's impatience and downright scorn.

"My chief source of trouble is with the Army of the Cumberland," Sherman informed Grant by telegraph this week. "A fresh furrow in a plowed field will stop the whole column and all begin to intrench. I have again and again tried to impress on Thomas that we must assail and not defend; we are on the offensive, and yet it seems that the whole Army of the Cumberland is so habituated to be[ing] on the defensive that from its commander down to its lowest private I cannot get it out of their heads."

He turned snappish in reaction to the delays and disadvantages involved in fighting what he called "a big Indian war" against an opponent whose army remained elusively intact and who, as Sherman complained in a letter to his brother in Washington, could "fight or fall back, as he pleases. The future is uncertain," he wound up gloomily, "but I will do all that is possible."

Aside from another unwanted sidle on muddy roads, not much seemed possible just now except to keep up the pressure, dead ahead, in hope that something would give. Nothing did. Johnston had contracted, somewhat retired, and thereby strengthened his line of defense, pulling Hardee in around Gilgal Church and Hood behind Noonday Creek, astride the railroad; Lost and Brush mountains were left to the protection of the cavalry, and Polk reinforced the center, on call to help cover not only the Western & Atlantic but also the wagon roads between Acworth and Marietta.

For outpost and observation purposes, a brigade from Bate's division remained on Pine Mountain, occupying what had become a salient when the line was readjusted in its rear. Called Pine Top by the natives, it was not so much a mountain as it was an overgrown hill, detached from the others roundabout and bristled atop with pine trees. Steepest on its northern face, it afforded a fine view of all three Federal armies and thus was well worth holding onto; Johnston had posted two batteries on its crest to help defend it, including one from South Carolina commanded by Lieutenant René Beauregard, the Creole general's son. Hardee was apprehensive, however, that both troops and guns were too far in advance of the main position for support to reach them before they were gobbled up by a sudden blue assault, and he asked his chief to go with him next morning, June 14, to judge in person the risk to which the salient was exposed.

Johnston agreed and the two set out on horseback as arranged, accompanied by their staffs and also by Polk, who wanted to come along for a look at the country from the hilltop. The rain had slackened and a cool breeze made the ride and the climb up the south slope a pleasant interlude, although Johnston had not gone far before he agreed that Hardee's fears were well founded; he told him to withdraw Bate's brigade and the two batteries after nightfall. Reaching the crest, however, he decided to avail himself of this last chance to study the enemy position from Pine Top, despite a warning that a battery of rifled Parrott guns, about half a mile in front, had been firing with deadly accuracy all morning at anyone who exposed himself to view.

Sure enough, the three generals had no sooner mounted the parapet and begun adjusting their binoculars than they were greeted by a bursting shell.

Sherman himself, riding out on a line inspection down below, had seen them, although without personal recognition at that range, and had taken offense at their presumption. "How saucy they are," he said, and he turned to Howard, who held this portion of the front, and told him to have one of his batteries throw a few shots in their direction to "make 'em take cover." He rode on, and Howard passed the word to Battery I, 1st Ohio Light Artillery, whose commander, Captain Hubert Dilger, had already acted on the order before it reached him.

Dilger was something of a character, well known throughout the

---

Aside from another unwanted sidle on muddy roads, not much seemed possible just now except to keep up the pressure, dead ahead, in hope that something would give. Nothing did.

---

army, partly because of the way he dressed, immaculate in a white shirt with rolled sleeves, highly polished top boots, and doeskin trousers — hence the nickname "Leatherbreeches" — and partly because of his habit of taking his guns so close to the front in battle that one general had proposed to equip them with bayonets. On leave from the Prussian army, in which he was also an artillerist, he had been visiting New York in 1861 and had joined the Army of the Potomac, fighting in all its battles through Gettysburg before coming west with Hooker to join the Army of the Cumberland. Perhaps because he spoke with a heavy German accent, he trained his crews to respond to hand claps, rather than voice commands, and had won such admiration as an expert, famed for the rapidity and precision of his fire, that he was allowed to function largely on his own, roving about as a sort of free lance and posting his battery wherever he judged it could do the most good. Today he was within half a mile of Pine Top, and when he saw the cluster of saucy Confederates mount the parapet on its crest he ran forward to one of his rifled Parrotts, sighted it carefully, then stepped back. "Shust teeckle them fellers," he told the cannoneer on the lanyard, and clapped his hands.

★

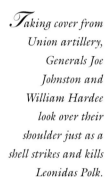

Taking cover from Union artillery, Generals Joe Johnston and William Hardee look over their shoulder just as a shell strikes and kills Leonidas Polk.

That was the first shot, a near miss. Johnston gave the order to disperse, and all three generals and their staffs had begun to do so when a second projectile landed even closer.

Hardee and Johnston moved briskly, heading for shelter behind the crest of the hill, but Polk, a portly figure apparently mindful of his dignity, walked off slowly by himself, hands clasped behind his back as if in deep thought. Just then the third shell came shrieking; Dilger had been quick to find the range. It struck the churchly warrior squarely in the side, passing through his left arm and his body and his right arm before emerging to explode against a tree. Johnston and Hardee turned and hurried back through other shell-bursts to kneel beside the quivering corpse of the bishop general. "My dear, dear friend," Hardee groaned, tears falling. Johnston too was weeping as he laid his hand upon the dead man's head. "We have lost much," he said, and presently added: "I would rather anything but this."

An ambulance, summoned by wigwag from the Pine Top signal

★

station, brought Polk's mangled remains down off the mountain that afternoon, followed that night, in accordance with Johnston's evacuation order, by the men of the two batteries and the infantry brigade, who filed down in a long column not unlike a funeral cortege.

Indeed, the whole army mourned the fifty-eight-year-old bishop's passing; he had been with it from the outset, before Shiloh, and at one time or another had commanded nearly every soldier in its ranks. There were, of course, those who doubted that his clerical qualities justified his elevation to the leadership of a corps. "Thus died a gentleman and a high Church dignitary," one of his division commanders wrote. "As a soldier he was more theoretical than practical." Though there was truth in this, it overlooked the contribution he made to the army's moral tone, which was one of the factors that enabled it to survive hardships, defeats, retreats, and Bragg. Northerners might express outrage that a man of the cloth, West Point graduate or not, should take up the sword of rebellion; Southerners took his action as strong evidence that the Lord was on their side, and they on His. That was part of what Jefferson Davis meant when he later referred to his old friend's death as "an irreparable loss" and said that the country had sustained no heavier blow since the fall of Sidney Johnston and Stonewall Jackson.

One service Polk's maiming performed, at any rate, and that was to break up the pattern of Sherman's incipient depression. He had small use for the clergy anyhow, as a class, let alone this one who had joined in the current unholy attempt to dissolve the finest government the world had ever known, and when the news reached his headquarters at Big Shanty that afternoon — Federal signalmen decoded a wigwag appeal from atop Pine Mountain: "Send an ambulance for General Polk's body" — he took it as a sign that things were going better than he had thought.

Sure enough, morning showed the enemy gone from the troublesome salient opposite his center. The rain had resumed its drumming on his tent, still further increasing the depth of the mud on all the roads, but Sherman did not let that keep his rising spirits from taking another mercurial jump. Ordering Thomas to close the gap in front while McPherson and Schofield stepped up the pressure on the flanks, he rode out to see it done and returned much pleased with the events of the past two days. Though he was careful, then and down the years, to deny the rumor that it was he, not Leatherbreeches Dilger, who had laid with his own hands the gun that sniped the militant churchman off of Pine Top, he was delighted with the result produced on this fortieth day of his campaign to "knock Jos. Johnston."

"We killed Bishop Polk yesterday," he wired Halleck, once more in high feather, "and made good progress today."

★ ★ ★

★

*French Impressionist Edouard
Manet's interpretation of the battle
between the U.S.S. Kearsarge and
the C.S.S. Alabama pictures the
rebel ship sinking by the stern.*

FIVE

Brice's; Lincoln; "Alabama"

1864 ★ ★ ★ ★ ★ ★ Not that, in his revived ebullience, Sherman had dismissed all fear for what he called "that single stem of railroad 473 miles long," back through Nashville and Bowling Green, hurdling rivers and burrowing under mountains to reach his base on the Ohio; "Taxed [as it was] to its utmost to supply our daily wants," he said flatly that without it "the Atlanta campaign was an impossibility." It was as much on his mind as ever, along with the two famed raiders who threatened its unbroken operation. "Thus far we have been well supplied, and I hope it will continue," he wrote his wife this week from Big Shanty, "though I expect to hear every day of Forrest breaking into Tennessee from some quarter. John Morgan is in Kentucky, but I attach little importance to him or his raid. Forrest is a more dangerous man."

Even as he wrote, events were proving him right in both assessments. Morgan, after his victory at Crockett's Cove in the second week of May, reverted to his plan for a return to his homeland, which had been interrupted by the need for keeping Averell away from the salt works and lead mines in the Department of Southwest Virginia. His application for permission to make the raid had been turned down by the Richmond authorities, on the grounds that he was needed where he was, but he did not let that stop him now any more than he had done ten months ago, when he set out on the "ride" that landed

★

him in the Ohio Penitentiary. Besides, having just learned that Brigadier General Stephen Burbridge, Union commander of the District of Kentucky, and a subordinate, Brigadier General Edward Hobson, were even then assembling troops in separate camps for a march across the Cumberlands to visit on Saltville and Wytheville the destruction Averell had failed to accomplish, Morgan believed he now had a more persuasive argument in favor of a quick return to the Bluegrass. Their combined forces were better than twice the size of his own, which amounted to fewer than 3000 men, and he was convinced that the only way to stop them was to distract them before they got started. "This information has determined me to move at once into the State of Kentucky," he informed the War Department on the last day of the month, "and thus divert the plans of the enemy by initiating a movement within his lines."

Forestalling another refusal, he set out that same day. By the time the message reached Richmond, two days later — "A most unfortunate withdrawal of forces from an important position at a very critical moment," Bragg indorsed it, and Seddon added: "Unfortunately, I see no remedy for this movement now" — Morgan was through Pound Gap and back on the soil of his native state.

That was June 2. It took him another five days to complete the rugged 150-mile trek across the mountains to within sight of the Bluegrass, and then on the morning of June 8 he approached the town of Mount Sterling, a day's ride west of Lexington. His strength was 2700 men, less than a third of them veterans from his old command, while another third were unmounted recruits for whom he hoped to find horses and equipment in the stock-rich country up ahead. A beginning was made at Mount Sterling, which he surrounded and captured, along with 380 Federals posted there to guard a large accumulation of supplies, including some badly needed boots.

While the prisoners were being paroled and Morgan was preparing to move on, looters began to break into shops, plunder homes, and even rough up citizens to relieve them of watches and wallets. "It was a general robbery," one merchant later protested, and though officers did what they could to stop the pillage, the undisciplined recruits, many of whom had spent the past two years avoiding conscription and stealing to make a living while on the run, were so far beyond control that some even drew pistols on women to rob them of their jewelry — an outrage the blood-thirstiest guerilla in Missouri had not perpetrated up to now. Confederates had mostly been greeted joyously on previous raids through this section of Kentucky, of which Morgan himself was a boasted product, but they were not likely to be welcome in the future, if indeed there was to be a future for them. A sort of climax was reached when a group of townspeople called indignantly on Morgan to show him an order, issued over the name of one of his brigade commanders, demanding immediate delivery of all the money in the local bank, under penalty of having "every house in the place" put to the

★

At the beginning of June 1864, John Hunt Morgan launched what was to be his final ride into Kentucky without waiting for approval from his superiors.

torch; $72,000 in gold and greenbacks had been handed over. Morgan paled and turned to the colonel in question, who pronounced the signature a forgery and asked who had presented it. A light-haired officer with a blond beard and a German accent, he was told. Surgeon R. R. Goode answered that description, but when he was sent for he did not appear. He was missing — and remained so, though afterwards he was rumored to be living high in his native Germany.

Morgan could afford no time for an investigation, however desirable one was to clear his name, and set out without further delay for Lexington, his home town just over thirty miles away, leaving the foot-sore, horseless troopers behind to complete the distribution and destruction of the captured stores before taking up the march to join him.

Only about half of them ever did, the rest being killed or captured as the result of a miscalculation. "There will be nothing in the state to retard our progress except a few scattered provost guards," Morgan had predicted on setting out, and this opinion had been bolstered by reports from scouts that the heavy Union column under Burbridge, unaware of what was in progress across

★

the way, had begun its eastward march toward the Cumberlands just before the Confederates emerged from them, headed west. Morgan's announced purpose was to oblige the blue invaders to turn back, but he had not thought they would react with anything like the speed they did. When Burbridge learned at Prestonburg that his adversary had passed him en route, by way of Pound Gap to the south, he not only countermarched promptly; he did so with such celerity that he was on the outskirts of Mount Sterling before daylight, June 9, and launched a dawn attack that caught the scantly picketed gray recruits so completely by surprise that many of them, still groggy from their excesses of the previous day and night, were shot before they could struggle out of their blankets. The survivors — about 450 of the original 800 — managed to fall back through the town and down the road to the west, thankful that the Federals were too worn by their hard return march to pursue.

During Morgan's brief stay in his home town,
Lexington, Kentucky, his unruly troopers
joined in the looting, burning, and bank robbery.

★

Morgan was halfway to Lexington when he found out what had happened, and though his first reaction was to turn back and counterattack with his whole command, on second thought (Burbridge had about twice as many men, well supported by artillery, and Morgan had been able to bring no guns across the mountains) he decided to wait for what was left of the horseless brigade to join him, then continue on to his home town. He approached it that night, made camp astride the pike, and rode in next morning to find, along with much else in the way of supplies and equipment, enough horses in its several government stables to mount all of his still-dismounted men and replace the animals broken down by the long march from Virginia.

Despite this valid military gain, June 10 was another stain on the reputation the raid had been designed, in part, to burnish. "Though the stay of Morgan's command in Lexington was brief, embracing but a few hours," the local paper reported next day, "he made good use of his time — as many empty shelves and pockets will testify." Once more looters took over, and this time veterans joined the pillage. Another bank was robbed, though more forthrightly than the one two days ago; the celebrants simply put a pistol to the cashier's head and made him open the vault, from which they took $10,000. Several buildings were set afire and whiskey stores were stripped, with the result that a good many troopers, too drunk to stay on a horse, had to be loaded into wagons for the ride to Cynthiana, thirty miles northeast. Morgan had learned there were supplies and a 500-man garrison there, and he was determined to have or destroy them both.

He marched by way of Georgetown to arrive next day, demanding surrender. This was declined, at first, but then accepted after a house-to-house fight in which, Morgan informed Richmond, "I was forced to burn a large portion of the town." Before he could enjoy the fruits of victory, lookouts spotted a blue column, 1200 strong, approaching from the east. It was Hobson; he too had turned back, well short of the Virginia line, on hearing from Burbridge that the raiders were in his rear. Headed for Lexington, he marched hard for Cynthiana when he saw the smoke and heard the firing. As it turned out, he was marching to join the surrender. Morgan threw two brigades directly at him and circled around to gain his rear with the other. This being done, Hobson was left with no choice except to be slaughtered or lay down his arms. He chose the latter course; which was doubly sweet for Morgan, Hobson having been widely praised for his share in the capture, near Buffington on the north bank of the Ohio River last July, of about half of Morgan's "terrible men," including the raider's second in command and two of his brothers, whom he later joined in prison as a felon. Now with Hobson himself a captive the tables were turned.

Proud of this latest exploit — as well he might be; he now had more prisoners than troopers — Morgan refused to be alarmed when scouts rode in at nightfall to report that Burbridge, having learned of his appearance at Cynthiana,

*Morgan's men loved Enfield rifles such as
this one. They refused to give them up for others, even
if they ran low on cartridges for the Enfields.*

was on the way from Mount Sterling with close to 5000 men. That was three times the strength of the Confederates, who were down to about 1400, half their original force, as a result of casualties, stragglers, and detachments sent out to mislead the numerous Union garrisons roundabout. Even more serious, perhaps, was a shortage of cartridges for the Enfield rifles his raiders favored so much that they declined to exchange them for captured Springfields, even though there was plenty of ammunition for the latter. But Morgan's mind was quite made up. Determined to give his weary men a good night's rest, he announced to his brigade commanders that he would meet the bluecoats next morning on ground of his own choosing, two miles south of town, and whip them as he had whipped Hobson today, whatever the odds. When one colonel protested that Burbridge was too strong to be fought without full cartridge boxes, the Alabama-born Kentuckian replied curtly: "It is my order that you hold your position at all hazard. We can whip him with empty guns."

Preceding another victory, the words would have had a defiant, martial ring, fit for the books and altogether in keeping with his earlier career; but followed as they were by a defeat, they took on the sound not of bravery, but of bravado. Burbridge attacked at dawn, June 12, and though Morgan was prevented from employing his accustomed flanking tactics by the need for putting all his men in line, he managed to stem the assault successfully until the shout, "Out of ammunition!" came from the right and was taken up next by the center, then the left. "Our whole command was soon forced back into the streets of the town, routed and demoralized," one raider would recall. "The confusion was indescribable. . . . There was much shooting, swearing, and yelling. Some from sheer mortification were crying."

Morgan did what he could to accomplish an orderly withdrawal, but what was left of his force by now had been split in two, with the halves presently blasted into fragments, some men fleeing southwest across the Sinking River to Leesburg, others northeast to Augusta. Many, caught on foot, surrendered; others were shot down. Not over half escaped, including their leader. "While falling back on the town," the same trooper wrote, "I saw General Morgan, on his step-trotting roan, going toward the Augusta road. He was skimming along at an easy pace, looking up at our broken lines and — softly whistling. I was glad to see him getting away, for had he been captured he would doubtless have fared badly."

He fared badly enough as it was. Back in Virginia before the month was out — minus half his troopers, even after all the stragglers had come in by various routes across the mountains, and considerably better than half his reputation — he put the raid in the best light he could manage in composing his report, stressing the frustration of Burbridge's expedition against the salt works and lead mines, the capture and parole of almost as many soldiers as he took with him, the procurement of nearly a thousand horses for men afoot and the exchange of roughly the same number of broken-down mounts for fresh ones, the destruction of "about 2,000,000$ worth of U.S. Govt. property," and the disruption of Federal recruitment in central and eastern Kentucky.

All this was much; but it was not enough, in the minds of his Richmond superiors, to offset his unauthorized departure in the first place, the misbehavior of his raiders wherever they went, and his second-day defeats at Mount Sterling and Cynthiana. Moreover, he now faced all his old problems, with only about half as many troops, and the confirmed displeasure, if not the downright enmity, of the Confederate War Department. It was fairly clear, in any case, that John Morgan had taken his last "ride," that his beloved home state had seen its last of him and his terrible men.

*S*herman was pleased, but hardly surprised, by Morgan's failure. Indeed, aside from having work crews standing by to make quick repairs in case the Kentuckian broke through to damage the railroad below Louisville, he feared him so little that he had scarcely planned for his coming beyond warning local commanders to be on the lookout. The other raider was another matter. After telling his wife, "Forrest is a more dangerous man," the red-haired Ohioan added: "I am in hopes that an expedition sent out from Memphis about the first of June will give him full employment."

It certainly should have done at least that, preceded as it was by a top-to-bottom shakeup of department personnel, beginning with Major General Stephen Hurlbut, commander of the District of West Tennessee. A Shiloh veteran and prewar Republican politician, Hurlbut had high-placed friends — Lincoln himself had made him a brigadier within a month of Sumter — but Sherman, far from satisfied with the "marked timidity" of his attempts to keep Forrest out of the region this past year, replaced him, less than a week after the fall of Fort Pillow, with Major General Cadwallader C. Washburn, who also had lofty Washington connections, including his brother Elihu, Grant's congressional guardian angel. Washburn had shown aggressiveness at Vicksburg, and Sherman chose him for that quality, which he encouraged by sending him a new chief of cavalry who shared it, Brigadier General Samuel D. Sturgis.

Seasoned by combat in Missouri as well as in Virginia (where he had contributed at least one famous quotation to the annals of this war: "I don't care for John Pope one pinch of owl dung") Sturgis had graduated from West Point alongside Stonewall Jackson and George McClellan. That he was more akin militarily to the former than to the latter was demonstrated by the manner in which he took hold on arrival in late April. Forrest by then was returning to North Mississippi from his raid to the Ohio; Sturgis pursued him as far as Ripley, seventy-five miles southeast of Memphis, before turning back for lack of subsistence for his 6400-man column.

"I regret very much that I could not have the pleasure of bringing you his hair," he wrote Sherman on his return to Tennessee, "but he is too great a plunderer to fight anything like an equal force, and we have to be satisfied with driving him from the state. He may turn on your communications . . . I rather think he will, but see no way to prevent it from this point and with this force."

In part — the remark about Forrest's hair, for example — this had a true aggressive ring, confirming the choice of Sturgis for the post he filled, but Sherman did not enjoy being told there was no way to keep the raider off his life line. His Georgia campaign had opened by then, and the farther he got from his starting point (Dalton to Resaca; across the Oostanaula to Kingston; then finally over the Etowah for the roundhouse swing through Dallas) the more vital that supply line became, and the more exposed it was to depredation. Concerned lest Forrest give Washburn the slip, he wired orders for the West Tennessee commander to launch "a threatening movement from Memphis," southeast into Mississippi, to prevent Forrest "from swinging over against my communications" in North Georgia or Middle Tennessee.

Sturgis was to have charge of the expedition, but Washburn himself saw to the preparations, taking two full weeks to make certain nothing was omitted that might be needed, either in men or supplies or equipment. "The force sent out was in complete order," he later reported, "and consisted of some of our best troops. They were ordered to go in the lightest possible marching order, and to take only wagons for commissary stores and ammunition. They had a supply for twenty days. I saw to it personally that they lacked nothing to insure a successful campaign. The number of troops deemed necessary by General Sherman, as he telegraphed me, was 6000, but I sent 8000."

He sent in fact 8300: three brigades of infantry, totaling 5000, under Colonel William L. McMillen, the senior field officer in the district, and two of cavalry, totalling 3300, led by Brigadier General Benjamin Grierson, who had come into prominence a year ago with the 600-mile raid that distracted Vicksburg's defenders while Grant was beginning the final phase of the campaign that accomplished its surrender. In over-all charge of the two divisions, Sturgis also had 22 guns, of various calibers, and 250 wagons loaded with the

★

twenty-day supply of food and ammunition. Grierson's troopers were equipped with repeating carbines of the latest model, which would give them a big advantage in firepower over their butternut opponents, and part at least of McMillen's command was armed with a zeal beyond the normal, one of his brigades being made up of Negro soldiers who had taken an oath to avenge Fort Pillow by showing Forrest's troops no quarter. "In case of an action in which they are successful," Hurlbut had stated on the eve of his departure, "it will be nearly impracticable to restrain them from retaliation." Now they and their white comrades, mounted and afoot, were on the march toward a confrontation with the man from whom they had sworn to exact vengeance.

They left Memphis on June 1, and as they set out from Collierville next day the rain began to fall, drenching men and horses and drowning fields and roads, much as it was doing 300 miles away in Georgia. Here, as there, the result was slow going, especially for the wagons lurching hub-deep through the mud. Five days of slogging about seven miles a day brought the marchers as far as Salem, a North Mississippi hamlet whose only historical distinction was that it had been Bedford Forrest's boyhood home. A disencumbered flying column of 400 troopers was detached there for a forty-mile ride due east to strike the Mobile & Ohio at Rienzi, a dozen miles below Corinth, in hopes that breaking the railroad at that point would delay the concentration, somewhere down the line, of the Confederates who no doubt by now had begun to gather in the path of the main column. Another three days of heavy-footed plodding, through June 8, covered another twenty miles of the nearly bottomless road to Ripley, where Sturgis had turned back from his pursuit of the plunderer a month ago.

Discouraged by the slowness of his march, as well as by the thought of all those graybacks probably gathering up ahead, he was inclined toward doing the same thing tomorrow, and that night he held a conference with his division commanders to get their views on the matter. Grierson felt much as his chief did. Delay had most likely enabled the rebs "to concentrate an overwhelming force against us," and he was impressed as well by "the utter hopelessness of saving our train or artillery in case of defeat." McMillen, on the other hand, declared that he "would rather go on and meet the enemy, even if we should be whipped, than to return again to Memphis without having met them." The key word here was again, Sturgis having turned back at this same point the month before. He thought it over and decided, on balance, that "it would be ruinous on all sides" — not least, it would seem, to the aggressive reputation that had won him his present post — "to return again without first meeting the enemy."

"Under these circumstances, and with a sad foreboding of the consequences," he afterwards summed up, "I determined to move forward, keeping my force as compact as possible and ready for action at all times."

★

His fears were better founded than he knew, although he was completely wrong about the odds he thought he faced. The Confederates were indeed preparing to oppose him, but it could scarcely be with an "overwhelming force," since the number of men available to the defenders was barely more than half as many as were in the blue column toiling toward them through the rain. On the day Sturgis left Memphis, June 1, Forrest had left Tupelo with 2200 troopers and six guns, bound at last for Middle Tennessee and a descent on Sherman's life line below Nashville. He was in North Alabama on June 3, preparing to cross the Tennessee River, when an urgent message from Stephen Lee summoned him back to meet Sturgis's newly developed threat to the department Lee had inherited from Polk.

Forrest returned to Tupelo on June 5, the day the Federals reached his boyhood home fifty miles northwest. Uncertain whether they were headed for Corinth or Tupelo — the 400-man flying column, detached that day for the strike at Rienzi, contributed to the confusion — Lee told Forrest to dispose his men along the M&O between those two towns, ready to move in either direction, while he himself did what he could to get hold of more troops to help ward

Unsure where the Federals were heading, Stephen Lee had Forrest dispose his men along the M & O between Corinth, shown here, and Tupelo, ready to move in either direction.

★

off the 8300-man blow, wherever it might land. His notion was that, if the enemy moved southward, the cavalry should retire toward Okolona, about twenty miles below Tupelo, in order to protect the Black Prairie region just beyond, where most of the subsistence for his department was grown and processed, and also to draw Sturgis as far as possible from his base of supplies and place of refuge in Memphis before giving him battle with whatever reinforcements had been rounded up by then. Lee made it clear before they parted, however, that Forrest was left to his own devices as to what should be done in the meantime, and Forrest took full advantage of the discretion thus allowed him.

He had at the time some 4300 troopers within reach: 2800 in Colonel Tyree Bell's brigade, which was part of Abraham Buford's division, and about 750 in each of two small brigades under Colonels Hylan Lyon and Edmund Rucker. While waiting for Sturgis to show his hand, Forrest spent the next two days posting these commands in accordance with Lee's instructions to cover both Tupelo and Corinth. Bell, with considerably better than half the available force, was sent to Rienzi, which he reached in time to drive off the 400 detached bluecoats before they did any serious damage to the railroad. Rucker and Lyon,

with 1500 between them, moved to Booneville, nine miles south of Rienzi, accompanied by Captain John Morton's two four-gun batteries, all the artillery on hand. Forrest was there on June 8 when he received word that Sturgis was at Ripley, twenty miles away, and when he learned next morning that the mud-slathered Union column was continuing southeast, there was no longer any doubt that it was headed not for Corinth but for Tupelo, twelve miles below Guntown, a station on the M&O at the end of the road down which Sturgis was marching. A brigade remnant of 500 men under Colonel William A. Johnson arrived that day from Alabama, raising Forrest's strength to 4800. That was all he was likely to have for several days, but he figured it was enough for what he had in mind. He told Johnson to rest his troopers near Baldwyn, twenty miles down the track from Booneville, having decided to hit Sturgis, and hit him hard, before he got to Guntown.

In fact, he had already chosen his field of fight, twenty miles from Ripley and six miles short of the railroad — a timber-laced low plateau where the Ripley-Guntown road, on which the Federals were moving southeast, was intersected at nearly right angles by one from Booneville that ran southwest to Pontotoc — and when he learned that evening that Sturgis had called an overnight halt at Stubbs Farm, nine miles from the intended point of contact, his plan was complete. Orders went out to all units that night, June 9, and the march began before dawn next morning. Forrest led the way with his hundred-man escort company and Lyon's small Kentucky brigade; Rucker and Bell were to follow, along with Morton's guns, and Johnson would come in from the east. The result, that day, was the battle variously celebrated as Guntown, Tishomingo Creek, or Brice's Crossroads.

The enemy had close to a two-to-one advantage in men, as well as nearly three times as many guns, but Forrest believed that boldness and the nature of the terrain, which he knew well, would make up for the numerical odds he faced. "I know they greatly outnumber the troops I have at hand," he told Rucker, who rode with him in advance of his brigade, "but the road along which they will march is narrow and muddy; they will make slow progress. The country is densely wooded and the undergrowth so heavy that when we strike them they will not know how few men we have."

His companion might have pointed out, but did not, that the road they themselves were on — called the Wire Road because in early days, before the railroad, the telegraph line to New Orleans had run along it — was as muddy and as narrow as the one across the way. Moreover, all the Federals were within nine miles of the objective, while aside from Johnson's 500 Alabamians, seven miles away at Baldwyn, all the Confederates had twice as far to go or farther; Lyon, Rucker, and Morton had eighteen miles to cover, and Bell just over twenty-five. Forrest had thought of that as well, however, and here too he saw

★

compensating factors, not only in the marching ability of his troopers, but also in the contrasting effect of the weather on their blue-clad adversaries. The rain had stopped and the rising sun gave promise that the day would be a scorcher.

"Their cavalry will move out ahead of their infantry," he explained, "and should reach the crossroads three hours in advance. We can whip their cavalry in that time. As soon as the fight opens they will send back to have the infantry hurried in. It is going to be hot as hell, and coming on the run for five or six miles, their infantry will be so tired out we will ride right over them."

Aside from the temperature estimate, which was open to question in the absence of any thermometer readings from hell, Rucker was to discover that this was practically a blow-by-blow account of what would follow; but the general quickly returned to present matters. "I want everything to move up as soon as possible," he said. "I will go ahead with Lyon and the escort and open the fight."

Sturgis rose at Stubbs Farm in a better frame of mind, encouraged by the letup of the rain and the prospect that a couple of days of mid-June heat would bake the roads dry, down through Tupelo and beyond. The flying column had returned from Rienzi the night before, and though their mounts were badly jaded the 400 troopers were doubly welcome as replacements for about the same number of "sick and worn-out men" he started back toward Memphis this morning in forty of the wagons his two divisions had eaten empty in the past nine days. These ailing bluecoats would miss a signal experience this hot June 10 at Brice's Crossroads, nine miles down the Guntown road, but their commander — round-faced and rather plump, Pennsylvania-born and a former Indian fighter, with a thick shock of curly hair, a trim mustache, and an abbreviated chin beard, he would be forty-two years old tomorrow: Forrest's age — did not know that, yet. All he knew, for the present, was "that it was impossible to gain any accurate or reliable information of the enemy and that it behooved us to move and act constantly as though in his presence."

This last, however, was precisely what he failed to do. Despite his previous resolution "to move forward, keeping my force as compact as possible and ready for action at all times," compassion for his weary foot soldiers led him to give them an extra couple of hours in camp to dry their clothes and get themselves in order for another hard day's march. Grierson and his troopers rode off for Guntown at 5.30 but McMillen's lead brigade did not set out till 7 o'clock, thus giving Forrest a full measure of the time he estimated he would need to "whip their cavalry" before the infantry "hurried up."

His plan, whose execution today would advance his growing reputation as "the Wizard of the Saddle," was for a battle in three stages: 1) holding attack, 2) main effort, and 3) pursuit. But Sturgis, riding with McMillen at the head of the infantry column, knew nothing of this — not even that Forrest was nearby — until shortly after 10 o'clock, when a courier from Grierson came

Forty-two years old and a former Indian fighter, the Pennsylvania-born Samuel D. Sturgis would face a humiliating and utter rout by Forrest's rebel raiders.

pounding back with news that the cavalry was hotly engaged, some five miles down the road, with a superior hostile force; he had, he said, "an advantageous position," and could hold it "if the infantry was brought up promptly." Leaving orders for McMillen to proceed "as rapidly as possible without distressing the troops," Sturgis galloped ahead to examine the situation at first hand.

It did not look at all good from the rear, where a nearly mile-long causeway across a stretch of flooded bottomland led to and from a narrow bridge over Tishomingo Creek; "artillery and ambulances and led horses jammed the road," he observed, and when he reached Brice's about noon, another mile and a half toward Guntown, he found the cavalry hard pressed, fighting dismounted amid "considerable confusion." One brigade commander declared flatly that he "would have to fall back unless he received some support," while the other, according to Sturgis, was "almost demanding to be relieved."

Grierson was more stalwart. Though the rebels were there "in large numbers, with double lines of skirmishers and heavy supports," he was proud to report that he and his rapid-firing troopers had "succeeded in holding our own and repulsing with great slaughter three distinct and desperate charges." The sun by now was past the overhead. How much longer he could hang on he did not say, but it could scarcely be for long unless he was reinforced, heavily and soon, by men from the infantry column toiling toward him through the mud

★

and heat. Sturgis reacted promptly. With no further mention of concern about "distressing the troops," he sent word for McMillen to hurry his three brigades forward and save the day. "Make all haste," he told him, and followed this with a second urgent message: "Lose no time in coming up."

Grierson was wrong in almost everything he said, and Sturgis was fatally wrong in accepting his estimate of the situation. Those three "desperate charges," for example, had simply been feints, made by Forrest — a great believer in what he called "bulge" — to disguise the fact that his troopers, dismounted and fed piecemeal into the brush-screened line as soon as they came up, were badly outnumbered by those in the two blue brigades, who overlapped him on both flanks and had six pieces of horse artillery in action, unopposed, and four more in reserve. He opened the fight, as he had said he would do, by attacking with Lyon astride the Wire Road, then put Rucker and Johnson in on the left and right, when they arrived, for a second and a third attack to keep the Federals off balance while waiting for Morton's guns and the rest of his command to complete their marches from Booneville and Rienzi. "Tell Bell to move up fast and fetch all he's got," he told a staff major, who rode back to deliver the message.

It was just past 1 o'clock when this last and largest of his brigades came onto the field, close behind Morton; by which time, true to his schedule, Forrest had the enemy cavalry whipped.

Convinced, as he said then and later, that he had been "over-whelmed by numbers," Grierson was asking to have his division taken out of line, "as it was exhausted and well-nigh out of ammunition" for its rapid-firing carbines. McMillen rode up to the crossroads at that point, in advance of his lead brigade, and was dismayed to find that "everything was going to the devil as fast as it possibly could." Like Sturgis earlier, he threw caution to the winds. Though many of his troops had already collapsed from heat exhaustion on the hurried approach march, and though all were blown and in great distress from the savage midday, mid-June Mississippi sun, he sent peremptory orders for his two front brigades to come up on the double quick and restore the crumbling cavalry line before the rebels overran it.

They were hurrying to destruction, and hurrying needlessly at that; for just as they came into position, every bit as "tired out" as Forrest had pre-dicted, a lull fell over the crossroad. It was brief, however, and lasted only long enough for the Confederate commander, now that all his troops were on the field, to mount and launch his first real assault of the day. Giving direction of the three brigades on the right to Buford, a Kentucky-born West Pointer two years his senior in age, he went in person to confer with Bell, whose newly arrived brigade comprised the left. This done, he came back to the right, checking his line along the way. In shirtsleeves because of the heat, with his coat laid over the pommel of his saddle, he "looked the very God of War," one soldier would remember, and as he rode among them on his big sorrel horse, saber in hand, he spoke to the dismounted troopers lying about for some rest in the blackjack thickets. "Get up, men," he told them. "I have ordered Bell to charge on the left. When you hear his guns, and the bugle sounds, every man must charge, and we will give them hell." Other things he said, then and later, went unrecorded. "I notice some writers on Forrest say he seldom cursed," one watcher was to recall. "Well, the fellow who writes that way was not where the 7th Tennessee was that day. . . . He would curse, then praise and then threaten to shoot us himself, if we were so afraid the Yankees might hit us."

Drawing rein at Morton's position, Forrest told him to double-shot four of his guns with canister and join the charge when the bugle sounded, then keep pace with the front rank as it advanced. Afterwards, the young artillerist, who had celebrated his twenty-first birthday on the field of Chickamauga, told his chief: "You scared me pretty badly when you pushed me up so close to their infantry and left me without protection. I was afraid they might take my guns." Forrest laughed. "Well, artillery is made to be captured," he said, "and I wanted to see them take yours."

But that was after the third stage ended, two days later; now the second, the main effort, was just beginning, and there was a grim struggle, much of it hand to hand, before the contest reached the climactic point at which Forrest judged the time had come to go all-out. Returning to the left, where he believed the resistance would be stiffest, he put an end to the thirty-minute lull by starting Bell's advance up the Guntown road. McMillen's second brigade was posted there, sturdy men from Indiana, Illinois, and Minnesota who, winded though they were from their sprint to reach the field, not only broke the gray attack but launched one of their own, throwing the Tennesseans into such confusion that Forrest had to dismount his escort troopers and lead them into the breach, firing pistols, to stop what had the makings of disaster. Over on the right, Buford too was finding the enemy stubborn, and had all he could do to keep up the pressure along his front. Finally, though, the pressure told. Orders came from Forrest — who fought this, as he did all his battles, "by ear" — that the time had come to "hit 'em on the ee-end." It was past 4 o'clock by now, and simultaneous attacks, around the flanks and into the rear of the Union left and right, made the whole blue line waver and cave in, first slowly, then with a rush.

"The retreat or rout began," in Forrest's words, or as Sturgis put it: "Order gave way to confusion and confusion to panic. . . . Everywhere the army now drifted toward the rear, and was soon altogether beyond control."

Fleeing past the two-story Brice house at the crossroads, the fugitives sought shelter back up the road they had run down, four hours ago, to reach the battle that now was lost. But conditions there were in some ways worse than those in what had been the front: especially along the causeway

Yet again confounding a Yankee commander, Nathan Bedford Forrest triumphed at Guntown and chased routed Federals throughout the afternoon and long into the night.

through the Tishomingo bottoms and on the railless bridge across the creek, the narrow spout of the funnel-shaped host of panicked men, who, as Sturgis said, "came crowding in like an avalanche from the battlefield." Morton's batteries had the range, and their execution was increased by the addition of four Federal guns, captured with their ammunition. Presently a wagon overturned on the high bridge and others quickly piled up behind it, creating what a retreating colonel described as "one indiscriminate mass of artillery, caissons, ambulances, and broken, disordered troops."

Some escaped by leaping into the creek, swollen neck-deep by the rains, and wading to the opposite bank. But there was no safety there either. Though Sturgis had hoped to form a new line on the far side of the stream, the rebels were crossing so close in his rear that every attempt to make a stand only brought on a new stampede. The only thing that slowed the whooping gray-backs was the sight of abandoned wagons, loaded with what one hungry pursuer called "fresh, crisp hardtack and nice, thin side bacon." They would pause for plunder, wolf it down, and then come on for more.

This continued, well past sundown, to within three miles of last night's bivouac, where there was another and still worse stretch of miry road across one of the headwater prongs of the Hatchie River. It was night now and the going was hard, one officer noted, "in consequence of abandoned vehicles, drowned and dying horses and mules, and the depth of the mud." Despairing of getting what was left of his shipwrecked train through this morass, Sturgis went on to Stubbs Farm, where he was approached before midnight by Colonel Edward Bouton, whose Negro brigade had served as train guard during the battle and had therefore suffered less than the other two infantry commands had done.

"General, for God's sake don't let us give up so," he exclaimed.

But Sturgis, quite unstrung, was at his wit's end. "What can we do?" he said, not really asking.

Bouton wanted ammunition with which to hold Forrest in check, on the far side of the bottoms, while the remaining guns and wagons were being snaked across to more solid ground beyond. Sturgis was too far in despair, however, to consider this or any other proposal involving resistance. Besides, he had no ammunition to give.

"For God's sake," he broke out, distraught by the events of this longest day in his life and the prospect of a sad birthday tomorrow, "if Mr Forrest will let me alone, I will let him alone! You have done all you could, and more than was expected. . . . Now all you can do is to save yourselves."

Mr Forrest, as Sturgis so respectfully styled the man he had said a month ago was "too great a plunderer to fight anything like an equal force," had no intention of letting him alone so long as there was profit to be gained from pressing the chase. Heaving the wreckage off the Tishomingo bridge and into the creek, along with the dead and dying animals, he continued to crowd the rear of the retreating bluecoats. "Keep the skeer on 'em," he told his troopers, remounted now, and they did just that, past sunset and on into twilight and full night. "[Sturgis] attempted the destruction of his wagons, loaded with ammunition and bacon," Forrest would report, "but so closely was he pursued that many of them were saved without injury, although the road was lighted for some distance." Furious at this incendiary treatment of property he considered his already, he came upon a group of his soldiers who had paused, still mounted, to watch the flames. "Don't you see the damned Yankees are burning my wagons?" he roared. "Get off your horses and throw the burning beds off." Much toasted hardtack and broiled bacon was saved that way, until finally, some time after 8 o'clock, "It being dark and my men and horses requiring rest" — they did indeed, having been on the go, marching and fighting, for better than sixteen hours — "I threw out an advance to follow slowly and cautiously after the enemy, and ordered the command to halt, feed, and rest."

By 1 a.m. he had his troopers back in the saddle and hard on the equipment-littered trail. Within two hours they reached the Hatchie bottoms, where they came upon the richest haul of all. Despite Bouton's plea, Sturgis had ordered everything movable to proceed that night to Stubbs Farm and beyond, abandoning what was left of his train, all his non-walking wounded, and another 14 guns, all that remained of the original 22 except for four small mountain howitzers that had seen no action anyhow. This brought Forrest's total acquisition to 18 guns, 176 wagons, 1500 rifles, 300,000 rounds of small-arms ammunition, and much else. He himself lost nothing, and though he had 492 killed and wounded in the battle — a figure larger in proportion than the 617 casualties he inflicted — his capture of more than 1600 men on the retreat brought the Federal loss to 2240, nearly five times his own.

Many of the enemy, especially from Bouton's brigade, which had the misfortune to bring up the rear and suffered heavily in the process, were picked up here in the Hatchie bottoms. A Tennessee sergeant later recalled the scene. "Somewhere between midnight and day, we came to a wide slough or creek bottom; it was miry and truly the slough of despair and despond to the Yanks. Their artillery and wagons which had heretofore escaped capture were now bogged down and had to be abandoned. This slough was near kneedeep in mud and water, with logs lying here and there. On top of every log were Yanks perched as close as they could be, for there were more Yanks

> *"For God's sake, if Mr Forrest will let me alone, I will let him alone! You have done all you could, and more than was expected. . . . Now all you can do is to save yourselves."*
>
> — Samuel D. Sturgis

than logs." They put him in mind "of chickens at roost," he said, but added: "We who were in front were ordered to pay no attention to prisoners. Those in the rear would look after that."

Four miles short of Ripley at dawn, the pursuers came upon a rear-guard remnant, which Forrest said "made only a feeble and ineffectual resistance." He drove its members back on the town, where they were reinforced and rallied briefly, only to scatter when attacked. "From this place," Forrest's report continued, "the enemy offered no organized resistance, but retreated in the most complete disorder, throwing away guns, clothing, and everything calculated to impede his flight." Beyond Ripley he left the direct pursuit to Buford and swung onto a roundabout adjoining road with Bell's brigade, intending to cut the Federals off at Salem. But that was a miscalculation. Buford pressed them so hard the interception failed; the blue column cleared the hamlet before Forrest got there around sundown. He called off the chase at that point and turned back to scour the woods and brush for fugitives, gather up his spoils, and give his men and mounts some rest from their famous victory, which would be studied down the years, in war colleges here and abroad, as an example of what a numerically inferior force could accomplish once it got what its commander called "the bulge" on an opponent, even one twice its size.

There was no rest, though, for Sturgis and his men, who continued to flee in their ignorance that they were no longer pursued except by rumors of gray-backs hovering on their flank. "On we went, and ever on," a weary colonel was to write, "marching all that day and all that interminable [second] night. Until half past ten the next morning, when we reached Collierville and the railroad, rein-forcements and supplies, we marched, marched, marched, without rest, without sleep, without food." At any rate they made excellent time. The march down had taken more than a week, but the one back took only a night and a day and a night. In Collierville that morning (June 12; Morgan's troopers were scattering from Cynthiana, 300 miles northeastward in Kentucky) the wait for the train that would take them on to the outskirts of Memphis, seventeen miles away, was in some ways even harder than the 90-mile forced march had been. Relieved of a measure of their fright, they now knew in their bones how tired they were and how thor-oughly they had been whipped. An Ohio regimental commander reported that, in the course of their wait beside the railroad track, his troops "became so stiffened as to require assistance to enable them to walk. Some of them, too foot-sore to stand upon their feet, crawled upon their hands and knees to the cars."

Sturgis's hurts were mainly professional, being inflicted on his career. Back in Memphis, amid rumors that he had been drunk on the field — a con-clusion apparently reached by way of the premise that no sober man could be so roundly trounced — he put the disaster in the best light he could manage. Winding up his official report with "regret that I find myself called upon to record a defeat," he added: "Yet there is some consolation in knowing that the army fought nobly while it did fight, and only yielded to overwhelming numbers." Just over 8000 troops had been thrown into a rout and driven headlong for nearly a hundred miles by just under 5000, but he persisted in claiming (and even believing, so persuasive were Forrest's tactics) that the odds had been the other way around, and longer. "The strength of the enemy is variously estimated by my most intelligent officers at from 15,000 to 20,000 men."

So he said; but vainly, so far as concerned the salvation of his career. For him, the war ended at Brice's Crossroads. Despite the board's finding no sub-stance in the charge that he had been drunk, either in battle or on the birthday re-treat, Sturgis spent the rest of the conflict on the sidelines, awaiting orders that did not come. Disconsolate as he was, he only shared what those who had served under him were feeling. Though in time their aching muscles would find relief and their wounds would heal, the inward scars of their drubbing would remain. "It is the fate of war that one or the other side should suffer defeat," a cavalry major who survived the battle was to write, more than twenty years later. "But here there was more. The men were cowed, and there pressed upon them a sense of bitter humiliation, which rankles after nearly a quarter of a century has passed."

Sherman was disappointed, of course, but he was also inclined to give Sturgis credit for having achieved his "chief object," which had been "to hold Forrest there [in Mississippi] and keep him off our [rail]road." There was truth in a participating colonel's observation that the expedition had been "sent out as a tub to Forrest's whale," and though the price turned out to be high, both in men and equipment, it was by no means exorbitant, considering the alternative. Learning that the raider had been in North Alabama, poised for a strike across the Tennessee River before Sturgis lured him back, the red-haired Ohioan wired the district commander instructions designed to discourage a return: "You may send notice to Florence that if Forrest invades Tennessee from that direction, the town will be burned, and if it occurs you will remove the inhabitants north of the Ohio River, and burn the town" — adding, as if by afterthought: "and Tuscumbia also."

He would send both places up in smoke, along with much else, if it would help to keep "that devil Forrest" off his life line. But that was only an interim deterrent. He had it in mind to follow through, as soon as possible, with a second expedition into northern Mississippi, stronger and better led, to profit by the shortcomings of the first. "Forrest is the very devil," he declared, "and I think has got some of our troops under cover." He proposed to correct this in short order. A. J. Smith's three divisions were on their way back from service up Red River with Banks, hard-handed veterans whose commanders had been closely observed by Sherman in the course of the fighting last year around Vicksburg. He had intended either to bring them to Georgia as reinforcements or else to send them against Mobile; but now, he notified Washington, he had what he considered a better, or in any case a more urgent, use for them. "I will order them to make up a force and go out and follow Forrest to the death, if it costs 10,000 lives and breaks the Treasury. There will never be peace in Tennessee till Forrest is dead."

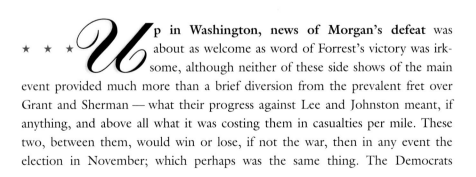

★ ★ ★ *U*p in Washington, news of Morgan's defeat was about as welcome as word of Forrest's victory was irksome, although neither of these side shows of the main event provided much more than a brief diversion from the prevalent fret over Grant and Sherman — what their progress against Lee and Johnston meant, if anything, and above all what it was costing them in casualties per mile. These two, between them, would win or lose, if not the war, then in any event the election in November; which perhaps was the same thing. The Democrats would convene in August to nominate a candidate who would run on the issue of ending the conflict by declaring peace, whatever accommodations might be required by their late fellow countrymen down South, and it was generally agreed that the Republicans could not survive a prolongation of the bloody three-year stalemate through the five months between now and the election.

Lincoln had declared himself "only a passenger" on the juggernaut of war, but his hand was still on the tiller of the ship of state and he intended to keep it there if he could. Public attention was mainly fixed on the fighting in Virginia, where the casualties had been awesome from the start, and he tried to offset the civilian reaction by stressing his admiration for Grant's refusal to be distracted by the bloodshed and by recommending that his listeners do likewise.

"I think, without knowing the particulars of the plans of General Grant, that what has been accomplished is of more importance than at first appears," he told a crowd that came to serenade him on hearing that the Army of the Potomac had resumed its southward march after two days of cataclysmic battle in the Wilderness. "I believe I know — and am especially grateful to know — that General Grant has not been jostled in his purposes, that he has made all his points, and today he is on his line as he purposed before he moved. . . . I commend you to keep yourselves in the same tranquil mood that is characteristic of that brave and loyal man."

Tranquillity was easier to prescribe than to attain. Hemmed in as he was by cares from all directions, including the importunities of incessant office seekers — "Too many pigs for the tits," he said wryly — Lincoln found the sight of the wounded, returning in their thousands from where he had sent them to get hit, a heavy burden on his spirit. "Look yonder at those poor fellows," he said one day when a long line of ambulances creaked past his halted carriage. "I cannot bear it. This suffering, this loss of life is dreadful." It was during this dark time that a White House visitor watched him pace the dawn-gray corridors in his nightshirt and long wrapper, hands clasped behind his back, head bent low, and with black rings under his eyes from loss of sleep.

By no means all the strain was of a purely military nature. While it was true that some events which normally would have awakened a sharp sense of national loss were muted by the uproar of the guns — the death of Nathaniel Hawthorne, for example, was barely noted amid the excitement over Grant's shift from Spotsylvania to the North Anna — others were so closely tied to the conflict that they stood out in stark relief against its glare. One was the so-called Gold Hoax, perpetrated on May 18, the day before Hawthorne died, by Joseph Howard, the journalist who three years ago had written of Lincoln's furtive passage through Baltimore in a "Scotch cap and long military cloak" to avoid assassination on the way to his inauguration. At 4 a.m. that morning Howard distributed anonymously to all the New York papers a bogus proclamation, complete with the forged

Lincoln's uneasy relationship with the press was underscored by the so-called "Gold Hoax" of 1864.

signature of the President, fixing May 26 "as a day of fasting, humiliation and prayer," and calling for an additional draft of 400,000 men required by "the situation in Virginia, the disaster at Red River, the delay at Charleston, and the general state of the country."

Defeat, it seemed from the doleful tone of the document, was just around the corner. Only two papers, the *New York World* and the *Journal of Commerce*, were on the street with the story before the forgery was detected; bulletins of denial promptly quashed its effect on the gold market, defeating the scheme. With Lincoln's approval, Stanton moved swiftly in reprisal, padlocking the offices of both papers and clapping their editors into military arrest, along with Howard, who was soon sniffed out. Within three days the editors were released and their papers resumed publication; even Howard was freed within about three months, on the plea that he was "the only spotted child of a large family" and had been guilty of nothing worse than "the hope of making some *money*." No real harm was done, except to increase the public's impression of Stanton — and, inferentially, his chief — as a tyrant, an enemy of free speech and the press. One witness declared, however, that the affair "angered Lincoln more than almost any other occurrence of the war period." His ire was aroused in part by the fact that the country's reaction to the bogus proclamation obliged him to defer issuing an order he had prepared only the day before, calling, in far less doleful words, for the draft of 300,000 additional troops.

They were likely to be needed sooner, not later, at the rate men were falling in Grant's attempt to overrun Lee and Sherman's to outflank Johnston. And on top of these losses, before the month was out, there occurred a hemispheric provocation that seemed likely to bring on a second war, this one with a foreign power: France. Following up his occupation of Mexico City a year ago, purportedly to collect a national debt, Napoleon III landed his puppet Maximilian, whom he had persuaded to assume the title of Emperor of Mexico, at Vera Cruz, May 28; the Austrian archduke and his wife Charlotte were on their way to the capital, where they would reign over an empire designed to stand, with the help of still more French soldiers than the 35,000 already sent, as a bulwark against Anglo-Saxon expansion in Central and South America. This continued defiance of the Monroe Doctrine was hard for Lincoln to abide, but not so hard that he did not manage to do so, deferring action until he could afford to give it his full attention, preferably with a reunited country at his back; "One war at a time" was as much his policy now as it had been on the occasion of his near confrontation with England over the *Trent* affair, more than two years ago.

Some Republican radicals bolted the party and nominated John C. Frémont for President on May 31, 1864.

Besides, a domestic concern of a far more urgent nature than any posed by the latter day Napoleon — specifically, the double-barreled problem of getting renominated and reëlected — was hard upon him at the time. Three days after Maximilian stepped ashore at Vera Cruz, the radicals of Lincoln's own party, aware that they lacked the strength to dominate the regular Republican convention at Baltimore on June 7, called a convention of their own in Cleveland on May 31, one week earlier, and by acclamation nominated John C. Frémont as their candidate for President in the November election.

For some time Jacobinic disaffection had been growing, especially among New England abolitionists and German-born extremists in Missouri, who resented Lincoln's "manifest tendency toward temporary expedients," and com-

plained bitterly that he had "*words* for the ultras and *acts* for the more con-
servative." Now their opposition had taken this form; they were out in the open,
determined to bring him down. Frémont, the party's first presidential candidate in
1856 — he had polled a respectable 1,300,000 votes, as compared to James
Buchanan's 1,800,000 — accepted the nomination "with a view to prevent the misfortune of [Lincoln's] reëlection," which he said "would be fatal to the country."
Glad to be back in the public eye, after nearly two years of promoting railroads in
New York State, the Pathfinder looked forward to a vigorous campaign. The trouble
was that his most influential backers had to avoid giving him open support, for fear
of committing political suicide, and this had been evident at the convention in
Ohio, which one critic described as a "magnificent fizzle," attended mainly by
"disappointed contractors, sore-head governors, and Copperheads."

Thousands had been expected, but only about four hundred showed
up. Informed of this, Lincoln reached for the Bible on his desk, thumbed briefly
through I Samuel until he found what he was seeking, then read it out: *And
every one that was in distress, and every one that was in debt, and every one that
was discontented, gathered themselves unto him; and he became a captain over
them: and there were with him about four hundred men.*

A joke had its uses, particularly as therapy for a spirit as gloomy by
nature as this one, but the million-odd votes Frémont might poll in November
were no laughing matter. Before then, there would probably be ways to lure the
Jacobins back into the fold. Some piece of radical legislation hanging fire in
Congress for lack of Executive pressure, say, could be put through; or the scalp
of some Administration stalwart they had singled out as an enemy could be
yielded up. Meantime, however, the thing to do, if possible, was to solidify what
was left of the party and broaden its base to attract outsiders, meaning those
hard-war Democrats who would be repelled by the peace plank their leaders
were sure to include in the platform at their Chicago convention in late August,
nearly three months after the Republicans gathered next week in Baltimore.

Lincoln of course did not attend, despite the proximity to Washington;
nor did David Davis, his manager at the convention four years ago and now a
Supreme Court justice. Not since Andrew Jackson's reëlection, thirty-two years
ago, had any man been chosen to serve a second term as President, although
several had tried and failed to get renominated and Van Buren had even succeeded,
only to be defeated at the polls. But Davis foresaw no difficulty requiring his
considerable talent for maneuver, so far as the place at the top of the ticket was
concerned, and he was right; there was no real opposition, only some wistful
talk about "the salutary one-term principle," and no trouble. On the first ballot,
Missouri's delegates rocked the boat a bit by casting their 22 votes for Grant,
but switched when all the other 484 went to Lincoln, whose nomination thus
was made unanimous. This done, the convention was free to turn to the business

of solidification and broadening; which could be done, at least in part — so it was hoped — by the selection of the right man to replace Vice President Hannibal Hamlin, who not only lacked luster but also had sided with the radicals on most of the whipsaw issues before Congress.

A beginning had been made in this regard, first by changing the name of the party to National Union, which helped to reduce the onus of sectionalism, and then by adopting a platform that had, as one observer put it, "a radical flavor but no Radical planks." Appealing for unity in continuing the national effort to put down the rebellion, it called for the extirpation of slavery as the root cause of the war, promised to visit upon all rebels and traitors "the punishment due to their crimes," thanked soldiers and civilians alike for their sacrifices over the past three years, and wound up by favoring the encouragement of immigration and the construction of a transcontinental railroad.

Now came the vice-presidential nomination, and though Lincoln kept aloof from the contest, not wanting to anger the friends of disappointed candidates — "Convention must judge for itself," he indorsed a letter requesting a statement of his wishes as to the contest for second place on the ticket — he had confidants on the scene, including his secretary Nicolay and Henry J. Raymond, editor of the friendly *New York Times* and chairman of the platform committee. When Raymond saw to it that the name of Andrew Johnson, former senator and now military governor of Tennessee, was presented at a critical juncture, scarcely anyone failed to see that here was the best possible way of strengthening the ticket by giving simultaneous recognition to the claims of loyal men from the South, especially the border states, as well as to War Democrats all across the land. Johnson was both, and with an outburst of enthusiasm so vociferous that one delegate later testified that he "involuntarily looked up to see if the roof were lifted," his nomination too was made unanimous.

Lincoln learned informally of the outcome that afternoon, when he happened to walk over to the War Department and was congratulated as he entered the telegraph office. "What! Am I renominated?" he exclaimed, smiling, and when the operator showed him a confirming telegram his first thought was of his wife: "Send it over to the Madam. She will be more interested than I am."

He perhaps wanted to brace her for things to come, and they were not long in coming. Next day the *New York World*, back on the streets after being shut down for its unwitting share in the Gold Hoax three weeks ago, served notice that this was to be the bitterest of campaigns. Commenting on the nominations of Lincoln and Johnson — who like his running mate was a self-made man, having started out as a tailor before he studied law and entered politics — the *World* clucked its tongue over the come-down the national tone had suffered with the selection by the opposition party of this ungracious pair of candidates for the two most honored posts in all the land. "The age of statesmen is gone," the lead

★

editorial lamented; "the age of rail-splitters and tailors, of buffoons, boors, and fanatics, has succeeded. . . . In a crisis of the most appalling magnitude, requiring statesmanship of the highest order, the country is asked to consider the claims of two ignorant, boorish, third-rate backwoods lawyers, for the highest situations in the government. Such nominations, in such a conjecture, are an insult to the common-sense of the people. God save the Republic!"

Lincoln hoped God would, but he was modest in his judgment of why he had been chosen to compete again for the task of serving as God's chief helper in the search for that salvation. "I do not allow myself to suppose that [the delegates] have concluded to decide that I am either the greatest or best man in America," he replied to formal congratulations which presently followed, "but rather they have concluded it is not best to swap horses while crossing the river, and have further concluded that I am not so poor a horse that they might not make a botch of it in trying to swap."

Renomination was only the first, and much the lower, of the two formal hurdles to be cleared if he was to retain his post. The second was reëlection, and that would be a far more difficult matter, requiring not only a great deal of skill in maneuvering his way along the thorny path of politics — skill,

Andrew Johnson, the military governor of Tennessee, was nominated as Vice President by pro-Lincoln Republicans calling themselves the National Union party.

that is, such as he had just shown while skimming the first hurdle — but also a great deal of ability on the part of his hand-picked commanders in the field. In short, they would have to convince the public that he and they could win the war; otherwise, neither he nor the war would continue. Up to now, whatever admiration he might express for their refusal to be "jostled," their progress had been made at a price the voters were likely to find excessive, particularly if they were obliged to continue paying it over the course of the next five months. Even as the delegates converged on Baltimore, Grant was engaged in the grisly and belated task of burying his dead at Cold Harbor — a position McClellan had reached two years ago, the opposition press was pointing out, with the loss of less than a tenth as many soldiers — and Sherman, after his fruitless round-house swing through Dallas, was just getting back astride the railroad at Big Shanty, having also suffered checks about as abrupt, though not as bloody, along the way at New Hope Church and Pickett's Mill. As a result, in his continuing attempt to bolster national morale, Lincoln was reduced to the necessity of making what he could of such minor victories as Cynthiana, which at least disposed of John Morgan for a season, more or less.

That was on the Sunday ending the week of the Republican convention, and one week later there occurred another side-show triumph which more or less disposed of another Confederate raider; one even more famous, or infamous, than Morgan.

★ ★ ★ *S*unday, June 12; U.S.S. *Kearsarge*, a thousand-ton sloop named for one of New Hampshire's rugged mountains, was anchored off the Dutch coast, in the mouth of the River Scheldt near Flushing, when her skipper, Captain John A. Winslow, received word from his government's minister in Paris that the Confederate cruiser *Alabama*, which had eluded him throughout a year-long search of European waters, had steamed into Cherbourg the day before to discharge prisoners, take on coal, and perhaps refit. If he hurried, the telegram said, she might still be there when he arrived.

Winslow hurried. Firing a gun to recall his men on shore, he had the *Kearsarge* under weigh within two hours. Two days later he entered Cherbourg harbor, three hundred miles to the west, and there "lying at anchor in the roads" was the rebel vessel, just as he had prayed she would be. He stopped engines and lay to, looking her over and being in turn looked over; which done, he left to assume a position in the English Channel, beyond the three-mile limit required by international law, for intercepting her when she ventured out. He took precautions against a sudden night attack, knowing the enemy to be tricky, but his principal fear was that the raider might slip past him in the dark and thus avoid the fate he had in mind for her.

He need not have worried on that score, he discovered next day when the American vice consul sent him a message just received from the skipper of the *Alabama:* "My intention is to fight the *Kearsarge* as soon as I can make the necessary arrangements. I hope these will not detain me more than until tomorrow evening, or after the morrow morning at furthest. I beg she will not depart before I am ready to go out. . . . I have the honor to be, respectfully, your obedient servant, *R. Semmes*, Captain."

Winslow made no reply to this except to maintain station beyond the breakwater; which, after all, was answer enough, and spared him moreover the loss of dignity involved in exchanging cards, as it were, with a "pirate" who by now had captured, burned, or ransomed 83 U.S. merchant vessels, worth more than five million dollars, and sunk the heavier gunboat *Hatteras* in short order. Raphael Semmes, for his part, gave all his attention to trimming ship, drilling his gun crews, and otherwise preparing to meet the challenge extended by the *Kearsarge* when she steamed into the harbor, looked him over from stem to stern, then turned with the same cool insolence and steamed back out again to await his response, if any, to the insult. "The combat will no doubt be contested and obstinate," he wrote in his journal that night, "but the two ships are so evenly matched that I do not feel at liberty to decline it. God defend the right, and have mercy upon the souls of those who fall, as many of us must."

Fame aside — for Winslow had none whatever, and the *Kearsarge* had never been within gunshot of a foe; whereas Semmes and the *Alabama* were better known around the world than any other sailor or vessel afloat — the two warships and their captains were indeed quite evenly matched. Messmates for a time in the Mexican War, both men were southern-born, the Confederate in Maryland, Winslow farther south in North Carolina; Semmes was fifty-five, his opponent less than two years younger, and both had close to forty years of naval service, having received appointments as midshipmen in their middle teens. Alike as they were in their histories up to the outbreak of the current war, they were altogether different in looks. Winslow, going blind in his right eye, was rather heavy-set and balding, with a compensating ruff of gray-shot whiskers round his jaw, while Semmes was tall and slender, with a full head of hair, a tuft of beard at his lower lip, and a fantastical mustache twisted to needle points beyond the outline of his face; "Old Beeswax," his men called him.

Conversely, it was not in their histories, which were about as mutually different as could be, but in their physical attributes that the two ships were alike. Both were three-masted and steam-propelled, just over two hundred feet in length and a thousand tons in weight. *Kearsarge* had a complement of 163,

*Captain John A. Winslow (third from left)
gathers with his officers on the U.S.S. Kearsarge's main
deck before the fight with the C.S.S. Alabama.*

Alabama about a dozen less. The Federal carried seven guns, the Confederate eight — though this implied advantage was deceptive, mainly because of a pair of 11-inch Dahlgrens mounted on pivots along the center line of the *Kearsarge*, which, combined with the 32-pounders on each flank, enabled her to throw a 365-pound broadside, port or starboard. *Alabama*'s heaviest guns were an 8-inch smoothbore and a 7-inch Blakely rifle, also pivot-mounted, so that, in combination with three 32-pounders on each flank, her broadside came to 264 pounds, a hundred less than her adversary's. Two other disadvantages she had, both possibly dire. One was the state of her ammunition, which had not been replenished since she was commissioned, nearly two years ago; percussion caps had lately been failing to explode the shells, whose powder had been weakened by exposure to various climates on most of the seven seas. The other disadvantage had to do with the vessel's maneuverability and speed. Entering Cherbourg harbor, Semmes declared, she was like "the weary foxhound, limping back after a long chase, footsore and longing for quiet and repose." He had intended to put her in dry dock and give all aboard a two-month holiday; her bottom, badly fouled, needed scraping and recoppering, and her boilers had begun to leak at the seams. *Kearsarge*, on the other hand, though nine months older, had been refitted only three months ago and was in trim shape for the contest. Semmes, however, had confidence in his crew, which he affectionately referred to as "a precious set of rascals," his Blakely rifle, which not only had more range but also provided greater accuracy than did Winslow's outsized Dahlgrens, and his luck, which had never failed him yet.

Concern for this last but by no means least of the things in which he put his trust caused him to defer the promised action three days beyond the "morrow morning at furthest" he had fixed in his Wednesday note begging Winslow not to depart. He wanted to fight on Sunday, considering that his lucky day. It was a Sunday when he ran the *Sumter*, his first raider, past the Union gauntlet below New Orleans, out of the mouth of the Mississippi and into the Gulf of Mexico to begin his career as the scourge of Yankee commerce; a Sunday off the Azores, back in August '62, when he christened the *Alabama*, and a Sunday when he sank the *Hatteras*, as well as many of the other prizes he had taken in the course of the past three years.

His crew found the waiting hard, being anxious for the duel and the shore leave that would follow, but Semmes and his officers kept them busy. They cleaned and oiled the guns and other weapons, including cutlasses and pikes, sorted powder and shot from the magazines and laid them out in relays, took down the light spars, disposed of top hamper, and stoppered the standing rigging. They polished brasswork and holystoned the decks as for a ball, and while they worked they roared out a chantey a British seaman composed for the occasion:

> *We're homeward bound, homeward bound,*
>
> *And soon shall stand on English ground.*
>
> *But ere that English land we see*
>
> *We first must fight the Kearsargee!*

Such work continued through Saturday, June 18, when Semmes, aware that "the issue of combat is always uncertain," put ashore four sacks containing 4700 gold sovereigns, the ransom bonds of ten ships he had released for lack of space for their crews aboard the *Alabama*, and the large collection of chronometers taken from his victims, which he periodically wound by way of keeping tally or counting coup. After notifying the port authorities that he would be steaming out next morning, he went ashore for Mass, then came back and turned in early as an example for his officers and men, who did so too, despite many invitations to dine that night in Cherbourg with admirers.

Sunday dawned bright and nearly cloudless, cool for June, with a calm sea and a mild westerly breeze to clear the battle smoke away. After a leisurely breakfast, the crew weighed anchor at 9.45 and headed out, cheered by crowds along the mole and in the upper windows of houses affording a view of the Channel and the *Kearsarge*, still on station beyond the breakwater. News of the impending duel had been in all the papers for the past three days and excursion trains had brought so many spectators from Paris and other cities that there was no room left in the hotels; many sportsmen-excursionists had slept on the docks, as if at the entrance to a stadium on the night before a game between archrivals. They fluttered handkerchiefs and cheered, some waving small Confederate flags hawked by vendors along with spyglasses and camp stools. "Vivent les Confederates!" they cried, looking down at the trim and polished raider, all of whose sailors were dressed in their Sunday best except the gun crews, who were stripped to the waist, like athletes indeed, and stood about on decks that had been sanded to keep them from slipping in their blood when the contest opened. "Vivent les Confederates!" the crowd shrilled, flourishing its home-team pennants triumphantly when the *Kearsarge*, seeing the *Alabama* emerge from around the western end of the breakwater, turned suddenly and steamed away northeastward, as if in unpremeditated flight.

Semmes knew better: knew, indeed, that this maneuver signified that his adversary meant to give him the fight-to-a-finish he was seeking. Engaged in reading the Sunday service when a yardarm watchman sang out the warning, "She's coming out and she's headed straight for us!" Winslow closed the prayer book, ordered the drum to beat to quarters, and brought his ship about in a run for bluer water, his intention being to lure the rebel well beyond the three-mile limit, inside which she could take sanctuary in case she was disabled. This applied as well to the *Kearsarge*, of course, but Winslow was thinking of punishment he would inflict, rather than of damage he might suffer; his aim was not just to cripple, but to kill.

The warning had been given at 10.20; at 10.40, some seven miles out, he once more came about and bore down on the *Alabama*, just over two miles away, wanting to bring his two big Dahlgrens within range of his adversary.

Semmes held his course, closing fast. Resplendent in a new gray uniform, long-skirted and with a triple row of bright brass buttons down the breast, epaulets and polished sword making three fierce glints of sunlight, he had had all hands piped aft as soon as he cleared the breakwater, then mounted a gun carriage to deliver his first speech since setting out from the Azores. "Officers and seamen of the *Alabama*!" he declaimed, pale but calm behind the fantastical mustache whose spike-tips quivered as he spoke. "You have, at length, another opportunity of meeting the enemy — the first that has been presented to you since you sank the *Hatteras*. . . . The name of your ship has become a household

★

word wherever civilization extends. Shall that name be tarnished by defeat? The thing is impossible! Remember that you are in the English Channel, the theater of so much of the naval glory of our race, and that the eyes of all Europe are at this moment upon you. The flag that floats over you is that of a young Republic who bids defiance to her enemies, whenever and wherever found; show the world that you know how to uphold it. Go to your quarters!" Having said as much, he set the example, while the crew still cheered, by taking station on the horseblock abreast the mizzenmast, a vantage point from which he could see and be seen by the enemy throughout the fight to come.

Watch in hand, he waited until there was barely a mile between the two ships bearing down on each other, then at 10.57 turned to his executive, Lieutenant John Kell, a six-foot two-inch Georgian who, like himself, was a veteran of the old navy: "Are you ready, Mr Kell?" Kell said he was. "Then you may open fire at once, sir."

The Blakely roared. Its 100-pound shell raised a sudden geyser, well short of the target, and was followed within two minutes by another, which, over-corrected, went screaming through the Federal's rigging. By now the other guns had joined, but their shots too were high, fired without proper calculation of the reduction of space between the rapidly closing vessels. Not until the range was down to half a mile did Winslow return fire, sheering to bring his starboard battery to bear. All the shots fell short, but Semmes had to port his helm sharply to keep from being raked astern. He succeeded, though at the cost of having *Kearsarge* close the range. As the Confederate swung back to starboard, Winslow followed suit and the two warships began to describe a circle, steaming clockwise around a common center and firing at each other across the half-mile diameter.

Alabama drew first blood with a shell that exploded on the Union quarterdeck and knocked out three of the after Dahlgren's crew. Then came what Semmes had prayed for, ashore at church last night. A shell from the Blakely struck and lodged itself in the sternpost of the *Kearsarge*. But as he watched through his telescope, awaiting the explosion that would signal the end of the enemy vessel — "Splendid! Splendid!" he exclaimed from his perch on the horseblock — the long moment passed with no sign of smoke or flame in that vital spot. The projectile, a dud, accomplished nothing except to make the helmsman's job a little harder by binding the rudder, which was already set to starboard anyhow. *Alabama*'s gunners kept hard at it, firing fast while straining for another, luckier hit.

Winslow's gunnery was methodical by contrast, and a good deal more effective; he would get off a total of 173 shots in the course of the engage-ment, only about half as many as Semmes, but the accuracy in both cases, a tally of hits and misses would show, was in inverse ratio to the rate of fire. As the two sloops continued their wheeling fight, churning along in one another's wake, a three-knot current bore them westward so that they described a series of overlapping circles, each a little tighter than the one before, with the result that the range was constantly shortened, from half a mile on the first circle, down to little more than a quarter-mile on the seventh, which turned out to be the last.

From the outset, once the blue crews got on target, the damage inflicted by the 11-inchers was prodigious; *Alabama* was repeatedly hit and hulled by the 135 1/2-pound shells aimed at her waterline by the Dahlgrens, in accordance with Winslow's orders, while the 32-pounders swept her decks. The combined effect was devastating: as for example when a projectile breached the 8-inch smoothbore's port, disemboweling the first man it struck, then plunging on to mangle eighteen others when it blew. Survivors and replacements cleared away the wounded and heaved the corpses overboard, but resumption of fire had to wait for a shovel to be used to scrape up the slippery gobs of flesh and splinters of bone; only then, with the deck re-sanded, could the crew secure a proper footing for its work.

Meantime, Semmes had seen the most discouraging thing he had encountered since the shot lodged in the enemy sternpost failed to explode. Observing that shells of all sizes were bouncing ineffectively off the Federal's sides, like so many tennis balls, he told Kell to switch to solids for better penetration. Yet these too either splintered or rebounded, and it was not until after the battle that he found out that the cause lay in anything more than the weakened condition of his powder. *Kearsarge* was armored along her midriff with 120 fathoms of sheet chain, suspended from her scuppers to below her waterline, bolted down and boxed out of sight with one-inch planking. Indignant at the belated disclosure that his adversary was "iron-clad," Semmes protested that this violation of the code duello had produced an unfair fight. "It was the same thing as if two men were to go out and fight a duel, and one of them, unknown to the other, were to put on a suit of mail under his outer garment."

However true or false the analogy — and Old Beeswax, one of the trickiest skippers ever to prowl the sea lanes, was scarcely in a position to protest the use of a stratagem that had been common in all navies ever since Farragut employed it, more than two years ago, to run past the forts below New Orleans — the *Alabama*, with all her timbers aquiver from the pounding being inflicted by the *Kearsarge,* was clearly nearing the end of her career. Semmes, nicked in the right hand by a fragment of shell as the raider went into her seventh circle, had a quartermaster bind up the wound and rig a sling, never leaving his perch on the horseblock. From there he could see better than anyone the damage being done his ship and the ineffectiveness of his return fire. This seventh circle must be the last. The only course left was to attempt a run for safety. Accordingly, he told the exec: "Mr Kell, as soon as our head points to the French coast in our circuit of action, shift your guns to port and make all sail for the coast."

★

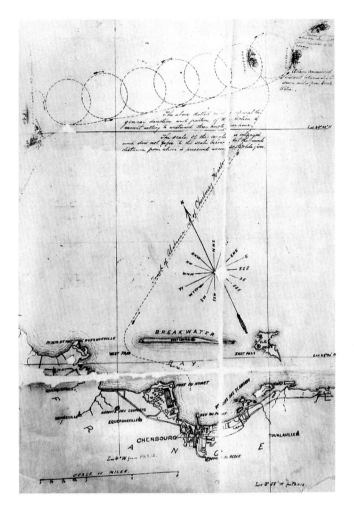

This Union map of the English Channel on June 19, 1864, traces the course of the running battle as the Kearsarge chased the Alabama through seven full circles.

Kell tried, but Winslow quickly interposed the *Kearsarge*, slamming in shots from dead ahead and at a shorter range than ever. At this point the *Alabama*'s chief engineer came topside to report that his fires were being flooded by rising water from holes the Dahlgrens were blasting in the hull. "Go below, Mr Kell," Semmes said grimly, "and see how long the ship can float."

The Georgian went, and on his way through the wardroom saw a sight he would never forget. Assistant Surgeon David Llewellyn, a Briton and the only non-Southerner among the two dozen officers aboard, stood poised alongside where his operating table and patient had been until an 11-inch solid crashed through the adjoining bulkhead, snatching table, wounded seaman, and all his instruments from under the ministering hand of the doctor, who stood there, abruptly alone, with a dazed expression of horror and disbelief. Kell continued down to the engine room, where he saw through the steam from her drowned fires that the ship could scarcely remain afloat another ten minutes. He picked his way back up, through the wreckage and past the still-dazed surgeon, to report to the captain that the *Alabama*'s ordeal was nearly over.

"Then sir," Semmes replied, "cease firing, shorten sail, and haul down the colors. It will never do in this nineteenth century for us to go down, and the decks covered with our gallant wounded."

Across the water, less than 500 yards away, Winslow saw the rebel flag come down, but being, as he later explained, "uncertain whether Captain Semmes was using some ruse," called out to his gun crews: "He's playing a trick on us. Give him another broadside." They did just that, adding to the carnage on *Alabama*'s bloody, ripped-up decks with every gun that could be brought to bear; whereupon a white flag was run up from the stern. "Cease firing!" Winslow cried at last.

Through his telescope he observed on board the sinking raider a pantomime that called up within him, in rapid sequence, mixed emotions of pity, mistrust, sympathy, and resentment. Settling fast, with only a thread of

---

"Cease firing, shorten sail, and haul down the colors. It will never do in this nineteenth century for us to go down, and the decks covered with our gallant wounded."

— Raphael Semmes

---

smoke from her riddled stack, the *Alabama* had lost headway; Semmes, though still on his horseblock, obviously had given the order to abandon ship. While some of the crew milled about in confusion, engaging Winslow's pity by their plight — which, after all, might have been his own if the 100-pound shell lodged in his sternpost had not turned out to be a dud — others aroused his mistrust by piling into a dinghy and shoving off, apparently in an attempt to avoid capture. This was disproved, however, when the dinghy made for the *Kearsarge* and he saw, when it came within hailing distance, that it was filled with wounded men, including a master's mate who shouted up a request that boats be sent to rescue survivors gone over the side and thrashing about in the water.

Winslow had only two boats not smashed in the course of the fight, but he ordered them lowered without further delay and gave permission, moreover, for the rebel dinghy to be used as well, once the wounded had been unloaded. Obviously, though, these three small boats would not hold all the men in the water; so he called through his speaking trumpet to a nearby English pleasure yacht whose owner had sailed out of Cherbourg that morning for a close-up view of the duel: "For God's sake, do what you can to save them!" The yacht responded promptly, and as she did so Winslow turned his telescope back to the final scene of the tableau being enacted on *Alabama*'s canted deck.

The rebel skipper by now had descended from his perch, and he and another officer, a large, heavily bearded man — John Kell — began to undress for their leap into the Channel. The big man stripped to his underwear, but Semmes, apparently mindful of his dignity, retained his trousers and waistcoat. He seemed to part reluctantly with his sword. After unbuckling it rather awkwardly with his unhurt left hand, he held it above his head for a long moment, flashing brightly in the noonday sunlight, before he did the thing that brought Winslow's resentment to a boil. He flung it whirling and glinting into the sea, thereby making impossible the ceremony of handing it over to his vanquisher. Winslow could scarcely expect him to bring it along while he swam one-handed across four hundred yards of choppy water to the *Kearsarge* to surrender, but it seemed to the Federal captain that his adversary took a spiteful pleasure in this gesture which deprived him of a customary right.

Semmes followed Kell and his sword into the Channel, and the two men struck out as best they could, the former clutching a life preserver, the latter a wooden grating, to avoid the suction that might pull them under when the *Alabama* sank. She was filling fast now, air gurgling, hissing, chuckling under her punctured decks while the sea poured in through rents in her hull. Her stern awash, her prow was lifting, and suddenly it rose higher as her guns, still hot from battle, tore loose from their lashings and slid aft. The breeze freshening, she recovered a little headway with her sails, and as she moved she left behind her a broad ribbon of flotsam, broken spars and bodies, bits of tackle and other gear. Fifty yards off, Semmes turned to watch her die. Backward she went, beginning her long downward slide, anchors swinging wildly in the air below her bow; the main-topmast, split by a solid in the fight, went by the board when she paused, nearly vertical; then she was gone, the Channel boiling greenly for a time to mark the place where she had been.

It was 12.24, just under ninety minutes since she fired her first shot at the *Kearsarge*. For all his grief, Semmes was glad in at least one sense that she was on the forty-fathom bottom with his sword. "A noble Roman once stabbed his daughter, rather than she should be polluted by the foul embrace of a tyrant," he later wrote. "It was with a similar feeling that Kell and I saw the *Alabama* go down. We had buried her as we had christened her, and she was safe from the polluting touch of the hated Yankee!"

By now the trim British yacht *Deerhound* — whose captain-owner John Lancaster, a wealthy industrialist on vacation with his family, had had her built up the Clyde by the Lairds two years ago, at the same time they were at work on the sloop that became the *Alabama* — was within reach of the crewmen bobbing amid the whitecaps. She lowered her boats and began fishing them out,

including Semmes and Kell and Marine Lieutenant Beckett Howell (Varina Davis's younger brother) but not Dr Llewellyn; a nonswimmer, he had drowned. Forty-two men were saved in all by the *Deerhound* in response to Winslow's plea; another dozen by the captains of two French pilot boats, who needed no urging; while seventy more were taken and made captive aboard the *Kearsarge*.

Semmes himself might have been among these last except for Kell's quick thinking. Exhausted, the Confederate skipper was laid "as if dead" on the sternsheets of one of *Deerhound*'s boats when the *Kearsarge* cutter came alongside. "Have you seen Captain Semmes?" a blue-clad officer asked sharply. Kell, who had put on a *Deerhound* crewman's cap and taken an oar to complete the dis-

As rebel sailors struggle into a lifeboat and the British yacht Deerhound (far left) steams to rescue Captain Raphael Semmes, his Alabama sinks beneath the waves.

guise, had a ready answer. "Captain Semmes is drowned," he said, to the Federal's apparent satisfaction. Aboard the yacht, after the shipwrecked men had been given hot coffee and shots of rum to counter the chill and exhaustion, Lancaster put the question: "Where shall I land you?" This time it was Semmes who had the answer that meant salvation. "I am now under English colors," he said, "and the sooner you put me, with my officers and men, on English soil the better."

Well before nightfall the *Deerhound* put in at Southampton, where, news of the battle having preceded them, Semmes and his men were given a welcome as hearty as if they had won; "A set of first-rate fellows," the London *Times* pronounced them. As soon as he had rested from his ordeal, the

★

Maryland-born Alabamian used the gold left at Cherbourg to pay off the survivors and send allotments to the nearest kin of the nine men killed in action
and twelve drowned. He was banqueted by admirers, including officers of the
Royal Navy, who united to present him with an elegant, gold-mounted sword,
engraved along the blade to signify that it was a replacement for the one he had
flung into the Channel after his "engagement off Cherbourg with a chain-plated
ship of superior power, armament, and crew."

However, when Confederate officials tendered him a new command
with which to continue the record begun aboard the *Sumter*, he declined, needing
time to absorb the shock of his "impossible" defeat. Though he was promoted
to rear admiral and eventually made his way, via Cuba and Mexico, back to the
Confederacy (none of whose ports the *Alabama* ever touched) he had done all
he would do afloat. Other raiders would continue to strike at Yankee shipping
around the globe, but not Raphael Semmes. "I considered my career upon the
high seas closed by the loss of my ship," he later explained.

As for Winslow, he too was being lionized by now as the man who
had abolished in single combat the myth that the *Alabama* was invincible. After
clearing his decks and assembling the crew for thanksgiving prayers — which
helped to ease his dudgeon at having seen the British yachtsman make off
with his prize of prizes, Semmes — he steamed into Cherbourg, flags aflutter
from every mast of the *Kearsarge,* and was promptly surrounded by boatloads
of people out to greet the ship whose victorious crew had somehow been
transformed into the home team.

Her casualties were limited to the three men hit early in the duel,
one of whom died a few days later; *Alabama*'s came to 43, just under half of
them drowned or killed in action. Once he had paroled his prisoners and
patched up superficial damage, Winslow went to Paris to consult a specialist
about his failing eye, only to learn that he had waited too long for treatment to
be of any use. A victory banquet, tendered by patriotic fellow countrymen in
the French capital, helped to dispel the medical gloom of the occasion, and a
letter from Gideon Welles was even more effective in that regard. "I congratulate
you," the Secretary wrote, "on your good fortune in meeting the *Alabama*,
which had so long avoided the fastest ships and some of the most vigilant and
intelligent officers of the service, and for the ability displayed in the contest you
have the thanks of the Department. . . . The battle was so brief, the victory so
decisive, and the comparative results so striking that the country will be reminded
of the brilliant actions of our infant Navy, which have been repeated and illus-
trated in the engagement."

Presently this was followed, upon the President's recommendation, by
a vote of thanks from Congress and a promotion to date from June 19. Commodore Winslow returned to the United States by the end of the year, and while

★

the *Kearsarge* was being refitted in the Boston Navy Yard carpenters removed a section of her sternpost, still with the 100-pound dud embedded in the oak, and boxed it for shipment to Washington, the Commander in Chief having expressed a desire to see for himself what a close call the ship and all aboard had had on that famous Sunday, six miles out in the English Channel, when she sank the *Alabama*.

Lincoln was indeed glad to learn that the most famed of rebel raiders had been struck from the list of woes to be endured until the war had run its course. Lately, though, he had begun to perceive that while striving to keep up national morale he would also have to deal with national impatience, which mounted with every indication, true or false, that the end might not be far off. Earlier that week, on June 14 — the day Bishop Polk was cannon-sniped on Pine Top and Grant began crossing the James — he had confessed to a friendly newsman that the country's tendency to "expect too much at once" was, for him, a matter of considerable private anxiety: "I wish, when you write or speak to people, you would do all you can to correct the impression that the war in Virginia will end right off and victoriously. . . . As God is my judge, I shall be satisfied if we are over with the fight in Virginia within a year. I hope we shall be 'happily disappointed,' as the saying is; but I am afraid not. I am afraid not."

This was something new, this concern lest the public, in its ebullience, demand an end to the war before it was won, and Lincoln bore down to counteract it two days later, nine days after his renomination, when he went to attend and address a sanitary fair in Philadelphia. "It is a pertinent question often asked in the mind privately, and from one to the other: When is the war to end? Surely I feel as deep an interest in this question as anyone can, but I do not wish to name a day, or month, or a year when it is to end. I do not wish to run any risk of seeing the time come, without our being ready for the end, and for fear of disappointment because the time had come and not the end. We accepted this war for an object, a worthy object, and the war will end when that object is attained. Under God, I hope it never will until that time."

Cheers went up at this, and he pressed on to warn his hearers that the approach of victory might call for more, not fewer sacrifices. "If I shall discover that General Grant and the noble officers and men under him can be greatly facilitated in their work by a sudden pouring forward of men and assistance, will you give them to me?"

"Yes! Yes!" the crowd roared, catching fire.

"Then I say, stand ready," Lincoln told the upturned faces about the rostrum, as well as those that would be downturned over tomorrow's newspapers all across the land, "for I am watching for the chance."

★ ★ ★

★

*The Army of the Cumberland's
Company A, 52d Ohio was part
of McCook's brigade, which
spearheaded the assault on the Dead
Angle at Kennesaw Mountain.*

S I X

Kennesaw to Chattahoochee

1864 ★ ★ ★ ★ ★ ★ *N*ow that Johnston had relinquished Pine Top, retiring down its rearward slope with the corpse of Bishop Polk, Sherman followed close on his heels, determined to keep up the pressure which, so far, had gained him eighty of the critical hundred air-line miles between Chattanooga and Atlanta, his base and his objective. He did so with caution, however, being confronted on the left and right by the loom of Brush and Lost mountains, both occupied by butternut marksmen who asked nothing more, in the way of compensation for their pains, than one quick glimpse down their rifle barrels at blue-clad soldiers moving toward them, within range and without cover. "We cannot risk the heavy loss of an assault at this distance from our base," the red-haired Ohioan had wired Halleck on the day before Polk's mangling. But on June 16, two days after that event, he changed his mind and began to consider trying what he had said he could not risk. "I am now inclined to feign on both flanks and assault the center," he told Old Brains. "It may cost us dear, but in results would surpass any attempt to pass around."

Presently, though, he changed his mind again — or, more strictly speaking, had it changed for him by Johnston, who gave him the slip the following night with another of his "clean retreats." This one was not so much an outright withdrawal, however, as it was a rectification, an adjustment whereby

★

the foxy Confederate not only shortened his rather extended line but also
shored up the sagging center Sherman
had planned to assault. Turning loose
of the high ground on his flanks, he
fell back to Kennesaw Mountain, two
miles in rear of the abandoned Pine
Top salient. Polk's corps — temporarily
under Major General W. W. Loring,
the senior division commander — was
posted there, dug in along its northern
face, with Hood on the right, astride
the Western & Atlantic, and Hardee
on the left, denying the Federals access
to Marietta by blocking the roads
coming in from Dallas and Burnt
Hickory. Johnston's line, which had
been concave after he gave up Pine
Top, was now convex, and its center,
which had been its weakest element
when Sherman contemplated launching a headlong strike, was now its

*M*ajor General W. W. Loring
commanded Polk's old corps
at Kennesaw Mountain.

stoutest part. In point of fact, the graybacks had occupied no stronger position in the course of their six-week retreat.

"Kennesaw Mountain is, I should think, about 700 feet high," an
Illinois major wrote home in reaction to his first sight of this forbidding piece of
geography reared up in the army's path, "and consists of two points or peaks, separated by a narrow gorge running across the top. The mountain itself is entirely
separated from all mountain ranges, and swells up like a great bulb from the plain."
Sherman too was impressed and given pause by what he called "the bold and striking twin mountain." Rebel signalmen were at work on its two bulbous peaks, both
of which were "crowned with batteries," while "the spurs were alive with men busy
felling trees, digging pits, and preparing for the grand struggle impending." As he
stood and looked, awe gave way to determination. "The scene was enchanting; too
beautiful to be disturbed by the harsh clamor of war," he was to say, years later;
"but the Chattahoochee lay beyond, and I had to reach it."

He had to reach it; but how? In an attempt to find some easier
means than a headlong assault, which seemed foredoomed, he brought up his
guns and began to pound away at the fortified slopes of the mountain, hoping
to fix the enemy in position there while he probed both flanks of the rebel line
in search of a way around it, one that would enable him to menace the railroad

★

in Johnston's rear and thus provoke him into abandoning his present all-but-impregnable position, as he had done so many others in the course of his long retreat, rather than risk a fight whose loss would mean the severance of his supply line. The result was a series of skirmishes, some of which attained the dignity of engagements, first at Gilgal Church, where the graybacks fought a holding action to cover their withdrawal, and then along Mud and Nose (or Noyes) creeks, both of which had to be crossed if Sherman was to turn the rebel left for a strike at Marietta, Johnston's base, two miles back of Kennesaw, or at Smyrna Station, another four miles down the railroad.

While Schofield, reinforced by Hooker, was doing all he could in that direction, McPherson, strengthened by Blair's return the week before, was feeling out the Confederate right, but with little success, being under the guns and surveillance of the enemy on the taller of Kennesaw's two peaks. Thomas mean-time kept up the pressure dead ahead, firing so many rounds from his massed batteries — he had 130 guns in all: half a dozen more than McPherson and Schofield combined — that his soldiers, watching the bombardment from dug-in positions on the flat, began to tell each other that Uncle Billy was determined to take the double-crested mountain in their front, or else "fill it full of old iron."

For three days this continued, neither Thomas nor McPherson achieving much with their pounding and probing, and then on June 22, having proceeded well to the south around Kennesaw's western flank, Schofield too was brought to a sudden halt.

It happened at a place called Culp's (or Kolb's) Farm, four miles southwest of Marietta on the road from Powder Springs, and it came about because Johnston, in reaction to Sherman's continuing effort to reach around his left, had issued instructions the night before for Hood, whose intrenchments on the right would be occupied temporarily by Wheeler's dismounted troopers, to march at daylight across the rear of Kennesaw and go into position beyond Hardee on the far left, south of the mountain's western flank, in order to block the Federal turning movement. Hood did this, and more. Within a mile of his objective by midday, he encountered troops from Schofield's corps advancing up the Powder Springs Road, and with soldierly instinct, but without taking time for reconnaissance, attacked at once.

Assuming he had the flankers outflanked, he figured that a prompt assault would "roll them up," drive them back with heavy casualties, and abolish this threat to Johnston's life line. The result was heavy casualties, all right, though not for Schofield, who had taken the precaution of having his and Hooker's men dig in while awaiting reports from patrols sent out to find the best route up the valley of Olley's Creek for a strike at the Western & Atlantic above Smyrna, three miles across the way. Hood drove these forward elements rapidly back, giving chase with the two divisions on hand, but at Culp's Farm the pursuers came

This Harper's Weekly engraving, from a Theodore Davis sketch, depicts Union General Alpheus S. Williams' division of the XX Corps at the battle of Culp's Farm.

unexpectedly upon the enemy main body, stoutly intrenched, and were bloodily repulsed. A second assault, launched near sundown, only added to the carnage; Stevenson's division alone lost more than 800 men, and Hindman's brought the total to better than 1000. Schofield and Hooker, whose soldiers did their fighting behind earthworks for a change, suffered less than a third that many casualties in breaking the two attacks. Then at nightfall, while the graybacks dug in too along the line where the fighting stopped, Schofield and Hood sent word to their superiors at Big Shanty and Marietta of what had happened.

Johnston's anger at this loss of a thousand badly needed veterans, once more as a result of Hood's impetuosity, was exceeded by Sherman's when he received an out-of-channels dispatch that evening from Hooker, proudly reporting that he had "repulsed two heavy attacks" and calling urgently for reinforcements before he was overrun. "Three entire corps are in front of us," he added by way of lending weight to his proud cry for help.

"Hooker must be mistaken; Johnston's army has only three corps," Sherman noted in passing the message along to Thomas, who, knowing only too well that Hardee and Loring were still in position to his and McPherson's front, replied rather mildly: "I look upon this as something of a stampede." Sherman agreed and next morning, still miffed, rode down to Culp's Farm in a pouring rain to tell Fighting Joe he wanted no more of his boasts and misrepresentations. In reaction, Hooker went into a month-long pout; or, as his

★

superior later put it, "From that time he began to sulk."

This would have its consequences for all concerned; but the fact was, Sherman's anger had its source in something far more irksome than Hooker's inability to avoid exaggeration. Daylight showed the graybacks intrenched across Schofield's front. This meant that the army had gone as far as it could go in that direction without turning loose of its supply line, already under threat from rebel horsemen, and the drowned condition of the roads precluded any movement on them so long as the rain continued.

Confronted thus with the probability of a stalemate — which was not only undesirable on its own account, here in Georgia, but might also give Richmond the chance to reinforce Lee's hard-pressed Virginia army from Johnston's, biding its time north of the Chattahoochee — Sherman reverted to his notion, expressed a week ago, "to feign on both flanks and assault the center." The trouble was that the center now was Kennesaw Mountain, and Kennesaw seemed unassailable. But there, perhaps, was just the factor that might augur best; an attacker would greatly increase his chance for success by striking where the blow was least expected. Besides, continued probes by McPherson today showed that Loring's corps had been extended eastward to include a portion of the works abandoned yesterday by Hood when he set out westward to counter Schofield's flanking threat. That march, with its extension of the Confederate left while Loring spread out to cover the right, stretched Johnston's line to a width of about eight miles, exclusive of the cavalry on his flanks. It must be quite thin somewhere, and that somewhere was likely to be dead ahead on Kennesaw, whose frown alone was enough to discourage assault. So Sherman reasoned, at any rate, in his search for some way to avoid a stalemate. Moreover, he explained afterwards, he conferred with his three army commanders, "and we all agreed that we could not with prudence stretch out any more, and therefore there was no alternative but to attack 'fortified lines,' a thing carefully avoided up to that time."

Such a change in tactics, abruptly sprung, would also serve to increase the element of surprise, which figured largely in Sherman's calculations. But the outlook remained grim, if not downright awesome. "The whole country is one vast fort," he informed Halleck on June 23. "Johnston must have full fifty miles of connected trenches, with abatis and finished batteries. . . . Our lines are now in close contact and the fighting incessant, with a good deal of artillery. As fast as we gain one position, the enemy has another all ready."

These were minor adjustments, permitting no more than a closer look at the honeycombed slopes of the mountain up ahead, and a closer look only magnified the original impression of impregnability. One-armed Howard, studying the rebel line from a position well to the front, pronounced it "stronger in artificial contrivances and natural features than the cemetery at Gettysburg," which he had helped to hold despite Lee's all-out efforts to oust him. But Sherman refused to be distracted, let alone dissuaded. Determined, as he had told Grant the week before, to "inspire motion into a large, ponderous and slow, by habit, army," he believed that his soldiers, weary of roundabout marches that never quite managed to bring the enemy to bay, needed the stimulus the pending assault would provide, even if most of the blood that was shed turned out to be their own — and he was concerned, as well, lest Johnston's habitual caution, which had led him to give up so many stout positions in the course of the past seven weeks, should be replaced by a conviction that the Federals would never attack him once he was snugly intrenched. Both of these things counted heavily in the redhead's calculations, as did the promise of all that would be gained if the attack was anything like as successful as the one up Missionary Ridge, seven months ago, by many of these same men against many of these same opponents, but with the considerable difference that there had been no unfordable Chatta-hoochee in the rebel rear on that occasion.

Other factors there were too, no less persuasive because Sherman himself — defined by Walt Whitman as "a bit of stern open air made up in the image of a man" — was perhaps not even aware of their influence on him. For one, the Union army in Virginia was not only doing most of the bleeding in the double-pronged offensive, it was also getting most of the headlines, and despite his dislike of journalists, and indeed of the press in general, he could see that his troops would be heartened by a more equitable distribution of praise, such as the overrunning of Kennesaw would secure. Moreover, back in Nashville and Chattanooga, while preparing for the campaign, he had learned that certain observers snidely characterized him as "not a fighting general." He dismissed the charge without exactly denying it, saying: "Fighting is the least part of a general's work. The battle will fight itself." Still, the imputation rankled, containing as it did some grains of truth, and he welcomed the opportunity, now at hand, to refute it for once and for all. On June 24 he issued a special field order directing his army commanders to "make full reconnaissances and preparations to attack the enemy in force on the 27th instant, at 8 a.m. precisely."

That left two full days for getting set; Sherman, having decided to be rash, had also decided to go about it methodically, even meticulously, so as to minimize the cost if the breakthrough failed. For one thing, he would limit the weight of his assault to less than a fifth of the troops on hand, and for another, despite its regrettable but inevitable detraction from the element of surprise, the

"Fighting is the least part of a general's work.
The battle will fight itself."

— William Tecumseh Sherman

jump-off would be preceded by an hour-long bombardment from every gun that could be brought to bear on the critical objectives.

Of these there were two, main and secondary, neither of them, properly speaking, on the mountain that would give the battle its name, although the secondary effort, assigned to McPherson, would be made against — and, if successful, across — the gently rolling southwest slope of the lower of the two peaks, called Little Kennesaw to distinguish it from Big Kennesaw, the taller and more massive portion of the mountain to the east, overlooking the slow curve of the Western & Atlantic on that flank. This attack would be launched astride the Burnt Hickory Road, simultaneously with Thomas's main effort, along and to the right of the Dallas Road, one mile south; both commanders would assault with two divisions, their others standing by to exploit whatever progress was achieved. Schofield and Hooker would feint on the far right, Garrard's cavalry on the left, all at the same prearranged hour, hard on the heels of the softening-up artillery bombardment, so as to prevent Johnston from knowing which part of his line to reinforce from any other, or from his reserves if he had them, before it was swamped. "At the time of the general attack," the special order ended, foreseeing a happy outcome to the rashness so meticulously prescribed, "the skirmishers at the base of Kennesaw will take advantage of it to gain, if possible, the summit and hold it. Each attacking column will endeavor to break a single point of the enemy's line, and make a secure lodgment beyond, and be prepared for following it up toward Marietta and the railroad in case of success."

Throughout that two-day interim, although few along the eight-mile curve of intrenchments knew what they were waiting or getting set for — "All commanders will maintain reserve and secrecy even from their staff officers," the field order had cautioned — fire fights, picket clashes, and sudden cannonades would break into flame from point to point, then subside into sputters and die away, sporadic, inconclusive, and productive of little more than speculation. Whether off on the flanks or crouched near the critical center, men listened and wondered, unable to find a pattern to the action. The crash of guns would come from somewhere up or down the line, an Indiana soldier would recall, "then the hurrahing, sometimes the shrill, boyish rebel yell, sometimes the loud, full-voiced, deep-toned, far-sounding chorus of northern men; then again the roar of cannon, the rattle of musketry and the awful suspense to the listeners. If, as the noise grew feebler, we caught the welcome cheer, answering shouts ran along. But if the far-off rebel yell told of our comrades' repulse, the silence could be felt."

Across the way, within the horseshoe curve of works containing Kennesaw and Marietta, the reaction was much the same, but in reverse. No one there could discern a pattern either, including the men of Major Generals Samuel French's and Benjamin Cheatham's divisions of Loring's and Hardee's corps, respectively astride the Burnt Hickory and Dallas roads, up which the

two Union assaults were to be delivered on Monday morning, June 27, one week past the summer solstice.

The rain left off on Sunday and the sun came up in a cloudless sky next morning at 4.40 to begin its work of drying the red clay roads, the sodden fields and breathless woods. By the time it was three hours high the day was hot and steamy with the promise of much greater heat to come. Twenty minutes later, precisely at 8 o'clock and without preamble, 200-odd Union cannon roared into action, pounding away at the rebel line on the mountainside and across the flats beyond.

Crouched in their pits and ditches, jarred and shaken about by the sudden hurtle of metal exploding over and around them, the defenders marveled at the volume and intensity of the fire, which was to them still another manifestation of Yankee ingenuity and wealth. "Hell has broke loose in Georgia, sure enough!" one grayback shouted amid shellbursts, and as the bombardment continued, sustained by an apparently inexhaustible supply of ammunition, they began to snatch down the blankets pegged for shade across the open tops of their trenches, preparing for what they knew would come when the guns let up. Finally, close to 9 o'clock, the uproar reached a spasmodic end; the cannoneers stepped back from their pieces, panting, and the blue infantry started forward in two clotted masses, about a mile apart, to assail the Confederate center.

For a time they advanced in relative security, protected by the intervening woods and the butternut pickets trotting back to join their comrades

Just visible through the haze are the twin peaks of Kennesaw Mountain (at right) and Little Kennesaw (at left) as seen from a position behind the Confederate right.

along the main line of resistance. Then the attackers emerged into brilliant sunlight, silhouetted against the bright green backdrop of trees, and the rebel headlogs seemed to burst spontaneously into flame along their bottoms, all up and down that portion of the line. Sam French, whose left-flank division of Loring's corps was challenged first on Little Kennesaw's lower slopes, said later that the rattle and flash of musketry, combined with the deep-voiced boom of guns whose crews had held their fire till now, produced "a roar as constant as Niagara and as sharp as the crash of thunder with lightning in the eye."

Such was the fury of the sound that accompanied McPherson's attack, launched astride the Burnt Hickory Road by Brigadier General Morgan Smith, whose division was reinforced for the effort by a brigade from another division in Major General John A. Logan's corps. Sound and fury were all it came to, however, in the end. In the course of their plunge across a rocky, brush-choked gully, unexpectedly encountered in rear of the line abandoned by the gray pickets, 563 of the 4000 attackers fell before they could get to grips with the defenders intrenched on the far side. At one point "within about thirty feet of the enemy's main line," Smith reported, they came close; but there, receiving the full blast of massed rifles, they "staggered and sought cover as best they could behind logs and rocks." Stalled ("It was almost sure death to take your face out of the dust," one prone Federal declared, while another expressed a somewhat less gloomy view of the consequences, saying: "It was only necessary to expose a hand to procure a furlough") they were no longer much of a threat to French, who turned his high-sited batteries a quarter circle to the left and added the weight of the metal to Hardee's resistance, a mile away, astride and beyond the Dallas Road.

There Thomas was making a sturdier bid for a breakthrough, and Cheatham's division had all it could do to keep from being overrun by nearly twice as many Federals as French had had to deal with. "They seemed to walk up and take death as coolly as if they were automatic or wooden men," one defender was to say of these troops from two divisions under Jeff Davis and Brigadier General John Newton, respectively of Palmer's and Howard's corps.

Two of Cheatham's four brigades were posted where Hardee's line bent sharply to the south, creating a somewhat isolated salient, and it was here at the hinge, known thereafter as the Dead Angle, that Thomas struck. "The least flicker on our part would have been sure death to all," a Tennessee private who helped to hold it later declared. "We could not be reinforced on account of our position, and we had to stand up to the rack, fodder or no fodder." They did stand up, inflicting in the process — with the help of French's guns and Cleburne, whose marksmen brought their rifles to bear from up the line — a total of 654 casualties on Newton and 824 on Davis, both of whom notified their superiors that they hoped they could hang on where they were, if that was what was wanted, but that there was no further hope of carrying the position.

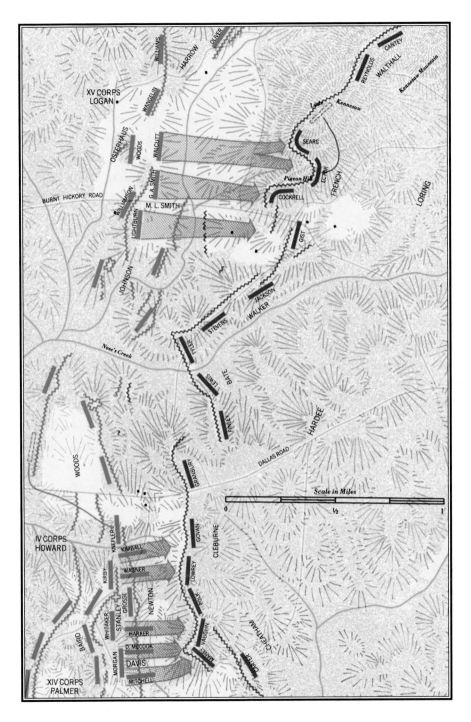

*This map depicts the Union's direct and costly assault
on Confederate-held Kennesaw Mountain,
which led Sherman to resume his flanking maneuvers.*

Howard put it strongest, some time later, looking back. "Our losses in this assault were heavy indeed," he wrote, "and our gain was nothing. We realized now, as never before, the futility of direct assault upon intrenched lines already well prepared and well manned." Thomas agreed, sending word around 11 o'clock for those who could fall back to do so at once, while those who could not were to dig in where they were and wait for darkness.

The sudden resultant drop in the intensity of the fighting came none too soon for the defenders of the Angle, one of whom was to testify that he fired no less than 120 rounds in the course of the repulse. "My gun became so hot that frequently the powder would flash before I could ram home the ball," he said, adding: "When the Yankees fell back and the firing ceased, I never saw so many broken down and exhausted men in my life. I was sick as a horse, and as wet with blood and sweat as I could be, and many of our men were vomiting with excessive fatigue, overexhaustion, and sunstroke; our tongues were parched and cracked for water, and our faces blackened with powder and smoke, and our dead and wounded were piled indiscriminately in the trenches."

Cheatham's loss came to 195, French's to 186; between them, they had shot down 2041 of the 12,000 Federals thrown against their works. Other losses, elsewhere in Loring's and Hardee's corps, as well as in Hood's, which had been skirmishing with Schofield all the while, brought the Confederate total to 552. Sherman put his at 2500 — a figure Johnston vowed was a good deal less than half the true one — but later revised it upward to "about 3000."

Even so, and despite the shock of the sudden double repulse, he had been willing to drive it still higher at the time. From Signal Hill, his command post on the left, he could see that McPherson had shot his wad, and word had come from Schofield that little could be done on the far right. That left Thomas, the Rock of Chickamauga. He too had been checked, losing two of his best brigade commanders in the process, but he might be willing to try again for a repetition of what he had achieved on Missionary Ridge despite conditions even more unfavorable. "McPherson and Schofield are at a deadlock," Sherman wired him at 1.30. "Do you think you can carry any part of the enemy's line today? . . . I will order the assault if you think you can succeed at any point." Thomas replied: "We have already lost heavily today without gaining any material advantage. One or two more such assaults would use up this army."

He recommended a change to siege methods, the digging of saps for a guarded approach. But Sherman, wanting no part of such a time-consuming business, preferred to maneuver the rebels out of position, as before. Encouraged by the let-up of the rain and the fast-drying condition of the roads, he telegraphed Thomas that evening: "Are you willing to risk [a] move on Fulton, cutting loose from our railroad?" Fulton was two miles beyond Smyrna Station, within three miles of the Chattahoochee and about ten miles in Johnston's rear;

★

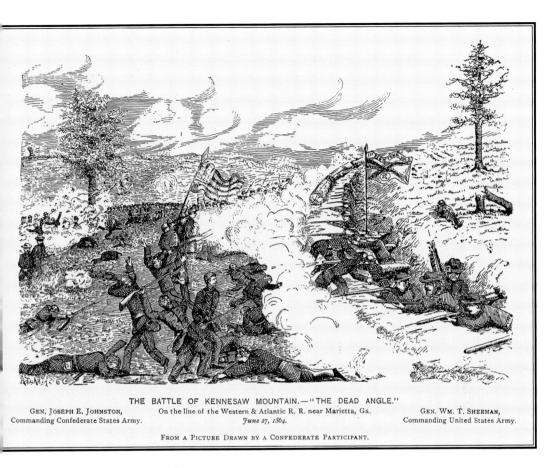

THE BATTLE OF KENNESAW MOUNTAIN.—"THE DEAD ANGLE."
On the line of the Western & Atlantic R. R. near Marietta, Ga.
June 27, 1864.

GEN. JOSEPH E. JOHNSTON,
Commanding Confederate States Army.

GEN. WM. T. SHERMAN,
Commanding United States Army.

FROM A PICTURE DRAWN BY A CONFEDERATE PARTICIPANT.

A battlefield guidebook published by the
Western & Atlantic Railroad included this engraving from
a sketch "drawn by a Confederate participant."

Sherman proposed to move by the right flank "with the whole army." Thomas considered the venture highly risky, exposing as it would the Union life line to Confederate seizure while the wheeling movement was in progress; but in any case, he replied before turning in for the night, "I think it decidedly better than butting against breastworks twelve feet thick and strongly abatised."

While waiting for the roads to finish drying Sherman worked on plans for his newest sidle and, eventually, on securing a truce for the burial of the unfortunates who had fallen in the double-pronged repulse. Undaunted — at least on paper — he took the offensive in defending his decision to strike at the rebel center, even though all it had got him was a lengthened casualty list. "The assault I made was no mistake; I had to do it," he wired Halleck, explaining that after nearly eight weeks of gingerly skirmishing, all the time conforming to a pattern about as precise as if he and Johnston were partners in a classic minuet, Federals and Confederates alike "had settled down into the conviction that the assault of lines formed no part of my game." Now that both sides knew better, having seen the dance pattern broken as if with a meat ax, he expected to find his adversary "much more cautious." That was his gain, as he saw it, and he continued to pursue this line of consolation. "Failure as it was, and for which I assume the entire responsibility," he would assert in his formal report of the lost battle, "I yet claim it produced good fruit, as it demonstrated to General Johnston that I would assault, and that boldly."

Earlier, while smoke still hung about the field and the wounded mewled for help between the lines, he had reminded Thomas: "Our loss is small compared with some of those in the East. It should not in the least discourage us. At times assaults are necessary and inevitable." However, his most forthright statement with regard to losses was reserved for his wife, to whom he wrote two days after the Kennesaw repulse. "I begin to regard the death and mangling of a couple of thousand men as a small affair, a kind of morning dash," he told her, adding: "It may be well that we become hardened. . . . The worst of the war is not yet begun."

During the Battle of Kennesaw Mountain, Confederates observe a brief truce as Federal troops carry their wounded and killed from the field.

★

That might well be, though there could be no denying that for a considerable number of his soldiers — young and old, recruits and veterans alike — the best was over, along with the worst. Their interment was a grisly thing to watch. "I get sick now when I happen to think about it," a Confederate wrote years later, remembering the June 30 burial armistice that was asked and granted "not for any respect either army had for the dead, but to get rid of the sickening stench." Although three days of festering midsummer Georgia heat had made the handling of the corpses a repugnant task, he recalled that Yankee ingenuity once more had measured up to the occasion. "Long and deep trenches were dug, and hooks made from bayonets crooked for the purpose, and all the dead were dragged and thrown pell mell into these trenches. Nothing was allowed to be taken off the dead, and finely dressed officers, with gold watch chains dangling over their vests, were thrown into the ditches. During the whole day both armies were hard at work, burying the Federal dead."

Thus June ended, bringing with it another pause for a backward look at the casualty count in each of the two armies. In both cases these were lower than they had been the month before, and they were similar in another way as well. Just as New Hope Church and Pickett's Mill, engagements fought near the bottom of the previous calendar leaf, had reversed the May tally, raising Sherman's losses above Johnston's, which had been higher than his opponent's before the clashes around Dallas, so now did Kennesaw Mountain reverse the count for June, which had been lower for the Union up till then. Sherman's loss for the past month was 7500, Johnston's around 6000. This brought their respective totals for the whole campaign to just under 17,000 and just over 14,000. Roughly speaking, to put it another way, one out of every four Confederates had been shot or captured, as compared to one out of seven Federals.

In time, when the guns had cooled and approximate figures from both sides became available in books, Sherman would take great pride in this reversal of the anticipated ratio of losses between attacker and defender (as well he might: especially in reviewing a campaign fought on ground as unfavorable to the offensive as North Georgia was, against an adversary he admired as much as he did Joe Johnston) but just now there was the war to get on with, the wheeling movement he had designed to flank the rebels off their impregnable mountain and back across the only remaining river between them and his goal, Atlanta. By July 1 the roads were baked about hard enough for marching; the sidle began next day.

Garrard's dismounted troopers replaced the infantry in the trenches astride the Western & Atlantic, blocking a possible track-breaking sortie by the graybacks on that flank, and McPherson set out across Thomas's rear to join Schofield for a lunge around Hood's left the following day. If successful, this would not only sever Johnston's life line, it would also oblige him to fight without the protection of intrenchments when he fell back, through Marietta and

Smyrna, to where the flankers would be waiting around Fulton, three miles short of the Chattahoochee and better than 50,000 strong. McPherson thus was given a chance to redeem his Resaca performance by repeating it without flaws, although Sherman's expectations were by no means as great as they had been eight weeks ago, some eighty miles back up the railroad. Warned by lookouts high on Kennesaw, which afforded a panoramic view of the country for miles and miles around, Johnston would probably choose to give up his present position rather than risk the consequences of fighting simultaneously front and rear, with a force about as large as his own in each direction. Anticipating this reaction the night before, Sherman told Garrard and Thomas to advance their pickets at daylight, July 3, and determine whether the Kennesaw trenches were occupied or abandoned; whether Johnston had chosen to stand his ground, despite the menace to his life line, or fall back, as he had always done in the face of such a threat.

On Signal Hill before dawn next morning, while the skirmishers were groping their way forward through the brush, Sherman waited impatiently for the light to grow enough to permit the use of a large telescope he had had mounted on a tripod and trained on the double-humped bulk of Kennesaw, looming blacker than the starless sky beyond it. Presently the sun broke clear and he saw, through the high-powered glass, "some of our pickets crawling up the hill cautiously. Soon they stood upon the very top, and I could see their movements as they ran along the crest."

Not a shot had been fired; the works were empty; the rebels had pulled out southward in the night.

The red-haired Ohioan caught fire at the notion that now they were out in the open, somewhere between the abandoned mountain and the river ten miles in its rear — his for the taking, so to speak, if he could overhaul them with his superior numbers before they reached whatever sanctuary their commander had it in mind to fortify. "In a minute I roused my staff, and started them off with orders in every direction for a pursuit by every possible road, hoping to catch Johnston in the confusion of retreat, especially at the crossing of the Chattahoochee River." Thomas could be depended on to descend at once on Marietta, but what was needed most just now, if the pursuers were to overcome whatever head start the Confederates might have gained, was cavalry. Sherman told Garrard to get his three brigades remounted and ride hard to bring the enemy to bay, short of the Chattahoochee, while McPherson and Schofield caught up to close in for the kill.

Events moved fast now, but not fast enough for Sherman. Without waiting for Garrard, he rode ahead with a small escort, around the eastern flank of the mountain and on into Marietta, nestled in its rear. He got there by 8.30 and was pleased to find that, although the graybacks had made a clean getaway with all their stores and had torn up several miles of railroad to the south,

★

Federal field artillery blasts away at Confederate breast-works — some of them seven feet high and nine feet thick — on Kennesaw Mountain during the June 27 battle.

Thomas already had soldiers in the town. As the minutes ticked off, however, and no troopers appeared, his impatience mounted. "Where's Gar'd?" he began to storm. "Where's Gar'd? Where in hell's Gar'd?" Finally the cavalryman — a fellow Ohioan, seven years his junior in age and eleven years behind him at West Point — arrived, explaining that it had taken time to bring his horses forward and get his men into column on the road. Dissatisfied to find still more time being wasted on excuses, Sherman yelled at him: "Get out of here quick!" Garrard was flustered. Transferred from the East on the eve of the present campaign, he was not yet accustomed to being addressed in this manner. "What shall I do?" he asked, and his red-haired chief barked angrily: "Don't make a damned bit of difference so you get out of here and go for the rebs."

Despite such urgency it was midafternoon before contact was reëstablished near Smyrna, five miles down the line, and reconnaissance used up the daylight needed for mounting an assault. Fortified in advance for ready occupation, its flanks protected east and west by Rottenwood and Nickajack creeks, the rebel position astride the railroad, midway between Marietta and the river crossing five miles in its rear, obviously called for caution if the Federals were to avoid blundering into a bloody repulse. Sherman was convinced, however, that his adversary had occupied it only in hope of delaying the blue pursuit, and he said as much in a message to Thomas near sundown: "The more I reflect the more I know Johnston's halt is to save time to cross his material and men. No general, such as he, would invite battle with the Chattahoochee behind him. . . . I know you appreciate the situation. We will never have such a chance again, and I want you to impress on Hooker, Howard, and Palmer the importance of the most intense energy of attack tonight and in the morning. . . . Press with vehemence at any cost of life and material. Every inch of line should be felt and the moment there is a give, pursuit should be made."

But there was no give, and no pursuit. In fact there was no attack. Vehemence yielded to prudence next morning — July 4: the first anniversary of Vicksburg's fall, Lee's retreat from Gettysburg, and Holmes's drubbing at Helena — when Sherman found the works in his front still a-bristle with bayonets and Johnston apparently desirous of nothing so much as he was of a blue assault that would permit a repetition of what had happened on the slopes of Little Kennesaw a week ago today.

On second thought, the Ohioan cancelled his sundown instructions to Thomas, which had called for "the most intense energy of action," and reverted instead to his time-tested method of attempting to maneuver, rather than knock, the graybacks out of fortifications established in his path. While the Cumberlanders kept up a noisy demonstration in front, banging away with all their guns as if in celebration of the Fourth, McPherson set out on another of his whiplash marches, down the near bank of Nickajack Creek, to threaten the Confederate left rear. Darkness fell before his troops were in position, and the following sunrise proved Sherman right after all. The Smyrna works yawned empty; the rebs once more had stolen away in the night. Eager as ever to catch them amid the confusion that always attended a river crossing, the northern commander took off fast, making excellent time on a march of about three miles; which ended unexpectedly, within two miles of the Chattahoochee, when he came upon Johnston, just beyond Vining Station, in occupation of what Sherman frankly called "the best line of field intrenchments I have ever seen."

Looking back on the experience, years later — mindful no doubt of what he had said, two nights before, about his adversary's unwillingness to "invite battle with the Chattahoochee behind him" — he expanded the compliment: "No officer or soldier who ever served under me will question the generalship of Joseph E. Johnston. His retreats were timely, in good order, and he left nothing behind."

One exhilarating gain there was at any rate, available from the crest of a hill inclosed by a loop of the railroad as it approached the Chattahoochee beyond Vining's. "Mine eyes have beheld the promised land," an Illinois major wrote home to his wife. "The 'domes and minarets and spires' of Atlanta are glittering in the sunlight before us, only eight miles distant." Sherman and Thomas were both on the hilltop for a Pisgah view of the prize beyond the river, and though the Union-loyal Virginian took it calmly, as always — to look at his deep-set eyes and massive brow, a newsman declared, "made one feel as if he were gazing into the mouth of a cannon; and the cannon said nothing" — the volatile Ohioan, as usual, let his exhilaration show. "Stepping nervously about, his eyes sparkling and his face aglow, casting a single glance at Atlanta, another at the river, and a dozen at the surrounding valley," he seemed to the major to be studying the rebel dispositions in order to "see where he could best cross the river, how best he could flank them."

Clearly this would take some doing: Johnston once more had chosen well. Faced with the problem of defending a stream whose low south bank was dominated by high ground on the side which a crossing would leave in enemy control, he had intrenched in advance a six-mile line along the north bank, above and below the critical railroad span. With this and five other bridges at his back — a pair for each of his three corps — he could withdraw quickly in case of a breakthrough, left or right, or counterattack without delay if the Federals were repulsed. His wagons were already over the river, parked in safety beyond a secondary line of south-bank works, preconstructed for instant occupation if needed, and so was his cavalry, posted upstream and down to guard against probes in either direction. Sherman, after a look at these canny dispositions from the Vining's hilltop, wired Halleck that he would have to "study the case a little" before proceeding. He foresaw delays and he wanted Washington braced for the disappointment they would bring.

"I am now far ahead of my railroad and telegraph, and want them to catch up," he explained; "[I] may be here some days. Atlanta is in plain view, nine miles distant. . . . The extent of the enemy's parallels already taken is wonderful, and much of the same sort confronts us yet, and is seen beyond the Chattahoochee."

Still, he was not long in deciding that he "could easily practice on that ground to better advantage our former tactics of intrenching a moiety in [Johnston's] front, and with the rest of our army cross the river [above or below] and threaten either his rear or the city of Atlanta itself." Accordingly, while repair gangs were hard at work restoring the railroad down to Vining's, he confronted the north-bank rebel *tête-du-pont* (as he called it) with the forces of Thomas and McPherson, posted Schofield rearward in reserve, under instructions to be ready to march at a moment's notice, and sent a division of cavalry in each direction, upstream and down, in search of a likely point or points for crossing.

Stoneman, who led the downriver column, found all the bridges destroyed and their sites covered by horse artillery on the opposite bank. Although Garrard, who rode all the way to Roswell, nearly twenty miles above, had no better luck with regard to bridges, in other respects he was fortunate indeed. Roswell was a manufacturing center; or it had been, anyhow, until Garrard's troopers put in a hard day's work with sledges and torches, wrecking and burning. One problem there was, of a somewhat diplomatic nature, but not for long. He came upon a cotton mill running full tilt, still turning out gray cloth for the rebel armies; a French flag flew above it and the Gallic owner claimed immunity from damage or interference on the grounds that he was not only not a Confederate but was of foreign allegiance.

Feeling rather beyond his depth in international waters, the cavalry-man referred the claim to Sherman, who reacted with predictable indignation. "Such nonsense cannot deceive me," he wired Halleck, a specialist in such matters. "I take it a neutral is no better than one of our own citizens." And to Garrard went instructions to proceed against the foreign-owned mill as he had done against the others. As for the Frenchman himself, Sherman was specific as to how he might be dealt with. "Should you, under the impulse of natural anger, natural at contemplating such perfidy, hang the wretch," he told Garrard, "I approve the act beforehand."

But there was neither a hanging nor another burning; Garrard let the Frenchman go and tore down his mill to provide material for rebuilding the nearby bridge, destroyed the week before. This took three days, which allowed plenty of time for one of McPherson's corps to arrive for a crossing on July 10, dry-shod and without rebel opposition, Schofield having crossed two days earlier, about midway between Roswell and the Confederate right at Pace's Ferry, and driven the butternut vedettes away from their picket posts on the south bank.

Sherman thus had been quick to solve the Chattahoochee problem, and Johnston's stand with his back to the river was correspondingly brief. Much of the credit went to Stoneman, whose downriver excursion had drawn the enemy's attention in that direction, but most of it went to Schofield, who showed for the first time in the campaign what he could accomplish when left to his own devices.

Ordered to carry out an upstream crossing, the New-York-born West Pointer — he had been a schoolteacher and a surveyor on the western plains by the time he was seventeen, and even now, though balding fast, was two years less than twice that age — arrived at daylight, July 8, reconnoitered briefly, and decided to cross where Soap Creek emptied into the river, seven miles below Roswell, the opposite bank being held at that point by a light force of gray cavalry, apparently not over-vigilant and equipped with only one gun. Silently he brought up his batteries, screened by brush along the north bank, and loaded infantry assault teams into pontoon floats launched well back from the creek mouth. "At the appointed time," he later reported, "the artillery was pushed quickly into position and opened fire, a line of battle advanced, rapidly firing, to the river bank, while the batteaux, loaded with men, were pulled down the creek and across the river. . . . The astonished rebels fired a single shot from their single gun, delivered a few random discharges of musketry, and fled, leaving

*F*ollowing the bridgehead created by Union General
Kenner Garrard's cavalry, Grenville Dodge's
XVI Corps fords the Chattahoochee at Roswell's Ferry.

their piece of artillery in our possession. The crossing was secured without the loss of a man." By dawn of July 9, the pontoon bridge having been installed the night before, "two divisions occupied a secure tête-de-pont a mile in depth, giving ample room for the *debouché* of the whole army."

Johnston reacted to Schofield's upstream crossing as expected, and with all his accustomed stealth and skill. Destroying or dismantling the six bridges in his wake — and, incidentally, provoking Sherman's one uncomplimentary post-war comment on the quality of his generalship throughout the long campaign: "I have always thought Johnston neglected his opportunity there, for he had lain comparatively idle while we got control of both banks of the river above him" — he withdrew his main body across the Chattahoochee that night, and after temporarily occupying the south-bank works, prepared in advance for just such an emergency, continued the pull-back the following day, July 10, to a line in rear of Peachtree Creek, apparently prompted by concern that if he took up a position any closer to the river the Federals might cut in behind him and seize the city. In any case he now was less than five miles from the heart of Atlanta.

Grateful though Sherman was for this development, which meant that he would be able to cross this last of North Georgia's three broad rivers without a battle that had seemed likely to prove costly both in casualties and time, he once more found himself confronted with the problem that had loomed with every major gain: What now? — meaning *how?* Should he swing left or right, upstream or down, for the accustomed flanking effort, or bull straight ahead for an end-all strike at an opponent whose back was at last to the gates of the city in his charge, with little room for maneuver unless he chose to give it up without a fight?

While the red-haired general pondered and pored over maps and reports, his troops moved up to the unguarded Chattahoochee, anticipating their first leisurely bath in ten weeks. Admiration for their commander had grown with every tactical leap or sidestep, and now it reached a climax in which almost anything seemed possible. "Charley," one dusty infantryman told a comrade as they approached this last natural barrier and saw smoke rising from the buildings along its banks, "I believe Sherman has set the river on fire."

Nor was the wonder limited to wearers of the blue. A butternut prisoner, conducted rearward past exuberant Federals in their tens of thousands, was so impressed by their multitude that he said to his captors: "Sherman ought to get on a high hill and command, 'Attention! Kingdoms by the right wheel!'" The general, in point of fact, was squatting naked in the Chattahoochee at the time, discussing the temperature of the water with a teamster who admired him from the bank, while all around them other soldiers lolled neck deep in the river, soaking away the grime of more than a hundred red-clay miles of marching and fighting and the caked sweat of seventy days of exertion and fear, or else whooped and splashed in pure delight at having nothing else to do.

But not for long. After the brief time-out for his dip in the Chatta-hoochee, Sherman returned to his maps and reports, designing the next, and he hoped final, move in the campaign to whip Joe Johnston and take Atlanta. With the two-weeks-old repulse at Kennesaw fresh in mind, he quickly rejected the notion of mounting an all-out frontal attack on the Confederates dug in behind Peachtree Creek — attractive though that would be as a slam-bang finish, if successful — and reverted instead to his accustomed practice of operating on or around one of the enemy flanks.

Mostly, before, he had moved by his right, in a series of mirror images, so to speak, of Grant's leftward sidles in Virginia; but in this case the choice was by no means simple. It was true, a downstream crossing would not only give him ground that favored the offensive (the south-bank creeks, below, ran into the Chattahoochee at right angles, affording Johnston no perpendicular ridges to defend but many to cross in changing position to meet the challenge, while permitting Sherman to advance on the city by moving up the ravines, unhindered in front and sheltered on the flanks); it would also place him in rear of his objective from the outset, within easy striking distance of the railroads leading southwest through Montgomery to Mobile and southeast through

Macon to Savannah, without which Atlanta could not long survive a siege. An upstream crossing, on the other hand, would give the advantage of terrain to the defenders; for there the creeks ran more or less parallel to the Chatta-hoochee, presenting Sherman with ridges to cross while advancing and Johnston with ravines to shelter his army while shifting to meet the threat. Geography clearly favored a downriver flanking operation.

Yet there was a good deal more to the problem than geography per se. For one thing, there was the risk of exposing the all-important Union supply line to depredations, and this would be a far greater danger if the crossing was made below the railroad bridge. Just above there, after receiving the waters of Peachtree Creek, the Chattahoochee swerved northward (on the map, that is; the flow, of course, was south) and ran alongside the Western & Atlantic all the way beyond Vining Station, the newly established Federal rail-head and supply dump, which would be within easy reach not only of rebel cavalry but also of rebel infantry, launched across the nearby river on a track-breaking sortie that could scarcely be blocked if most of the blue army moved below.

Union troops soaked off weeks' worth of red clay in the Chattahoochee. Here, a few naked troops patrol the shores for Confederate interlopers.

★

This gave Sherman pause, as well it might, and so did something else. Recent dispatches from Grant indicated that their previous concern, lest Johnston reinforce Lee for a blow at Meade, was now reversed; Lee's current problem, Grant explained, was not how he could get more troops, but rather how he could feed the ones he had, and under such circumstances it was not unlikely that he might detach a sizeable portion of them for service in far-off Georgia, just as he had done the year before, on the eve of Chickamauga. If he did so, they would come by rail: specifically, by way of Augusta on the Georgia Railroad, the one line into Atlanta that would not be threatened, let alone broken, if Sherman crossed downriver to close in on the city from the west.

Thus to define the problem was to solve it, so far at least as the choice of directions was concerned: Sherman decided to break the pattern of his campaign and move by the left, crossing the river well upstream for a preliminary strike at the Georgia Railroad. Schofield in fact had already begun the movement three days ago, when his improvised amphibious assault teams emerged from the mouth of Soap Creek to surprise the rebel pickets across the way, and Sherman had followed through by sending one of McPherson's corps to join Garrard at Roswell, seven miles beyond Schofield. On July 13, having reached a firm decision the night before, he continued the buildup by ordering McPherson to take his second corps upriver and reinforce the first, leaving the third in position on Thomas's right to maintain the downstream feint until Stoneman got back from the ride designed to mislead Johnston still further into thinking that the Federals were about to cross below.

"All is well," Sherman wired Halleck next day. "I have now accumulated stores at Allatoona and Marietta, both fortified and garrisoned points. Have also three places at which to cross the Chattahoochee in our possession, and only await General Stoneman's return from a trip down the river, to cross the army in force and move on Atlanta."

Stoneman got back the following night and McPherson's third corps set out for Roswell next morning, July 15. Reunited, the whiplash Army of the Tennessee would thus be on the rim of what Sherman described as "a general right wheel," designed to roll down on the city from the north and east, with Schofield about midway out the twelve-mile radius and Thomas holding the hub, or pivot, to confront and fix the Confederate main body in position for the crunch. McPherson would cross the river and march south to strike the railroad near Stone Mountain, six miles east of Decatur, Schofield's preliminary objective, about the same distance east of Atlanta. The two commands would then advance westward in tandem along the right-of-way, tearing up track as they went, and link up with Thomas for the final push that would assail Johnston along his front, outflank him on his right, and drive him back through the streets of the city in his rear.

★

"Each army will form a unit and connect with its neighbor by a line of pickets," the warning order read. "Should the enemy assume the offensive at any point, which is not expected until we reach below Peachtree Creek, the neighboring army will at once assist the one attacked. . . . A week's work after crossing the Chattahoochee should determine the first object aimed at, viz, the possession of the [Georgia Rail]road east of Decatur, or of Atlanta itself."

July 17 was the jump-off date, a Sunday, and everything went as ordered for all three armies involved in the grand wheel. Crossing with Schofield in the center, Sherman grew concerned, as usual, about what was happening out of sight: particularly in Thomas's direction, where the going was likely to be slow. "Feel down strong to Peach Tree and see what is there," he urged the Virginian. "A vigorous demonstration should be made, and caution your commanders not to exhibit any of the signs of a halt or pause." Next morning he rode over to check on the progress of the Cumberlanders, and found them crossing Nancy's Creek on schedule to descend on Buckhead, a crossroads hamlet where Thomas would set up headquarters before sundown, within a mile of Peachtree Creek and its intrenched defenders.

"I am fully aware of the necessity of making the most of time," Sherman wired Halleck, "and shall keep things moving." Accordingly, he kept prodding Thomas: "I would like you to get to Buckhead early today and then to feel down strong on Atlanta," meantime fretting about McPherson's progress on the far left: "I want that railroad as quick as possible and the weather seems too good to be wasted."

Informed after nightfall that both Schofield and McPherson had reached their objectives and would begin their wrecking marches westward along the railroad at daybreak, Sherman exulted: as well he might, having accomplished within two days what he had predicted would require "a week's work after crossing the Chattahoochee." He had control of the Georgia Railroad from Stone Mountain through Decatur, and now, secure against reinforcements sped from Virginia by Lee, he was out to take Atlanta by bringing his combinations to bear on its outflanked defenders. The question was whether Johnston would stand, as he had done at Kennesaw, or skedaddle, as he had done everywhere else in the course of the seventy-seven-day campaign.

Riding out to confer on the matter with Thomas next morning, July 19, the red-haired Ohioan encountered an answer of sorts in a copy of yesterday's newspaper, brought out of the semi-beleaguered city by a spy. Johnston, it seemed, would neither stand nor skedaddle. "At this critical moment," Sherman later put it, looking back, "the Confederate Government rendered us most valuable service."

★ ★ ★

★

Rebel earthworks, abandoned by the ever-retreating Joe Johnston, lie along a bluff above the Chatta-hoochee River near a railroad bridge rebuilt by Federal engineers.

SEVEN

Hood Replaces Johnston

1864 ★ ★ ★ ★ ★ ★ *T*n Atlanta, all this time, there had been growing consternation as Sherman's "worse than vandal hordes" bore down on the city, preceded by a stream of refugees in wagons and on foot, mostly old men and boys, below or beyond the conscription limits of seventeen and fifty-two, and "yellow-faced women and their daughters in long-slatted sunbonnets and faded calico," who had fled their upcountry farms and hamlets at the approach of the blue outriders. City parks were no longer parks; they bloomed instead with gray-white clusters of hospital tents, where the reek of disinfectants competed with the morbid stench of gangrene, and both combined to rival the predominant smell of horses. Trains chuffed into the station, day and night, loaded with sick and wounded soldiers, many of them dying, many dead before they got there. "Embalming: Free from Odor of Infection," signs proclaimed, soliciting business, and Bohnefield's Coffin Shop on Luckie Street had more orders than it could fill.

"Give us this day our daily bread," the Second Baptist minister had taken as his text the previous Sunday, when news came that Marietta had been abandoned in still another retreat. And before the dawn of another sabbath, so quickly did things move at this late stage of the campaign, word arrived that the gray army had retired across the Chattahoochee, burning in its rear the bridges

★

spanning the last natural barrier between Atlanta and destruction. "Stay a few days longer," a member of Hardee's staff advised a family he joined in town that afternoon for Sunday dinner. "I think we will hold this place at least a week."

They did not take the colonel's advice, but left next morning, scrambling with others like themselves for places on a southbound train. Places were hard to get now, for the military had commandeered most of the cars for removal of the wounded, along with all government stores and the vital machinery taken from outlying mills and factories, a salvage project assigned by Johnston to a high-ranking volunteer aide, Major General Mansfield Lovell, who presumably was experienced in such matters, having given up New Orleans two years back. Atlanta had not expected to share the fate of the Crescent City, but as the fighting grew nearer, week by week, the possibility seemed less and less remote, until finally even diehards had to admit that it had developed into a probability.

Loyal admirers of Old Joe — including an editor who maintained, even now, that his reputation had "grown with every backward step" — were hard put to defend the general from charges that he intended to give up the city without a fight. For the most part, he retained the confidence and above all the devotion of his soldiers, but there were those who questioned his Fabian strategy, which they saw as leading only to one end: especially after he turned loose of Kennesaw and fell back to the Chattahoochee.

"There was not an officer or man in this Army who ever dreamed of Johnston falling back this far," a young artillery lieutenant, whose home in Atlanta was then only seven miles in his rear, wrote his mother from the north bank of that river, "or ever doubted he would attack when the proper time came. But I think he has been woefully outgeneraled and has made a losing bargain."

Official concern had been growing proportionately as the Union forces closed down on Atlanta. "This place is to the Confederacy as important as the heart is to the body. We must hold it," Joe Brown wrote Jefferson Davis in late June, appealing for strategic diversions and substantial reinforcements to help Johnston avert what seemed certain to happen without them. The governor was in touch with other prominent men throughout the South, and he urged them to use their influence on the President to this end.

His chief hope was in a fellow Georgian, Senator Benjamin Hill, who occupied the unusual position of being the friend of both Davis and Johnston, a relationship they could scarcely be said to enjoy in reference to each other. Brown's hope was that Hill could serve as a go-between, if not to bring the two leaders together, then in any case to improve communications — particularly at the far end of the line, where Brown believed the messages were having the greater difficulty in getting through. He suggested that the senator write at once to the Commander in Chief, urging a more sympathetic response to the general's pleas now that the crisis was at hand. Hill said he would do better than that;

"Time is too precious and letters are too inadequate"; he would go to Richmond and talk with Davis face to face.

First, though, he thought it best to confer with Johnston for a clearer understanding of the hopes and plans he then would pass along. Accordingly, he rode up to the general's headquarters at Marietta next morning, July 1, and had what he later called a "free conversation" along these lines with the Virginian.

Reviewing the situation, Johnston declared that his principal aim, up to now, had been to defeat Sherman by obliging him to attack Confederate intrenchments, but after the limited effort which had been so decisively repulsed, four days ago at Kennesaw, he doubted that his adversary could be persuaded to try the thing again. As for himself, he certainly had no intention of wasting his outnumbered veterans in any such attempt. All he could do with his present force, he said, was block the direct path to Atlanta, thus delaying another Union advance until such time as Sherman again compelled his retreat by "ditching round his flank." Aside from the long-odds chance that the enemy mass would expose itself to piecemeal destruction by dividing into segments he could leap at, one by one, he saw but a single hope for reversing the blue tide, which even then was lapping the flanks of Kennesaw and would otherwise in time no doubt roll down to the Chattahoochee and beyond. This was that 5000 cavalry be thrown without delay against Sherman's life line up in Tennessee, either by Forrest or John Morgan; in which case, Johnston said, the Federals would have to accept battle on his terms — that is, attack him in his intrenchments — or else retreat to avoid starvation. Asked why he did not use his own cavalry for such a profitable venture, the general replied that all his horsemen were needed where they were. Observing that "I must go to Richmond, and Morgan must go from Virginia or Forrest from Mississippi, and this will take some time," Hill expressed some doubt whether either body of gray cavalry could reach the Federal rear before the Federals reached Atlanta.

"How long can you hold Sherman north of the Chattahoochee River?" he pointedly asked Johnston, who replied somewhat evasively that the bluecoats had covered less than a dozen

Georgia Governor Joseph E. Brown fretted that Johnston had not the will necessary to defend Atlanta.

southward miles in the past month, shifting their ground from around New Hope Church to Kennesaw Mountain, where they had made no progress at all in the past two weeks; Hill could figure for himself, the general said, how long it would take them to reach the river at this rate. Hill calculated, accordingly, that the Confederates could remain north of the Chattahoochee "at least fifty-four days, and perhaps sixty."

Johnston assented, but not Hood, who though present throughout the interview had held his peace till now. He disagreed, saying: "Mr Hill, when we leave our present line, we will, in my judgment, cross the Chattahoochee River very rapidly." Johnston turned on the tall blond Texan, who was twenty-four years his junior in age, as well as in length of service. "What makes you think that?" he asked, and Hood replied: "Because this line of Kennesaw is the strongest line we can get in this country. If we surrender this to Sherman he can reconnoiter from its summit the whole country between here and Atlanta,

---

"This line of Kennesaw is the strongest line we can get in this country. If we surrender this to Sherman he can reconnoiter from its summit the whole country between here and Atlanta . . ."

— John Bell Hood

---

and there is no such line of defense in the distance." Johnston demurred. "I differ with your conclusion," he said. "I admit this is a strong line of defense, but I have two more strong lines between this and the river, from which I can hold Sherman a long time."

Hill took his leave, pleased to learn that two more stout positions had been prepared for the army to defend before it retired across the Chattahoochee, some fifty-four to sixty days in the future, according to his Johnston-approved calculations, or in any case "a long time" from now. Delayed by personal matters, he took a train for Virginia before the end of the following week, passing en route a group of public men proceeding by rail on a mission similar to his own, except that the two were headed in opposite directions toward diametric goals. Hill was going from Atlanta to Richmond in hope of impressing Johnston's views on Davis, while they were going from Richmond to Atlanta in hope of impressing Davis's views on Johnston. Congressmen all, they had been delegated by their colleagues, as friends of the general, to warn him that his conduct of the Georgia campaign was under heavy attack in the capital and to urge him to disarm these

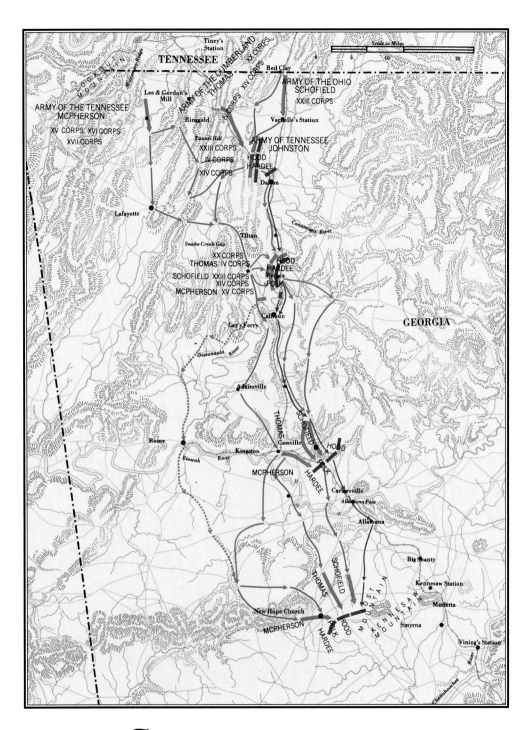

*This map, tracing Sherman's steady progress on
Atlanta, indicates why the South's leadership had lost
confidence in General Johnston's command.*

rearward critics by taking aggressive action against the enemy in his front.

Reaching Atlanta on the evening of July 8 they proceeded next morning to army headquarters for a conference with Johnston, who by then had fallen back through Smyrna, the first of his two stout positions south of Kennesaw, to his bridgehead on the north bank of the Chattahoochee, which was his second. The Virginian received them graciously, heard them out, and replied, alas, as if they had been dispatched for irksome purposes by the President himself: "You may tell Mr Davis that it would be folly for me under the circumstances to risk a decisive engagement. My plan is to draw Sherman further and further from his base in the hope of weakening him and by cutting his army in two. That is my only hope of defeating him."

There was silence at this until one delegate, a Missourian, remarked that what was required, both for the country's sake and the general's own, was for him to strike the Yankees "a crushing blow," and then went on — tactlessly,

"Mr Davis thinks he can do a great many things other men would hesitate to attempt. . . . He tried to do what God failed to do. He tried to make a soldier of Braxton Bragg . . ."

—Joseph Johnston

but apparently in hope of jogging Johnston into action — to say that lately he had heard the President quoted to the effect that "if he were in your place he could whip Sherman now." The general was jogged into action, all right, but not of the kind intended. He bridled and did not try to hide his scorn.

"Yes," he said icily, "I know Mr Davis thinks he can do a great many things other men would hesitate to attempt. For instance, he tried to do what God failed to do. He tried to make a soldier of Braxton Bragg, and you know the result. It couldn't be done."

This might have wound up the matter then and there, to no one's satisfaction, but a courier arrived at that point with news of a development to which Johnston's response provided the conference with an upbeat ending. Schofield had effected a south-bank lodgment yesterday, seven miles upriver, the courier reported, and this morning he had continued the crossing with what appeared to be most, if not all, of his command.

If the general's visitors expected him to react with dismay to this information that he had been flanked, they were agreeably disappointed. Pointing out that Sherman had thus divided his army, north and south of the

★

deep-running Chattahoochee, Johnston declared that the time at last had come to strike and "whip him in detail."

The delegates returned to Atlanta expecting to hear before nightfall the roar of guns that would signal the launching of the attack. It did not come, either then or the following morning, July 10, when all that broke the sabbath stillness was the peal of church bells, summoning the city's dwindling population to pray for a deliverance which Johnston himself seemed less and less willing to attempt.

Bells were tolling that Sunday morning in Richmond, too, when Benjamin Hill stepped off the train from Georgia. He went straight to his hotel and stayed there only long enough to wash up before going to the White House for the appointment he had secured by wiring ahead. Having, as he said, "repelled the idea that any influence with the President was needed, if

Jefferson Davis was once again faced with the necessity of removing a commanding general in the West.

the facts were as General Johnston reported them," the senator was convinced that all the situation required was for him to relay the general's requests to Davis; "I did not doubt he would act promptly."

He was ushered without delay into the Chief Executive's residential office, and as he advanced across the white rug that was said to provoke temerity in the breasts of men who called in unscraped boots, the Mississippian rose to greet him with a geniality that matched the Virginia general's own, nine days ago in Marietta. Davis heard him out, his smile fading when Hill spoke of Morgan and Forrest as presumably lying more or less idle in Southwest Virginia and North Mississippi.

As for Morgan, he replied, it was true that he was where Johnston said he was, having just returned, sadly depleted, from just such an expedition as Johnston recommended, whipped and in no condition for anything more than an attempt to pull his few survivors together for operations necessarily weeks in the future. Forrest too was unavailable, Davis said, although for different reasons. Having disposed of Sturgis at Brice's Crossroads in mid-June, he now was engaged in opposing a 15,000-man Union force that had left Memphis two weeks ago under A. J. Smith, bound either for Georgia to reinforce Sherman, in front or in rear of Atlanta, or for Mobile in conjunction with an even larger blue column reported to be on the march from New Orleans under Canby; he not only could not be spared for the proposed raid into Middle Tennessee, but his superior, Polk's successor Stephen Lee, was protesting hotly — as Johnston had only recently been informed — that he needed "his troops now with Johnston more than the latter can need Forrest."

Hill's hopes, which had been so high on the ride east, declined rapidly while he listened to this double-barreled refutation of the "facts" behind them. But presently they took an even sharper drop when Davis paused and asked: "How long did you understand General Johnston to say he could hold Sherman north of the Chattahoochee River?" Fifty-four to sixty days, the senator replied; whereupon Davis took up and read to him a telegraphic dispatch received just before his arrival. It was from Johnston and it announced that, a part of Sherman's army having crossed upriver two days ago, several miles beyond his right, he had begun his withdrawal across the Chattahoochee last night and completed it this morning.

Hill retired in some confusion, which was increased next day when the Secretary of War called on him "to reduce my interview with General Johnston to writing, for the use of the Cabinet."

He perceived now that his trip to Richmond, designed to help the Atlanta commander, had resulted instead in furnishing the general's Confederate foes with ammunition they could use in urging his removal from command. Three days later, after taking a still closer look at the attitude of those in high positions at the capital, he wired Johnston by way of warning: "You must do the work with your present force. For God's sake do it."

Just as the pressure had been greater, so now was Johnston's time even shorter than Hill knew — unless, that is, the general was somehow able to follow his friend's advice and "do the work." Atlanta, with its rolling mill and foundries, its munition plants and factories, its vital rail connections and vast store of military supplies, was the combined workshop and warehouse of the Confederate West, and as Sherman closed down upon it, Davis later wrote, the threat of its loss "produced intense anxiety far and wide. From many quarters, including such as had most urged his assignment, came delegations, petitions, and letters," insisting that the present army commander be replaced by one who would fight to save the city, not abandon it to the fate which Johnston seemed to consider unavoidable without outside help. "The clamor for his removal commenced immediately after it became known that the army had fallen back from Dalton," Davis added, "and it gathered volume with each remove toward Atlanta."

Nowhere was this clamor more vociferous than at meetings of the cabinet, not one of whose six members was by now in favor of keeping the

Virginia general at his Georgia post. Some had advised against sending him there in the first place: including the Secretary of State, who afterwards told why. "From a close observation of his career," the shrewd-minded Benjamin declared, "I became persuaded that his nervous dread of losing a battle would prevent at all times his ability to cope with an enemy of nearly equal strength, and that opportunities would thus constantly be lost which under other commanders would open a plain path to victory." Still, those who had opposed his selection were not nearly so strident in their demands for his removal, at this stage, as were those who had been his supporters at the outset. The Secretary of War, for example, explained that, having made "a great mistake" seven months ago, "he desired to do all he could, even at this late date, to atone for it."

Davis resisted — now as in the case of that other Johnston, two and a half years ago, after Donelson and on the eve of Shiloh — both the public and the private clamor for the general's removal; Seddon later revealed that though "the whole Cabinet concurred in advising and even urging" the change, the

Johnston called for redistributing Union prisoners held at overcrowded Andersonville, a hundred miles south of Atlanta, alarming anew his superiors.

President moved toward a decision "slowly and not without much hesitation, misgiving and, even to the last, reluctance." His concern was for Atlanta, for what it contained and for what it represented, not only in the minds of his own people, but also in the minds of the people of the North, who would be voting in November whether to sustain their present hard-war leader or replace him with one who might be willing, in the name of peace, to let the South depart in independence. A military professional, Davis knew only too well, as he put the case, "how serious it was to change commanders in the presence of the enemy," and he told Senator Hill flatly, in the course of their Sunday conference at the White House, that he "would not do it if he could have any assurance that General Johnston would not surrender Atlanta without a battle."

In this connection, he had sent his chief military adviser, Braxton Bragg, to determine at first hand, if possible, what the intentions of the western commander were. Bragg had left the previous day, July 9, but before he reached Atlanta — a three-day trip, as it turned out — the War Department received from Johnston himself, on July 11, a telegram which seemed to some to answer only too clearly the question as to the city's impending fate: "I strongly recommend the distribution of the U.S. prisoners, now at Andersonville, immediately."

Andersonville, a prisoner-of-war camp for enlisted personnel, established that spring near Americus, Georgia, and already badly crowded as a result of the northern decision to discontinue the exchange of prisoners, was more than a hundred miles due south of Atlanta. That distance, combined with the use of the word "immediately," gave occasion for alarm. For though Davis knew that what mainly caused Johnston to recommend the camp's evacuation was fear that Sherman, finding it within present cavalry range, might send out a flying column to liberate its 30,000 Federal captives — and thus create, as if by a sowing of dragon teeth, a ferocious new blue army deep in the Confederate rear — still, following hard as it did on the heels of news that Atlanta's defenders had retired in haste across the Chattahoochee, the telegram was an alarming indication of the direction in which Johnston's mind had turned now that Sherman was about to leap the last natural barrier in his path.

For the first time since the clamor for the Virginian's removal began, two months ago, Davis agreed that his relief seemed necessary, and he said as much next day in a cipher telegram asking R. E. Lee's advice in choosing a successor: "General Johnston has failed and there are strong indications that he will abandon Atlanta. . . . It seems necessary to remove him at once. Who should succeed him? What think you of Hood for the position?"

Lee replied, also by wire and in cipher: "I regret the fact stated. It is a bad time to relieve the commander of an army situated as that of Tenne. We may lose Atlanta and the army too. Hood is a bold fighter. I am doubtful as to other qualities necessary." That evening he expanded these words of caution and

Sent to check on Atlanta's defense, Braxton Bragg, shown here, wired back to Jeff Davis that General Johnston apparently intended to abandon the city.

regret in a follow-up letter. "It is a grievous thing," he said of the impending change. "Still if necessary it ought to be done. I know nothing of the necessity. I had hoped that Johnston was strong enough to deliver battle." As for the choice of his former star brigade and division chief as his old friend's successor out in Georgia, second thoughts had not diminished his reservations. "Hood is a good commander, very industrious on the battlefield, careless off, and I have had no opportunity of judging his action when the whole responsibility rested upon him. I have a high opinion of his gallantry, earnestness, and zeal." Further than this Lee would not go, either in praise or detraction, but he added suggestively: "General Hardee has more experience in managing an army. May God give you wisdom to decide in this momentous matter."

A series of telegrams and letters from Bragg, who reached Atlanta next morning, July 13, confirmed the need for early action, either by Johnston or the government. "Indications seem to favor an entire evacuation of this place," he wired Davis on arrival, and followed with a second gloomy message a few hours later, still without having ridden out to the general's headquarters in the field: "Our army is sadly depleted, and now reports 10,000 less than the return of the 10th June. I find but little encouraging." Two days later he was able to report more fully on conditions, having paid two calls on Johnston in the meantime. "He has not sought my advice, and it was not volunteered," Bragg wired. "I cannot learn that he has any more plan for the future than he has had in the past. It is expected that he will await the enemy on a line some three miles from here, and the impression prevails that he is now more inclined to fight. . . . The morale of our army is still reported good."

In a letter sent by courier to Richmond that same day he went more fully into this and other matters bearing on the issue. Johnston's apparent intention, now as always, Bragg declared, was to "await the enemy's approach and be governed, as heretofore, by the development in our front." What was likely to follow could be predicted by reviewing what had happened under similar circumstances at Dalton, Resaca, Cassville, and Marietta — or, indeed, by observing what had happened in and around Atlanta just this week; "All valuable stores and machinery have been removed, and most of the citizens able to go have left with their effects. . . . Position, numbers, and morale are now with the enemy."

Which said, Bragg moved on to the problem of choosing a successor to the general who had brought the army to this pass. Hardee had disqualified himself, not only because he had declined the post seven months ago (and thereby brought on Johnston) but also because he had "generally favored the retiring policy" of his chief. Alexander Stewart, who had been promoted to lieutenant general and given command of Polk's corps on the retreat to the Chattahoochee, was too green for larger duties yet, despite the commendable savagery he had displayed at New Hope Church. That left Hood, who had "been in favor of giving battle" all the way from Dalton and who, in fact — aside, that is, from the peculiar circumstances that prevailed at Cassville — had done just that whenever he was on his own. By way of evidence that this was so, Bragg included a letter he had received from the young Texan the day before, expressing regret that the army had "failed to give battle to the enemy many miles north of our present position."

"If any change is made," Bragg concluded, "Lieutenant General Hood would give unlimited satisfaction." Then, as if aware of the misgiving Lee had expressed three days ago, he added: "Do not understand me as proposing him as a man of genius, or a great general, but as far better in the present emergency than any one we have available."

Davis agreed that Hood was the man for the post, if its present occupant had to be replaced, but he would not act without giving Johnston one last chance to commit himself to a fight to save Atlanta, in which case he would keep him where he was. Accordingly, in a wire next day, July 16, he put the case to the general in no uncertain terms: "I wish to hear from you as to present situation, and your plan of operations so specifically as will enable me to anticipate events."

Johnston felt no more alarm at this than he had done at Hill's "For God's sake do it" telegram, received the day before. Busy with tactical matters, he did not take the time or trouble to outline for the Commander in Chief what he afterwards claimed was his plan for the overthrow of the blue host in his front: which — as he would set it forth some ten years later, after the guns had cooled but not the controversy — was to engage the enemy "on terms of advantage" while they were divided by Peachtree Creek. If this did not work he planned to hold the intrenchments overlooking the creek with 5000 state militia, lately sent him by Governor Brown, "and leisurely fall back with the Confederate troops into the town and, when the Federal army approached, march out with the three corps against one of its flanks." If this was successful, the bluecoats would be driven back against the unfordable Chattahoochee and cut to pieces before they could recross; if not, "the Confederate army had a near and secure place of refuge in Atlanta, which it could hold forever, and so win the campaign."

So he later said: "forever" — but not now. Now he merely responded, as before, that he would have to be governed by circumstances; circumstances which it was clear would be of Sherman's making. "As the enemy has double our number, we must be on the defensive," he replied to Davis's request for specific information. "My plan of operations must, therefore, depend on that of the enemy. It is mainly to watch for an opportunity to fight to advantage. We are trying to put Atlanta in condition to hold it for a day or two by the Georgia militia, that army movements may be freer and wider."

On the defensive. A day or two. The Georgia militia. Freer and wider movements. . . . Johnston would later maintain that just as he was about to deliver the blow that would "win the campaign," and which he had had in mind all along, his sword was wrenched from his grasp by the Richmond authorities; but the fact was, he signed his own warrant of dismissal when he put his hand to this telegram declaring, more clearly than anything else it said, that he had no plan involving a battle to save Atlanta.

Word came next morning — July 17, another Sunday — that Sherman's whole army was over the Chattahoochee, apparently engaged in an outsized turning movement designed to close down on the city from the north and east. After nightfall Johnston

*P*lanning to give up Atlanta after a series of retreats, Joe Johnston was relieved of his command.

was at his headquarters three miles out the Marietta Road, conferring with his chief engineer about work on the Atlanta fortifications, when a message for him from Adjutant General Samuel Cooper clicked off the telegraph receiver:

Lieutenant General J. B. Hood has been commissioned to the temporary rank of General under the late law of Congress. I am directed by the Secretary of War to inform you that as you have failed to arrest the advance of the enemy to the vicinity of Atlanta, far in the interior of Georgia, and express no confidence that you can defeat or repel him, you are hereby relieved from the command of the Army and Department of Tennessee, which you will immediately turn over to General Hood.

Old Joe spent most of the rest of the night in the throes of composition, preparing first a farewell address, in which he expressed his affection for the troops who had served under him, and then a response to his superiors, in which he managed to vent a measure of the resentment aroused by the backhand slap they had taken at him in the order for his removal.

"I cannot leave this noble army," he told its members, "without expressing my admiration of the high military qualities it has displayed. A long and arduous campaign has made conspicuous every soldierly virtue, endurance of toil, obedience to orders, brilliant courage. The enemy has never attacked but to be repulsed and severely punished. You, soldiers, have never argued but from your courage, and never counted your foes. No longer your leader, I will still watch your career, and will rejoice in your victories. To one and all I offer assurances of my friendship, and bid an affectionate farewell."

The other document was briefer, if no less emotional under its surface of ice. "Your dispatch of yesterday received and obeyed," it began, and passed at once to a refutation of the charges made in the dismissal order: "Sherman's army is much stronger compared with that of Tennessee than Grant's compared with that of Northern Virginia. Yet the enemy has been compelled to advance much more slowly to the vicinity of Atlanta than to that of Richmond and Petersburg, and has penetrated deeper into Virginia than into Georgia." Then at the end came the stinger. "Confident language by a military commander is not usually regarded as evidence of competency. J. E. Johnston."

Hood too got little if any sleep after he received at 11 p.m. the War Department telegram which, he said, "so astounded and overwhelmed" him

★

John Bell Hood, left, lionized for headlong charges at Gaine's Mills, Gettysburg, and Chickamauga, became the new rebel commander replacing Joseph E. Johnston.

that he "remained in deep thought throughout the night." He had in fact much to ponder, including a follow-up wire from Seddon: "You are charged with a great trust. You will, I know, test to the utmost your capacities to discharge it. Be wary no less than bold. . . . God be with you."

His appointment was plainly an endorsement of the aggressive views he had been propounding all the way south from the Tennessee line, and he was clearly expected to translate them into action. But he perceived that to do so here on the flat terrain south of the Chattahoochee, with his back to the gates of the city in his care, was a far more difficult undertaking than it would have been in the rugged country Johnston had traversed in the course of his long retreat from Dalton. "We may lose Atlanta and the army too," Lee had warned Davis five days ago, and though Hood had not seen the message, he was altogether aware of the danger pointed out — as well as of his own shortcomings, which Lee had by no means listed in full.

For one, there was his youth. He had just last month turned thirty-three, the crucifixion age, which made him not only younger than any of his infantry corps or division commanders, but also a solid ten years younger than the average among them. Then too there was his physical condition; Gettysburg had cost him the use of his left arm, paralyzed by a fragment of bursting shell as he charged the Devil's Den, and at Chickamauga his right leg had been amputated so close to the hip that from then on he had to be strapped in the saddle to ride a horse.

Worst of all, though, was the timing of the change now ordered by the War Department. Sherman's final lunge at Atlanta was in full career, and only Johnston knew what plans had been made, if any, to meet and survive the shock. Certainly Hood knew nothing of them, except as they applied to the disposition of his corps on the Confederate right, astride the Georgia Railroad. Emerging at last from the brown study into which the telegram had plunged him, the blond, Kentucky-born Texan came out of his tent before dawn, mounted his horse with the help of an orderly, and set out for Johnston's headquarters near the far end of the line.

On the way there, about sunrise, he encountered Stewart on the way there too. Old Straight, who had led a division under Hood until his recent promotion to head the corps that had been temporarily under Loring, was also disturbed by the untimely change. He proposed that they unite with Hardee "in an effort to prevail on General Johnston to withhold the order and retain com-

> *"A change of commanders, under existing circumstances, was regarded as so objectionable that I only accepted it as the alternative of continuing a policy which had proved so disastrous."*
>
> — Jefferson Davis

mand of the army until the impending battle has been fought." Hood readily agreed, and they rode on together.

At headquarters, where a candle flickered atop a barrel with the telegram beside it, Johnston received them courteously, but when Hood appealed to him to "pocket that dispatch, leave me in command of my corps, and fight the battle for Atlanta," the Virginian would have no part of such an irregular procedure. He was off the hook and he intended to stay off. "Gentlemen, I am a soldier," he said. "A soldier's first duty is to obey." So that was that.

Or perhaps not. Hardee having arrived by now, the three lieutenant generals dispatched a joint telegram to the President requesting that he postpone the transfer of command "until the fate of Atlanta is decided."

Davis's answer was not long in coming, and it was a flat No: "A change of commanders, under existing circumstances, was regarded as so objectionable that I only accepted it as the alternative of continuing a policy which had proved so disastrous. . . . The order has been executed, and I cannot suspend it without making the case worse than it was before the order was issued."

Hood made one last try, returning to plead a second time, "for the good of the country," that Johnston "pocket the correspondence" and remain in command, "as Sherman was at the very gates of the city." Old Joe again declined: whereupon Hood launched into a personal appeal, referring to "the great embarrassment of the position in which I had been placed." Not only was he in the dark as to such plans as had been made for meeting the enemy now bearing down on Atlanta and its defenders, he did not even know where the other two corps of the army were posted. "With all the earnestness of which man is capable," Hood later wrote, "I besought him, if he would under no circumstances retain command and fight the battle for Atlanta, to at least remain with me and give me the benefit of his counsel whilst I determined the issue."

Touched at last, and "with tears of emotion gathering in his eyes," Johnston assured his young successor that, after a necessary ride into Atlanta, he would return that evening and help him all he could. So he said. According to Hood, however, "he not only failed to comply with his promise, but, without a word of explanation or apology, left that evening for Macon, Georgia."

There was some fear, according to a number of observers, that the men in the ranks "would throw down their muskets and quit" when they learned of the transfer of command: not so much from distrust of Hood, who at this stage was little more than a damaged figurehead to most of them, as because of their "love for and confidence in Johnston," who many said "had been grievously wronged" by his superiors in Richmond. "A universal gloom seemed cast over the army," a lieutenant on Hood's own staff declared, and a Tennessee private — a veteran who remembered Bragg and the aftermath of Missionary Ridge — later told why the news was received with so much sorrow and resentment: "Old Joe Johnston had taken command of the Army of Tennessee when it was crushed and broken, at a time when no other man on earth could have united it. He found it in rags and tatters, hungry and broken-hearted, the morale of the men gone, their manhood vanished to the winds, their pride a thing of the past. Through his instrumentality and skillful manipulation, all these had been restored. . . . Farewell, old fellow!" he cried, breaking into an apostrophe of remembered grief as he approached the end of this "saddest chapter" of the war; "We privates loved you because you made us love ourselves."

Not all who felt that way about the Virginia general had to say goodbye from such a distance, either of time or space. Between the reading of his farewell address that Monday morning and his actual departure for Macon that afternoon, several units passed his headquarters on their way up to the lines on Peachtree Creek, and thereby got the chance to demonstrate their affection in his presence. A Georgia regiment happened to march out the Marietta Road, for example, and the colonel left a record of how he and his men reacted to what they thought would be their last look at their former commander, who

*U*nion commanders John Schofield (left) and
James McPherson (right), both West Point classmates of
Hood's, warned that he would fight aggressively.

came out of the house and stood by the gate to watch them pass. "We lifted our hats. There was no cheering. We simply passed silently, our heads uncovered. Some of the officers broke ranks and grasped his hand, as the tears poured down their cheeks."

Higher up the ladder of rank, the reaction was scarcely less emotional. Hardee, upset at having someone more than a year his junior in grade promoted over his head, promptly asked to be relieved, complaining that the President — who in the end persuaded him to withdraw his application for a transfer — was "attempting to create the impression that in declining the command [six months ago] at Dalton, I declined it for all future time." He doubted Hood's ability to fill the position to which he had been elevated, and others felt, as one of them put it, that the appointment was an "egregious blunder." Sam French called at headquarters that evening to assure the new commander of his full coöperation, but did not fail to add, with his usual forthrightness, that he regretted the change. "Although he took my hand and thanked me," he later said of Hood, "I was ever afterwards impressed with the belief that he never forgave me for what I said."

Still others, aware of the reason behind the shift, foresaw hard fighting and had mixed opinions concerning the fate of Atlanta, as well as their own. Undoubtedly, Hood being Hood, they were about to go over to the offensive;

Pat Cleburne, for one, believed that this was likely to take them far — in miles, at any rate. "We are going to carry the war to Africa," he predicted, "but I fear we will not be as successful as Scipio was."

Across the way, on the far side of Peachtree Creek and eastward out the Georgia Railroad, the reaction among Federals of rank was not dissimilar, so far as expectation of a step-up in the scale of fighting went, when it became known next day that the Confederates, in Lincoln's current campaign phrase, had "swapped horses in midstream."

McPherson and Schofield had been West Point classmates of Hood's, standing first and seventh respectively in a class of fifty-two, while he stood forty-fourth — ten places below even Sheridan, who had been held back a year for misconduct. Schofield in fact had been his roommate, and by coaching him in mathematics, which gave the Kentucky cadet a great deal of trouble, had managed to keep his military career from ending in academic failure and dismissal. "I came very near thinking once or twice that perhaps I had made a mistake," the Illinois general would remark in later years, though for the present he simply warned his chief: "He'll hit you like hell, now, before you know it."

McPherson agreed, and so did Thomas, under whom Hood had served five years ago in Texas. But perhaps the most convincing testimony as to this new opponent's boldness came from a Union-loyal fellow Kentuckian who had watched him play old-army poker. "I seed Hood bet $2500," this witness declared, "with nary a pair in his hand."

Warned from all sides that his adversary was "bold even to rashness, and courageous in the extreme," Sherman took the precaution of advising his unit commanders to keep their troops "always prepared for battle in any shape."

Not that he regretted the predicted shift in rebel tactics. His casualties would undoubtedly mount, but there was plenty of room for taking up the slack that was evident from a comparison of Union losses, east and west. In the eleven weeks of his campaign against Johnston and Atlanta, he had lost fewer men than Meade had lost in the two-day Wilderness battle that opened his drive on Lee and Richmond. Besides, as Sherman saw it, the heavier the casualties were — provided, of course, that they could be kept in ratio, Federal and Confederate — the sooner the fighting would end with him in occupation of his goal. That was what he meant, in part, when he wrote home the following week: "I confess I was pleased at the change."

★   ★   ★

Epilogue

★ ★ ★ **B**y late spring and early summer of 1864, the results of Grant's new "coordinated" war effort were apparent, and they were nowhere so good as he or Abraham Lincoln, in a battle for his political life, had hoped. While Phil Sheridan's cavalry had cost the South its premier horse soldier, Jeb Stuart, at Yellow Tavern, Franz Sigel's poor showing at New Market had led to his replacement. What was supposed to have been Benjamin Butler's bold foray up the James River had been bottled up and corked by Beauregard at Bermuda Hundred. If Bedford Forrest's wide-ranging raids in the West were strategically insignificant, they nevertheless seemed endless, and they posed a constant worry for Sherman as he brought his army to the gates of Atlanta. There, too, Sherman would stall, as it turned out, for the rest of the summer. And Grant's long forty days of fighting in the Wilderness and beyond had ended in a bloody stalemate at Cold Harbor.

Not surprisingly, Lincoln's chances for reëlection in the coming fall seemed to have dimmed considerably as a result. Not just Lee and Davis and the northern Copperhead Democrats longed for his defeat and now believed it certain, but also many in his own party had grown disaffected and were working toward his ouster. Some radicals had held a separate convention and nominated John C. Frémont, who might well siphon off enough loyal votes to elect the man everyone assumed would be the choice of the Democrats, George McClellan. Lincoln had redubbed his party the National Union party and chosen as his running mate a Tennessean named Andrew Johnson, and he would take more drastic measures in the coming months as even those closest to him began to consider nominating a replacement. The Union army leaders, especially Grant and Sherman, realized their star was tied to Lincoln's, and they would do all they could to help, but most of what they could do depended on their fortunes in battle.

All spring those fortunes had seemed to smile on Sherman as he rolled inexorably south, chasing rebel forces under Johnston out of one position after another, right up to heavily fortified Atlanta. When Johnston, with Sherman ensconced outside the city, hinted that he might abandon Atlanta, as he had every other position along the way, Jefferson Davis had replaced him with the fiery, if inexperienced John Bell Hood. Throughout the coming August, Sherman's cavalry and Hood's would raid each other to little effect, while Union infantry futilely probed south toward the railroad below Atlanta. Hood, taking a leaf from the book of Lee and Jackson, would launch a series of bold sorties whose major result was to raise the South's casualties in Georgia higher than Sherman's. In late August, when Sherman's army would suddenly disappear, Hood would rashly assume the Ohio general had retreated. By the time Hood came to realize that Sherman had swung south instead, it would be too late. To avoid being trapped, Hood would give up Atlanta.

Fortune had not smiled so warmly on Grant that spring. At Cold Harbor, where he was unwilling to ask for a truce to collect the wounded or bury the dead, nearly five acres were piled thick with bodies. A lucky few crawled to safety, but by the time litter bearers were finally let onto the battle-ground, only two of the nearly 7000 Union soldiers who had fallen were still alive. Grant would latter admit that he regretted nothing so much as the order he gave to attack at Cold Harbor, but more immediately he had changed his strategy. Under cover of darkness, Grant slipped his army out of its trenches and crossed the Chickahominy. Lee, assuming Grant was headed toward Richmond, rushed the majority of his troops to the outskirts of the city. But for once Lee was surprised, as Grant shifted left to the James River and his real target, Peters-burg. From there, Grant reasoned, he could choke off Richmond just as he had Vicksburg the year before.

As both sides settled in for a siege, Lincoln would stick by his commander and construe his task as persuading the North's electorate to "face the arith-metic" the way he and Grant already had. By summer's end there would be good news to shore up his campaigning, much of it from the sea — his navy had sunk the *Alabama* and would capture the *Florida*, sink the *Albemarle*, and take Mobile Bay — but most importantly from Sherman in occupied Atlanta. With that, and some high-handed political actions involving the first pocket veto, the suspension of *habeus corpus*, the culling of opponents from ballots and voting lists, and the use of Union troops furloughed home as voters, Lincoln would ultimately win his reëlection. And so, despite a few desperate but unofficial peace feelers, the sides would stay the same, one offering amnesty the other demanding independence, as they continued to wage civil war.

★   ★   ★

Picture Credits

Edouard Manet, John G. Johnson Collection, Philadelphia Museum of Art. **191:** Hunt-Morgan House, Lexington, Ky., copied by Mary S. Rezny. **192:** Audio-Visual Archives, Department of Special Collections and Archives, King Library, University of Kentucky, copied by Mary S. Rezny. **194:** Courtesy collection of Don Troiani. **198, 199:** From *The Photographic History of the Civil War*, Vol. 2, by Henry E. Elson, © 1911 Review of Reviews Co., New York. **202, 205:** Zenda, Inc. **211:** Courtesy Frank and Marie-Thérèse Wood Print Collections, Alexandria, Va. **212:** National Archives Neg. No. 111-B-3756. **215:** Library of Congress. **218:** National Archives Neg No. 111-B-448. **223:** U. S. Navy. **226, 227:** Chicago Historical Society, Neg. No. 1947.5 **230-232:** L. M. Strayer Collection. **234:** The Valentine Museum, Richmond. **236, 237:** Courtesy Frank and Marie-Thérèse Wood Print Collections, Alexandria, Va. **240, 241:** The Gilder Lehrman Collection on deposit at the Pierpont Morgan Library, New York, GLC 4610, No. 1 and No. 2. **243:** Map by Walter W. Roberts. **245:** Library of Congress. **246:** From *The Mountain Campaigns in Georgia,* by Joseph M. Brown, published by Matthews, Northrup & Co., Buffalo, N.Y., 1890. **249:** Library of Congress. **253, 255:** Courtesy Frank and Marie-Thérèse Wood Print Collections, Alexandria, Va. **258-260:** Library of Congress, Neg. No. B8184-10410. **263:** Library of Congress. **265:** Map by Walter W. Roberts. **267:** Zenda, Inc. **269:** Rochester Museum & Science Center, Rochester, N.Y. **271:** From: *Photographic History of the Civil War*, Vol. 10, Review of Reviews Co., New York, 1912. **273:** Cook Collection, The Valentine Museum, Richmond. **275:** Library of Congress. **278:** Massachusetts Commandery of the Military Order of the Loyal Legion of the United States and the U.S. Army Military History Institute (MASS-MOLLUS/USAMHI), copied by A. Pierce Bounds; Zenda, Inc.

Index

SHELBY FOOTE, THE CIVIL WAR, A NARRATIVE
VOLUME 11 YELLOW TAVERN TO COLD HARBOR

Library of Congress Cataloging-in-Publication Data
Foote, Shelby.
[Civil War, a narrative]
Shelby Foote, the Civil War, a narrative / by Shelby Foote and the editors of Time-Life Books. — 40th Anniversary ed.
p. cm.
Originally published: The Civil War, a narrative. New York : Random House, 1958-1974, in 3 v.
Includes bibliographical references and indexes.
Contents: v. 11. Yellow Tavern to Cold Harbor
ISBN 0-7835-0110-2
1. United States—History—Civil War, 1861-1865.
I. Time-Life Books. II. Title.
E468.F7 1999   99-13486
973.7—dc21   CIP

10 9 8 7 6 5 4 3 2 1

OTHER TIME-LIFE HISTORY PUBLICATIONS

Time-Life Books is a division of Time Life Inc.

TIME LIFE INC.
PRESIDENT and CEO: Jim Nelson

TIME-LIFE BOOKS
PUBLISHER/MANAGING EDITOR: Neil Kagan
SENIOR VICE PRESIDENT, MARKETING: Joseph A. Kuna
VICE PRESIDENT, NEW PRODUCT DEVELOPMENT: Amy Golden

EDITOR: Philip Brandt George
Art Director: Ellen L. Pattisall
Editorial Assistant: Patricia D. Whiteford

Correspondent: Christina Lieberman (New York)

ZENDA INC.

Editor: Charles Phillips
Managing Editor: Candace Floyd
Administration: Patricia Hogan
Design and Production:
Gore Studio, Inc.: Bruce Gore (cover)
The Graphics People: Susan Ellen Hogan, Mary Brillman, Roger Neiss

Separations by the Time-Life Imaging Department

NEW PRODUCT DEVELOPMENT: Director, Elizabeth D. Ward; Project Manager, Karen Ingebretsen; Director of Marketing, Mary Ann Donaghy; Marketing Manager, Paul Fontaine; Associate Marketing Manager, Erin Gaskins

MARKETING: Director, Peter Tardif; Marketing Manager, Nancy Gallo; Associate Marketing Manager, Kristen N. O'Shea

Executive Vice President, Operations: Ralph Cuomo
Senior Vice President and CFO: Claudia Goldberg
Senior Vice President, Law & Business Affairs: Randolph H. Elkins

Vice President, Financial Planning & Analysis: Christopher Hearing
Vice President, Book Production: Patricia Pascale
Vice President, Imaging: Marjann Caldwell
Director, Publishing Technology: Betsi McGrath
Director, Editorial Administration: Barbara Levitt
Director, Photography and Research: John Conrad Weiser
Director, Quality Assurance: James King
Manager, Technical Services: Anne Topp
Senior Production Manager: Ken Sabol
Manager, Copyedit/Page Makeup: Debby Tait
Chief Librarian: Louise D. Forstall